KIEFER SUTHERLAND

The biography

LAURA JACKSON

PORTRAIT

PIATKUS

First published in Great Britain in 2006 by Piatkus Books

Copyright © 2006 by Laura Jackson

Reprinted 2008

A CIP catalogue record for this book
is available from the British Library

ISBN 978-0-7499-5104-7

Typeset by Phoenix Photosetting, Chatham, Kent
Printed and bound in Great Britain
by MPG Books Ltd, Bodmin, Cornwall

Piatkus Books
An imprint of
Little, Brown Book Group
100 Victoria Embankment
London EC4Y 0DY

An Hachette Livre UK Company

www.piatkus.co.uk

PICTURE CREDITS

p.1(top) © Time Life Pictures/Getty Images; p.1(bottom) © TS/Keystone USA/Rex
Features; p.2(top) © Time Life Pictures/Getty Images; p.2(bottom) © Time Life
Pictures/Getty Images; p.3(top) © James Fraser/Rex Features; p.3(bottom) © Peter
Brooker/Rex Features; p.4(top) © Jim Ross/Reuters/Corbis; p.4(bottom) © Kip Rano/Rex
Features; p.5(top) © Warner Br/Everett/Rex Features; p.5(bottom) © Getty Images;
p.6(top) © Everett Collection/Rex Features; p.6(bottom) © SNAP/Rex Features; p.7(top)
© Warner Br/Everett/Rex Features; p.7(bottom) © Reuters/Corbis; p.8(top) © Mario
Anzuoni/Reuters/ Corbis; p.8(bottom) © Jen Lowery/Rex Features

*Every effort has been made to identify and acknowledge the copyright holders.
Any errors or omissions will be rectified in future editions provided that written
notification is made to the publishers.*

C O N T E N T S

This book is dedicated to David
– a quite extraordinary gem of a husband

ACKNOWLEDGEMENTS

The following helped with this book: Elgin Library staff; Falkirk Library; Clive Whichelow; *VH1*; *Daily Record*; *Time*; *Falkirk Herald*; *Rolling Stone*; *The Face*; *Cosmopolitan*; *Maxim*; *Emmy magazine*; *Playboy*; *Radio Times*; *Woman's Own*; *Red*; *DVD Review*; *Gibson Guitars*; *Details Magazine*; *Film Review*; *People Weekly*; *Sunday Mail*; *TV Guide*; *Sky Magazine*; *FHM*; *Cult Times*; *Interview*; *Flaunt*; *Inside Hollywood*; *Entertainment Weekly*; *USA Weekend*; *Los Angeles Times*.

Special thanks to David for all his patience, belief and assistance, to Stuart Rourke and Malcolm Bews for their welcome enthusiasm and to Alice Davis and all at Piatkus Books.

CHAPTER 1

IT'S A GENES THING

RIGHT NOW, THE FUTURE looks brighter than it ever has for one particularly vibrant, versatile and compelling young actor. Directors and scriptwriters in both film and television are clamouring to secure his services. His name is Kiefer Sutherland and starring as federal agent Jack Bauer, in the gritty, nail-biting hit TV drama *24*, he has come to encapsulate one of the finest screen heroes of our time. He has appeared in upwards of 60 films. At 17, Kiefer secured a Best Actor Genie Award nomination for his first major film role in the 1984 Canadian drama, *The Bay Boy*. In the late 1980s, while in his twenties, he rode the crest of a wave with striking performances such as an iconic vampire in *The Lost Boys*, a sensitive outlaw in *Young Guns*, and a driven medical student in *Flatliners*.

Although he continued to work, the bright spotlight throughout the 1990s more frequently fell on Kiefer's colourful off-screen activities, including his chequered love life. Two short-lived marriages bit the dust. Between them, his engagement to rising star Julia Roberts came to an abrupt, headline-grabbing end when their glitzy Hollywood wedding was sensationally called off in June 1991, only a handful of days before the actual ceremony. Kiefer's wild side surfaced with tales of long drinking sessions with friends, and occasional bar room brawling. An acquired passion for horses led him to sideline movie making in order to try out the rowdy, testosterone-soaked rodeo circuit. The counterbalance shows with his ingrained socialist principles, his prominent commitment to the preservation of Medicare (Canada's equivalent of the NHS), and his developing into a doting father to Sarah, his daughter by his first marriage.

Towards the end of the nineties, Kiefer again consciously opted out of frontline acting. More than one film critic was willing to write him off, but the resilience that is Kiefer's hallmark proved those doubters wrong when he returned to the screens with a vengeance in 2001 as the explosive star of the innovative drama, 24. By securing a slew of awards, including Best Actor trophies from the Golden Globes and the Screen Actors Guild, as well as countless award nominations, for his powerhouse portrayal of Jack Bauer, Kiefer has bounced back into the elite ranks of America's A-list actors and success tastes all the sweeter a second time around. He is an actor who brings intelligence, depth and vulnerability even to an unsympathetic role; this enviable talent gained further recognition in June 2005, when he was inducted into Canada's Walk of Fame. Kiefer's accomplishments, though, should come as no surprise, for he comes from a family of high achievers. His maternal grandfather, Tommy Douglas, was Premier of Saskatchewan between 1944 and 1961, before becoming leader of the New Democratic Party – the first elected socialist government in North America. He is revered as the father of Canada's government-funded health care system, and in 2004 he beat off rock stars and internationally famous statesmen in a nationwide poll, to be voted 'The Greatest Canadian of All Time'.

A remarkable man, of a calibre that is rare in today's society, Tommy Douglas was born in 1904 in Falkirk, Scotland, at Sunnybrae, Camelon, a house owned by the family of TV inventor John Logie Baird. For generations, the

Douglases of Falkirk had worked as iron moulders at the Carron Ironworks, which had made cannons for the Duke of Wellington during the Peninsular Wars. When Tommy was six, he fell and cut his right knee, a seemingly innocuous injury that yet refused to heal. He developed osteomyelitis, and a local doctor performed many a crude operation on him at home on the kitchen table, with Tommy's mother administering the chloroform. In 1910, his family emigrated to Winnipeg in Canada, where Tommy frequently landed in the Sick Children's Hospital. His condition became so desperate, that a decision to amputate his right leg loomed large.

After a cursory look-over by a busy duty physician, Tommy's prospects were alarmingly bleak. One day, by chance, an orthopaedic surgeon with students in tow passed through the overcrowded ward, and Tommy Douglas randomly drew the man's attention. Tommy was chosen as a guinea pig for an experimental operation, and the procedure was a success. His grateful parents were euphoric. It went deeper with Tommy. Years later he revealed: 'That experience had a profound effect on me. I thought, if my parents had been rich, I'd have had the best doctor in Winnipeg. Why was it that a poor boy almost lost his leg? That kept gnawing at me through the years.'

When World War I broke out in 1914, his father took the family back to Scotland, where he enlisted in the army. Tommy's mother and her children moved in with her parents in Glasgow, where Tommy spent four formative years becoming imbued with the political ferment that was rife on Clydeside. While children of his age played knockabout football in tenement back alleys, the young firebrand haunted Glasgow Green to soak up the fiery oratory of members of the Independent Labour Party. The finest orators of that era, in Tommy's opinion, were Lloyd George and Aneurin Bevan, the architect of Britain's cradle-to-the-grave NHS system. In 1919, the Douglas family returned to Winnipeg to find the city in the grip of a general strike, and it is little wonder that politics became Tommy Douglas's destiny.

In 1930, Tommy married Irma Dempsey and settled in Weyburn, Saskatchewan. Five years later, by which time a daughter, Shirley, had been born, he became MP for Weyburn, and within nine years was making a profound difference to the lives of ordinary working-class people. 'The first thing I did when I became Premier of Saskatchewan,' he recalled, 'was to make myself Minister of Health, and on January 1, 1947 the first hospital care programme in North America came into effect.' Tommy Douglas's number one concern was the creation of Medicare, and to implement it he took on fierce struggles with the North American medical establishment. At one stage he was faced with an all-out doctors' strike, but in the end the sheer force of his passionate argument won the day. He proved that through careful fiscal management it was possible to provide a universal government-funded health service. Tommy Douglas had many achievements, but his most notable was Medicare, and that passion has passed down the generations, ultimately to Kiefer himself.

In 1981, Tommy Douglas was made a Companion of the Order of Canada, and in 2003 his daughter Shirley became a member of that same prestigious Order. Universally accessible health care is of immense importance to Shirley Douglas. She has been a national spokesperson for the Canada Health Coalition lobby group, and it was perhaps inevitable that she would inherit her father's firebrand personality. Born in Weyburn in 1934, Shirley, a future committed activist on several fronts, only ever knew her father to be in the thick of the political arena. Ten years old when Tommy became Premier of Saskatchewan, she spent the next 17 years accustomed to him hitting the campaign trail. When not out on the stump with her parents, the young Shirley was drawn to music and theatre, becoming involved in church-staged amateur dramatics. By 16, now serious about acting, she enrolled at the Banff School of Fine Arts, and in the early 1950s she travelled to Britain to spend two years at London's Royal Academy of Dramatic Art, then working in UK theatre and television, and securing a role in the 1955 film, *Joe Macbeth*, directed by Ken Hughes, and starring Paul Douglas and Sidney James.

A stunningly beautiful young woman, a petite 5′2″, and radiating a noticeable vibrancy, Shirley appeared to have what it took to succeed in the crowded acting world, but her career plans had to be put on temporary hold in 1960 when, at the age of 26, three years after returning to Canada, she gave birth to a son she named Thomas, upholding a Douglas tradition of so naming first-born boys. When Tom was two, Shirley landed a second film role, this time in *Lolita*. Based on the novel by Vladimir Nabokov, directed by Stanley Kubrick and starring James Mason and Shelley Winters, the film dealt with the controversial subject of a middle-aged lecturer's infatuation with a 14-year-old girl. Shirley played a piano teacher, but although a certain luminous screen quality caught the eye, a movie career at that point still proved elusive, and by the following year Shirley had stepped away from front of camera to work as an assistant to director Warren Kiefer. By the early 1960s she had also relocated with her child to Italy, where she met the father of her second son, Kiefer. Donald Sutherland would go on to become a screen legend, but when he and Shirley met, he had yet to make his film debut.

A fellow Canadian, Donald McNichol Sutherland was born in 1934 in Saint John, New Brunswick, to Frederick Sutherland, a salesman, and his wife, Dorothy, and was raised in Bridgewater, Nova Scotia. Donald developed polio as a child, which rendered him virtually bed-bound for a year, yet his appetite for life could not be diminished. With a fertile imagination and a keen intelligence, he was always destined to break out of the mould. Donald was already a striking individual – a thin, lanky adolescent who ultimately shot up to 6'4", with eyes that were by turns nakedly roguish or thoroughly unreadable, and a smile that suggested imminent mischief. As an actor, his looks could never be labelled conventionally handsome. Indeed, a casting director once told Sutherland, hungry for a particular film role: 'Sorry, you're the best actor but this part calls for a guy-next-door type. You don't look as if you've ever lived next door to anyone!'

An urge to entertain prompted Donald at 14 to land a job as a disc jockey at CBC Radio in Halifax, Nova Scotia, but his overriding ambition was to become an actor. At 16, he latched on to a poem by Brecht called 'To The Worker Actors of Denmark', which he has described as having been his 'bible'. Said Sutherland: 'It was a key to what an actor was supposed to do. It was about observing and comparing your observations, distilling a truth out of that and bringing that to an audience.' When Donald went to study at Victoria College, University of Toronto, in his late teens, although he majored in engineering his heart lay firmly in drama. He wanted to work in Toronto's theatre land, so he joined a comedy troupe called UC Follies. It was less hilarious when he was allegedly expelled from his university residence for apparently throwing a sink out of a window.

While at university, Donald met and fell in love with a pretty, petite philosophy student named Lois Hardwick. They married in 1959, when Donald was 25, but times were tough. His preoccupation with acting had impacted on his engineering studies to the extent that he failed the course. He worked briefly as a croupier, and lived in a dingy, cramped Toronto apartment where the stingy landlord turned the heating off at weekends. In an attempt to get back on the acting track, Donald travelled to Britain, aiming to enrol at the London Academy of Music and Dramatic Art, but ended up immersing himself in UK repertory theatre and cadging the occasional television appearance. By the early 1960s, his marriage was disintegrating, and he and Lois separated and later filed for divorce.

In 1963, Donald made his movie debut portraying both a young soldier and an old man in the Italian horror film, *Castle of the Living Dead*, with Warren Kiefer at the helm. It was inevitable that while working on this film Donald's eye would fall on the director's vivacious assistant, Shirley Douglas. By the time *Castle of the Living Dead* was released in 1964, Shirley and Donald were lovers; they married in 1966, once Donald and Lois's divorce had come through. By then, the couple were in London, where Shirley became pregnant. Having fluctuated between forgettable horror films and brief TV appearances, Donald landed a role in the British TV mini-series, *A Farewell to Arms*, based on the Ernest Hemingway novel, starring Vanessa Redgrave and George Hamilton, and directed by Rex Tucker. For Donald, it was a welcome step up in calibre of work in an overall energised time.

1966 was a hugely volatile year, when there was a distinct divide between life in Britain and across the pond. President Lyndon B Johnson, who was sworn into office after the assassination of John F Kennedy in November 1963, had deepened his country's involvement in the Vietnam War, which was proving to be massively unpopular with a growing section of the American people. On 16 May 1966, 8,000 Vietnam War protesters encircled the White House for two hours, making the Washington authorities very nervous. Yet six weeks later, US bombers raided the North Vietnamese capital, Hanoi, and its port, Haiphong, for the first time. Racial tension was rife across the United States, too, and escalated into widespread urban race riots. In the ensuing years, both Shirley Douglas and Donald Sutherland would become active anti-Vietnam War protesters, but right then Britain was in a vastly different, buoyant mood.

Swinging London, with its epicentre in the Kings Road, was the music and fashion capital of the world. The Rolling Stones' classic album, *Aftermath*, hit the number one slot in April. The Beatles' *Revolver* promptly topped the charts in

August, and while Muhammad Ali reigned supreme as the heavyweight boxing champion of the world, England beat West Germany at Wembley to lift football's World Cup. It was in the thriving film industry, however, where the sharpest contrast was visible. In Britain, the box office smash hit film was the outrageous, Oscar-nominated sex comedy, *Alfie*, directed by Lewis Gilbert and starring Michael Caine, Shirley Anne Field and Jane Asher. In America, on the other hand, the movie that made uncomfortable but compelling viewing was *Who's Afraid of Virginia Woolf?* Adapted from the play by Edward Albee, and directed by Mike Nichols, it starred Richard Burton and Elizabeth Taylor as a violently warring husband and wife. Hailed as one of the most scathingly honest American films ever made, it secured Taylor an Academy Award. In a few years' time, Shirley Douglas would undertake the powerful portrayal of Martha in a Canadian stage version of the play, something that in turn would have a profound effect on her young son Kiefer, who made his entrance into the world in London on 21 December 1966 at St Mary's Hospital, Paddington. Seven minutes later, his twin sister Rachel followed.

Blond, with one blue and one green eye, Kiefer was a striking baby. He was given one of the longest names in showbiz – Kiefer William Frederick Dempsey George Rufus Sutherland. Regularly ribbed about this, as well as with the jest that Donald Sutherland had pledged to name his first-born after everyone he owed money to, years later Kiefer explained: 'I know my first name came from Warren Kiefer who directed my father's first film. Dempsey is my grandmother's maiden name. George was a friend of my father's and Frederick was my father's father, but William and Rufus? No one's ever told me where those came from.'

It was Rachel who inherited her father's towering height, while Kiefer reached 5'11". Their dainty mother recently recalled of her youngest pair: 'They've been very close. Although people get older, there's a sameness in their behaviour towards each other, whether it's the fight or the real affection – it's always there.' Kiefer particularly valued his mother's attitude towards himself and his twin. 'She made a point of allowing us to be different,' he said. 'She didn't get into that cutie thing of us wearing the same outfits. We had a strong sense of our own identities.'

In 1967, soon after Kiefer and Rachel were born, the Sutherland family, including Shirley's son Tom, moved to Los Angeles, California, as Donald's career was about to flourish. It was here that the young mother became embroiled in the vocal opposition to the Vietnam War, and began to champion the causes of the underprivileged – she is her firebrand father's passionately socialist daughter to the core.

That same year, Donald Sutherland shared the silver screen with Lee Marvin, Charles Bronson, George Kennedy and Telly Savalas, playing a mindless killer in the Robert Aldrich movie, *The Dirty Dozen*. Although these were the foothills of a long and distinguished career, his workload rapidly mushroomed, with roles in seven films in the next 18 months. Donald, therefore, had limited time to spend with his wife and children, but he vividly remembers one day at home when his growing young son was trying to attract his attention. Said Donald: 'When Kiefer was two, he ran in circles and hit his head against the wall. I told him to stop, but he said he was trying to make me laugh.'

Come 1969, the Sutherland family found very little cause for levity. First, while Donald was on location in Yugoslavia with Clint Eastwood and Telly Savalas, shooting the action war film, *Kelly's Heroes*, he fell seriously ill with spinal meningitis. He was flown to hospital in London, where Shirley joined him, to help nurse him through this health scare. Later that year, the Sutherlands' political views attracted trouble. Lyndon B Johnson's policy of military escalation in Vietnam proved to be his political undoing, and with his popularity at rock bottom in 1968, he decided not to run for re-election to the presidency. His successor in the

White House was 55-year-old Republican, Richard M Nixon. Nixon's tenure eventually saw the end of Americans fighting in Vietnam, but right then America was still a tinderbox. Indeed, simmering grievances over a wide range of emotive issues had created a cauldron of discontent that was ready to spill over into anarchy.

Prominent among the rising chorus of protesters, speaking out for the needy, the oppressed and against the war, was Shirley Douglas. She became involved in a scheme to provide food for poor children, but it transpired that somewhere far along the line the scheme was affiliated to a radical African-American group called The Black Panthers. All Shirley's efforts were channelled into purely peaceful humanitarian work, and she had no involvement with violence or with terrorist activity of any kind, but the authorities were jittery about anyone they suspected of being influential and potentially subversive, and in the early hours of 2 October 1969, around 70 heavily armed police officers stormed the Sutherlands' Beverly Hills home.

Kiefer and Rachel were just two years old, and their half-brother Tom nine, when this alarming raid on their home occurred. During the drama, furniture was upended and ripped open, cabinets and drawers were emptied out indiscriminately on to the floors as rooms were noisily ransacked. As the grim-faced, gun-toting policemen swarmed through the house, the occupants were kept corralled together in one spot in their nightclothes, wide-eyed and bewildered. Speaking of that dramatic dawn raid Shirley Douglas has revealed: 'Someone had told them that something fantastic was taking place and also, obviously, they were fearful that there was a great group of armed people in the house, but after a while they found out that there was me and three children and a housekeeper.' Shirley was cleared of all charges but it must have been a terrifying experience for everyone.

Although not guilty of any crime, Shirley was blacklisted in

America because of her passionate protesting, and Donald only became more prominent in voicing anti-Vietnam War sentiments. At the time Kiefer was too young to grasp what was behind the police raid, but he grew up respecting the stance his parents took. He defended: 'They're very passionate in their beliefs. Everybody in my family has followed an impulse they've felt. They're very rich in ideals, but they also follow through.' Sadly, the personal commitment Shirley and Donald had made to one another three years earlier was coming unglued, and their marriage began to dissolve. Kiefer's parents separated in 1970 and divorced a year later. Donald's colossal work commitments certainly bore some of the blame for the marriage break-up, and 1970 was indeed the year his stock rocketed, when he starred as Captain Benjamin Franklin 'Hawkeye' Pierce in *M*A*S*H*, the Robert Altman film centred around surgeons at a mobile field hospital in Korea, that became a worldwide smash.

It was an ensemble piece, also starring Elliott Gould, Robert Duvall and Tom Skerritt but it was Donald who stole the show as the iconoclastic surgeon 'Hawkeye', wearing glasses and a fishing bucket hat throughout. This role finally gained him professional respect and credibility, and made him much in demand as a leading man, albeit an unconventional one. First *Klute*, and then *Don't Look Now*, in which Donald and his leading lady, Julie Christie, enacted one of the most near-the-knuckle love scenes ever depicted in a non-porno movie, added further momentum to his runaway success. Kiefer was just three when his parents parted, but it was not a traumatic wrench for him because frankly he had no sustained conscious awareness of his parents being together. To his credit, Kiefer has never used his successful father leaving the nest as some kind of excuse for the destabilising episodes that occurred later in his own life. Instead, the boy developed an inner resilience that came primarily from the influence of his strong-minded, independent mother.

Shirley was now a single mother with three children – ten-year-old Tom, and twins not yet school age – whom she went on to raise in the southern flats of Beverly Hills. With her difficulty in getting a work permit, it was tough going, but she kept her children happy and on an even keel. When Kiefer was five, he started violin lessons and took up ice hockey, which became a passion. He was inquisitive and quick to learn. He later reflected: 'Parents of the sixties generation were very astute in knowing that the more you can expose a young person to, the better chance they have at learning a wide variety of things.'

It is inexplicably eerie, but although Kiefer was not raised with his father around him, he developed mannerisms and an indefinable air that is redolent of Donald. Even their speech patterns would prove to be remarkably similar. Sutherland senior's voice is one of his distinctive hallmarks. Equally, Kiefer's rich, deep timbre later led him to be dubbed 'The Velvet Whisper', and he is the opposite of vain. As Jack Bauer, Kiefer has never looked better. Yet from a young age, he took a somewhat pessimistic attitude towards his physical attributes. He has confessed candidly: 'I've never liked the way I look from the time I was in grade two when I saw a school photograph and I thought: "Oh god, you better start being funny or something because you're in a lot of trouble!"'

Although Kiefer did not pine for his absent father, in his late teens he would get his first real handle on Donald from watching videos of his films, and he always lapped up stories about him from others. Kiefer later related with relish: 'My father had no money when he first came to the US. He was a hippie. He didn't wear underpants and he had one pair of trousers, a black pair, and he ripped a hole in them but instead of sewing them up, he painted that part of his ass black!' Donald would see his twins whenever he could, and always at Christmas. Kiefer recalled: 'I remember Elliott Gould once bought me cap guns for Christmas. My family does not believe in guns, so Elliott got in trouble for it.'

12

In 1974, a new dimension was added to Kiefer's life. By now, Donald was involved with 27-year-old Quebec-born actress, Francine Racette. They had met on the Saskatoon set of *Alien Thunder*, in which Donald plays a Canadian Mountie. In years to come the couple would marry, after having had three sons, the first of whom, Roeg, was born in 1974. Kiefer accepted another half-brother with unruffled equanimity, but in other respects it was a confusing time for the eight-year-old. Spending quality time with his father was something Kiefer always looked forward to with a cheerful openness, but more often than not he would end the day bewildered. Kiefer revealed: 'As a kid, I knew my dad was really successful because I'd go to baseball games with him and people would ask for his autograph. I knew he was famous, but I didn't know why. I hadn't seen his movies.' Of course, at that age Kiefer wasn't about to show how thrilled he was to see the attention his father generated. 'I'd pretend it was embarrassing,' he admitted, 'but really, it was pretty cool!'

The touchstone to these heady experiences came both at home and on summer holidays, which Kiefer spent with his maternal grandparents, Tommy and Irma Douglas, in Ottawa, Canada. Although 70, Tommy Douglas had only stepped down from leading the New Democratic Party three years earlier, and he remained an influential MP until the end of the 1970s. Tommy's fiercely socialist principles were ingrained in his daughter, who in turn raised all her children with these same passionate ideals, and today Kiefer holds those principles dear. He has declared: 'It's my perception of what is common sense. If in a group of ten, one person has $9 and the others are splitting dimes, there's going to be a level of contempt towards the person holding $9.'

In 2002, Kiefer was out on the protest marches to try to preserve Medicare. He told reporters: 'My grandfather, Tommy Douglas, implemented a socialised health care system that was then adopted on a federal level, and I have a belief that we're responsible for helping each other.' Kiefer's ingrained maturity helped him cope with the usual trials and tribulations of growing up. At school he often got picked on because of his uncommon first name. 'When I was in fourth grade the older boys used to call me *"Reeeffeer!"* which was embarrassing,' he said. 'I didn't even know what they were talking about.'

Not much about school appealed to Kiefer. He was a boy whose unconventional home life rubbed off on him. His mother tenaciously chased and secured as much theatre work as she could. Kiefer recalled: 'We'd get carted off to whatever town she was working in and we'd have to do our homework in the dressing room, but it was amazing and inspirational.' Occasionally, Kiefer would visit his father on glamorous, bustling movie sets. Against this, he also saw the contrasting reality of theatres run on a shoestring. The acting fraternity itself, though, is a close one, and in his mother's professional world Kiefer, Rachel and Tom were enveloped in a friendly community, what Kiefer called a 'wonderful village'. Listening backstage to the thunderous applause that Shirley and the rest of the cast elicited was a rush for the young, thoughtful boy, but his mother had also drilled into him how fortunate she was to have work at all. 'Children are shaped by what's around them,' said Kiefer. 'So I was more aware of my mother's career than my dad's.'

Just before Christmas 1975, Kiefer turned nine, by which time it had become commonplace at home for him to join his mother and half-brother in reading scripts. Fifteen-year-old Tom was eyeing up the chances of an acting career, so it was a natural progression when Kiefer began doing acting workshops at school and getting his feet wet in amateur productions. He didn't hang around, either, and soon wanted to taste bigger stuff. At nine he made his stage debut at the Odyssey Theatre in Los Angeles with a role in the Warsaw ghetto story, *Throne of Straw*.

Despite Kiefer's lack of confidence in his looks, in truth he was an attractive lad with a developing bad-boy grin, and the light of his vivid personality shone from keen, curious, unusual eyes. It was early days, but Shirley saw more in Kiefer than just a precocious comfort with the limelight. She watched him closely in *Throne of Straw*, and later opined: 'It's a funny thing, talent. It's either there or it isn't, and when Kiefer did that play I knew, if he ever wanted to be actor, he could be.'

CHAPTER 2

KICKING OVER THE TRACES

BY THE TIME KIEFER was ten, he and his family had upsticked from Los Angeles and moved their home base to Toronto in Canada. Situated on the banks of Lake Ontario, the upbeat, cosmopolitan city spreads out on a grid around the Don and the Humber rivers. Although Kiefer initially took a little time to adjust, he came to adore the heaving metropolis and the country as a whole. Though British-born, Kiefer will proudly declare: 'I have a Canadian passport. I am very much a Canadian.'

At the outset of their new life away from America, the family lived in somewhat straitened circumstances. Forty-three-year-old Shirley had to integrate into a whole new acting sphere, in an already dog-eat-dog business. Culturally a rich city, Toronto was certainly teeming with theatres, but it would still take time to make her mark; until then, tightening the family belt was essential. It would later puzzle people to learn that Kiefer's family had had to struggle financially, given that in the mid-1970s Donald Sutherland was an internationally recognised Hollywood star. He had lately made his mark in the John Sturges-directed World War II spy melodrama, *The Eagle Has Landed*. Perhaps sensitive to an implied slight on his father, or maybe just determined to be even-handed, Kiefer combated such curiosity by saying: 'Maybe, he'd offered my mother an absolute fortune and she didn't want it. I do know that my brother and sister and I grew up on the first housing project in Canada and didn't have any money. For the longest time, we didn't have a couch so we sat on the floor.'

With the force of his mother's personality, though, it did not take her long to secure regular work and to accumulate a new, flamboyant circle of friends. Mixing so much with middle-aged actors meant there were social aspects of growing up that Kiefer later felt he had missed out on, but there were also definite benefits, and he would not have traded the way he was raised for anything. Being so much in adult company perhaps accounts for why, from a young age, Kiefer had a strange maturity and wisdom. At the same time he was always in a hyper hurry to grow up, to appear to others to be older than he was, and not just for the usual adolescent reasons. He certainly continued to cope with his father having embedded himself firmly in a new life, with a new partner. In 1978 another half-brother, Rossif, arrived and was followed the next year by Angus. Donald would have four sons and a daughter, and he and Francine always made Kiefer very welcome when his eldest boy came to visit.

Back in Toronto, by 1979 the family finances had so improved due to Shirley's hard endeavour that she was able to send Kiefer and Rachel to boarding school. With the itinerant nature of her working world she aimed to embed better stability in the twins' lives, but where Rachel welcomed this development, Kiefer remained utterly underwhelmed by school. There are 13 grades in the Canadian education system, taking pupils to 19 years old, and he had lately realised that he was not even midway through his school life. He recalled thinking that he couldn't contemplate another seven long dreary years of school – that he had better start looking for a way out.

So, in 1979 it was with a heavy step that, along with his

sister, 12-year-old Kiefer showed up for his first day at St Andrew's College in Aurora, near Toronto, where he was destined to leave his mark. Kiefer spent two years at this prestigious school, years that were watermarked by rebellious behaviour. He had expected to hate everything about being there, since academic study largely missed the spot with him, but in fact he found an intense love of English. 'I had a Jesuit priest English professor and he taught me to enjoy reading and made me feel very confident in my understanding of the material,' he said. For a future actor, this was invaluable.

Despite Kiefer's general disdain for school, at times life did not seem so arduous at St Andrew's College. On occasions, pupils were given the option of going on outward bound excursions or kicking back, taking it easy in their dorms. Rachel always opted for the field trips; the less energetic Kiefer loved a nap instead. As a Scots-Canadian college, St Andrew's expects its pupils to wear a kilt to chapel every Sunday and on special occasions. Kiefer took to the Highland traditional dress with gusto, regardless of the inherent dangers in windy weather of wearing the kilt like a true Scotsman. He recalled: 'One hot summer parade when a student passed out, the wind blew his kilt up to reveal all. It was quite a concern and a little embarrassing.'

Yet although Kiefer found certain aspects of life at St Andrew's surprisingly tolerable, he was developing into too colourful a character to fit into any institution. With a growing independent streak, he also had an irrepressible spirit that was forever ready to lead him astray. He had an entrepreneurial sense, and would turn a buck wherever he could, and his passionate personality could make him somewhat quick tempered. Over the years, he got into several fistfights; he was 12 the first time he came to blows with someone. It was prompted by his protectiveness towards his twin. Kiefer found Rachel being hassled in the school playground by an older boy. Warning the bully to leave his sister alone, and steering Rachel away, he turned his back on the pupil. The teenager promptly jumped on Kiefer from behind, startling the living daylights out of him. Kiefer reacted instinctively. He recalled: 'I reached over and grabbed him, got him in a headlock and kneed him. I fractured his cheekbone.' Kiefer would later create a screen image playing tough, ruthless characters, but in real life physical fighting never exhilarated him. Right then, it was a combination of panic and fear that produced such an effective response, but injuring this boy made Kiefer feel sick. At the same time, he quickly registered that, on that performance, word had swept through St Andrew's bullyboys – don't mess with Kiefer Sutherland!

Between squandering his academic intelligence and engaging in rascally rough-and-tumble behaviour, Kiefer's school reports made animated reading. His mother recalled of these periodic reports: 'They'd say: "It's been many years since we had a boy who showed so much leadership, but it's leading him in all the wrong directions!"' One direction Kiefer was happy to head for was rock music. Tom, his 18-year-old stepbrother, had a record collection that was turning him on to guitar-led hard rock bands like Led Zeppelin and Deep Purple. It is a love that has remained constant throughout Kiefer's life. He admitted: 'I'm a huge fan of Canadian rock. When I was growing up, Rush came out with a record called *Hemispheres* and I must have listened to that album for two years straight. Even when I was asleep, I had it on.' Rachel, who would go on to work in television post-production, declared: 'We never felt any pressure to become actors. In fact, Kiefer wanted to be a rock star.'

To that end, Kiefer plagued his mother to let him learn to play guitar. Shirley was keen for him to continue learning the violin, but eventually she gave in and bought him a classical guitar. A nylon-stringed acoustic wasn't quite what the lad had in mind, but he found a way round things. When his mother paid for him to have classical guitar lessons, he promptly sought people who could show him how to transpose those lessons to let him play lead rock guitar. Around this time, Kiefer was much struck by David Bowie's chameleon-like image, and a personal sense of style was seeping in. Acting, too, was about to impinge on his consciousness in a stronger way. He had been around the greasepaint, stages and props all his life, but always viewed from back of house. That was about to change. Said Kiefer: 'One year the school's theatre department put on *Anything Goes* and me and the guys in my class went to laugh at it, but it was really good. I was amazed.'

What truly knocked Kiefer out was a year later, at 13, seeing his mother let rip as Martha in Edward Albee's dramatic play, *Who's Afraid of Virginia Woolf?* Directed by Neil Munro, this production was staged at the National Arts Centre in Ottawa. Shirley became part of the permanent company at the NAC, where she was renowned for vivid portrayals of passionate and formidable women. Shocking in its day, Martha was a searingly emotional role in which Kiefer's mother triumphed on stage. At curtain up that first night in 1980 at the National Arts Centre, Kiefer sat hunkered down in the cheap seats with his eyes peeled. 'It was the first time I remember watching her come out on stage,' he recalled. 'I thought: Wow! That's my mom! This was the first thing I had seen either of my parents in. I couldn't see my father's films, because they were age restricted and we didn't have videos or DVDs back then.'

Kiefer was riveted. When she walked on stage and when she took her bow at the end, she was Shirley Douglas, his resourceful, strong-minded, familiar mother. What happened in between staggered the teenager. A metamorphosis took place somewhere near the end of act one, and by act two Kiefer was carried away. Looking back, he explained: 'I sat in the audience and watched this other character very slowly take over and by the end of the play I wasn't even aware of the fact that she was my mother anymore. That had a very profound effect.' Muttering on the night: 'Holy shit! How did she do that?' Kiefer sat in the empty, litter-strewn auditorium for a long time afterwards, alone with his thoughts. When he performed on stage, aged nine, in *Throne of Straw* at the Odyssey Theatre in Los Angeles, he had a strong sense that he would enjoy acting. It had given him a bigger buzz than any other experience he'd had at that time. Four years on, seeing his mother give an acting master class on the boards, it was as if a light bulb had been switched on inside his head, and in that moment he knew he wanted to be an actor.

Far from this invigorating Kiefer, however, it worried him. He felt it was complicated because his parents were such good actors, and his father so famous. 'I was too embarrassed to tell them this was what I wanted to do,' he confessed. He felt unable to tell anyone, and so kept it his burning secret ambition for the next two years. Instead, Kiefer channelled his energies elsewhere. A highly competitive streak made him a thrilling ice hockey player, and he learned to ski, but his rebelliousness reared its head from time to time as he continued to become embroiled in bouts of fisticuffs, and school was a rolling disaster. 'I was 14 years old and thought I was wicked cool,' said Kiefer. 'When they told me I couldn't have an earring, I chopped the stud off and left the pipe in, and when they told me to get a haircut, I shaved my head.' He has freely admitted to having been disruptive at St Andrew's College.

Having to smother his acting ambitions made room for his love of music to take stronger hold. He pawned a couple of Christmas presents he didn't care for, and with the cash dashed out and bought a Gibson Sonex electric guitar, of which he was immensely proud. He couldn't play it as well as he would like, but he treasured it. 'It was as light as a potato chip,' remembered Kiefer. 'It was almost like a Les Paul but with some very weird kind of body material and two double-coil pickups.' Years later, Kiefer would set up Ironworks, a recording studio to help budding musicians and music is extremely important to him. 'It really dictates a lot about my life, how I view things and feel things,' he has revealed. 'My whole mood or sense can change by virtue of the music that I'm listening to. It really does affect me on a visceral and emotional level.'

Around this time, Kiefer was especially emotionally close to his family. Tom Douglas was already an actor working in theatre, and occasionally Kiefer picked up a role alongside him. He never got the chance to be nervous of fluffing his lines, because his mother would make sure that he knew each role backwards before arriving at the stage door. Kiefer was also developing a clear physical resemblance to his father. He had indisputably inherited Donald's long thin sculpted mouth, the upper lip prominently dipping in the centre, and the sweeping, well defined jaw line. They also unwittingly shared an increasing number of mannerisms, even down to a certain way each has of propping his head in his hand. Kiefer has called it 'an aspect of DNA I find really spooky.'

What came as no surprise to all concerned was that, after two eventful years, Kiefer's days at St Andrew's College were numbered. His exuberant individuality and his distinct lack of willingness to knuckle down to anything remotely like the full breadth of studies, all compelled the school to ask Kiefer to leave. He had actually liked St Andrew's College, and in hindsight knew that he had screwed up. It's something he holds his hands up to: 'I was a horrible student, really awful.' According to Kiefer, not maintaining his grades was the catalyst for his ejection, but he admits that his expulsion was entirely his own fault. The disruptiveness that got Kiefer tossed out of St Andrew's College did not abate, however, and he entered a very unsettled period. Frustration that he had blown it at a good school made him even less prepared to toe the line anywhere else. He was enrolled at another boarding school, but didn't show up come Monday morning after spending a weekend with friends in Montreal, and over the next 12 months he went from one school to another in an effort to find the right environment to suit him.

It wasn't all misery, though. In 1982, his perennial passion for the guitar led him to join a succession of amateur rock bands, with names such as Broken Glass and the Crippled Christians. By the early 1980s, Kiefer had been turned on to the Rolling Stones. He liked the perceived machismo of Mick Jagger and Keith Richards, and he was also influenced stylewise by the punk rock movement. The whole edgy attitude look strongly appealed to him. It was a source of some affectionate amusement for Shirley, as Kiefer recalled: 'When I was 15, my mother used to laugh at what I used to wear. The shoes were so pointed and way too small. I used to hobble because I didn't want really long feet and the pants were so tight, you could barely get them round your ankles.' Paying the price of trying to look cool, he would also loiter at the mirror, meticulously applying dark eyeliner to create a dramatic effect that was lost on his family, who ribbed him irreverently. A studded leather belt slung low about his snake hips wasn't quite the expected accessory to go with a flashy white tuxedo jacket with black lapels, but Kiefer said: 'I thought, I was it!'

The Canadian education authorities within a sizeable radius of Toronto thought Kiefer Sutherland was a tough challenge. Shirley had done her best, but she was running out of options. At 16, Kiefer would be legally free to leave school, so they were really in the dying throes of his scholastic career. Still, in summer 1982, a place was found for him at a boarding school near Venta, just outside Ottawa. 'It was a real last resort,' confessed Kiefer. 'My mother said that if I didn't go to that school they might as well send me to the penitentiary and save the taxpayers some dollars.' Kiefer detested this school from day one, and knew he wouldn't even reign long enough to be tossed out – he would abscond. The school term had scarcely begun when, in October, the new boy made his getaway. 'Once I decided to take off, they'd have had to put me in jail to stop me,' he recalled.

Kiefer told no one of his plans. With practically only the

clothes he stood up in, he simply vanished from the school dormitory as his fellow pupils snored. As he boarded a deserted night train for Toronto, he was both exhilarated and terrified. 'When I got there I had maybe $46 or something frightening like that,' he recalled. 'The train station in Toronto is massive, like Grand Central Station. That morning it was glorious, it was empty. I remember walking out of the station seeing the pigeons take off and thinking: "This is the first day of the rest of my life."' Kiefer said he felt like the Sylvester Stallone screen character, Rocky, when he runs to the top of some steps in Philadelphia and jumps for joy, but in Kiefer's case the liberating sensation was quickly tempered by the desperate reality of his situation. His paltry few dollars would not stretch very far, and he had to be careful whom he contacted in Toronto, since his parents were in the dark about this latest escapade. He had two months to go before his 16th birthday, a landmark he saw as his emancipation. The problems of where to live, to sleep, how to afford to eat and how to keep clean and stay safe suddenly all crowded in on him.

Kiefer wasn't exactly a look-before-you-leap kind of guy. Indeed, this sort of headstrong behaviour is very much a cornerstone of his stubborn nature, but it is also a strength that has stood him in good stead, for he has had to work hard for his achievements. One long-standing friend, Jude Cole, who became Kiefer's business partner years later in the Ironworks venture, is adamant: 'One of the biggest misconceptions about Kiefer is that he ever got anything easy in life. He has done it on his own, every step of the way.' In the initial days, as a 15-year-old alone in a big city, Kiefer lived like a refugee. A couple of friends persuaded him to sleep over for the night at their family homes, but Kiefer was conscious of not wanting to impose, and so was reduced to kipping down under bridges or on park benches. He knew that living rough was not going to advance him in life, and besides, he hadn't escaped from school to dwindle into a mindless aimlessness. If he had to, he was ready to try to cut it on his own, but to have the best chance of gaining his feet he knew he would have to ask his parents for help. Making contact with them in the circumstances, though, was pretty daunting.

Tough guys roles or not, in his thirties Kiefer candidly confessed that his diminutive mother is the only person he is scared of. So, at half that age, it took him more than a couple of weeks to summon the courage to pick up the telephone. By this time, between stretched nerves, the perishing winter cold and pernicious hunger, he was rather prickly – not so much in the mood to take any lectures, as ready to issue an edict of his own. He knew what he wanted – to break into acting – and he presented his case by payphone separately to both parents. Shirley and Donald were angry, but worried out of their minds that Kiefer had run away from school into the night that way; both were grateful when he finally made contact, even if he would not at this stage divulge his whereabouts.

Kiefer recalled: 'I told them I would make them a deal. Either I could be gone for months until I was sixteen and legally an adult, or we could work something out.' Another boarding school was out as far as Kiefer was concerned. 'I said: "I guarantee that there is nowhere you can put me that I can't get out of." My father agreed right away, but my mother was like: "You are so dead when I find you!"' Kiefer's defiant stand paid off. Neither Shirley Douglas nor Donald Sutherland was cut from conventional cloth, and a compromise was quickly floated. Kiefer was relieved. 'Everyone in my life made decisions for themselves,' he defended. 'I ended up feeling, well now *I'm* making a decision for myself and you have to respect that, and they did.'

Donald offered to fly Kiefer down to Los Angeles for a talk. Confronted with how committed to his plan Kiefer was, between the three of them they thrashed out a way forward. Kiefer agreed to go to a regular school in Toronto and knuckle down. The trade-off was that his parents would let him try to get an agent and do auditions for, say, theatre work at first – anything, so long as he could enter the shallows of acting seriously. 'My parents weren't exactly pleased by my decision to act but I think my mother was so sure I was going to spend a large part of my life in prison that by this time she was relieved. I put that poor woman through a lot of trouble,' he confessed.

With his life beginning to take the shape he envisaged, Kiefer calmed down a great deal. He returned to Toronto. Donald gave him a $400 monthly allowance to help him get by, but it was years before Kiefer found out that his mother was actually responsible for him finding an acting agent so quickly. Although Kiefer re-enrolled at school, he couldn't wait to leave, and has since owned up to having few regrets about squandering those years. 'I think the thing I missed most was the emotional development, but I got a street education and as far as communicating with people, I picked that up quicker than most college graduates,' he said.

What Kiefer actively thrived on was throwing himself into Toronto's vivid entertainment scene. There were so many lively districts to choose from. He particularly fell in love with an area called the Annex, which he likens to New York's Greenwich Village, in that writers, musicians and artists frequent it. Then there is the Danforth, jam-packed with Greek restaurants, colourful bars and bustling dance halls. He learned to play billiards at the Silver Cue in Danforth. Still keen on playing in a rock band, Kiefer couldn't keep away from Queen Street West, where live bands playing everything from reggae to rock blasted well into the night. He haunted the vicinity of the El Mocambo bar, since he'd heard that the Rolling Stones had once played an impromptu gig there. It wasn't that easy to gatecrash bars in those days, and he could hardly wait to come of age to get in. Another of Toronto's favourite leisure attractions is a recreation area called Ontario Place. 'It has a beautiful amphitheatre. I kissed my first girl at Ontario Place,' recalled Kiefer.

Kiefer would go on to have a turbulent love life, and as part of his need to feel older than he was, he tried to make commitments before he was emotionally ready for them, but in his mid teens he was a footloose, red-blooded live wire who was hugely attractive to the opposite sex. Standing just short of six foot tall, and built along lean, athletic lines, with luxuriantly thick blond hair, Kiefer was handsome in an interesting way. His unruly smile could exude mischief or menace, and by now his unique, deep, velvety voice meant that you'd know him in the dark! Cheekily charismatic, his personality was already one of depth and complexity; although well capable of defending himself, he also possessed a strong core of gentle sensitivity. He was the kind of guy that girls were intrinsically drawn to.

Right then, girls were just a part of the tapestry of Kiefer's busy life. Music and acting were his main magnets, and Toronto's theatre land was to him the most vibrant place on earth. He said: 'There were nationally funded theatres and a lot of talent. You just knew that this was the place to be.' He dreamt of one day treading the boards at the hallowed Royal Alexander Theatre, and in the meantime landed a variety of roles in productions staged at the likes of the (now defunct) Bayview Playhouse.

Kiefer once said: 'My ambition was fuelled by fantasy rather than reality, and I got lucky.' Undoubtedly, every artiste needs a slice of luck, but to the discerning eye Kiefer Sutherland was a young, eager actor with far more than just burning enthusiasm. On stage, it was not so much his delivery of the well-rehearsed lines, but the way in which he listened closely to the other actors, tuning in to every nuance around him. This heightened and sharpened his responses, which in turn breathed increased life into his own portrayal.

The fertile hotbed of acting opportunities in Toronto gave Kiefer the scope to grow in these crucial stages, developing as a budding actor in a way that would have been more difficult had he been in the glare of Los Angeles's acting community, where he would have fallen under merciless scrutiny to see if he measured up as Donald Sutherland's son. In recent years, Donald had racked up more memorable performances in films such as the thriller, *Eye of the Needle*, and the highly emotive Robert Redford-directed drama, *Ordinary People*, for which he had been nominated for a best actor Golden Globe award.

That said, Kiefer was not shy about trying to follow in his parents' footsteps. On the contrary, the white-hot flame of his ambition was fed by looking back at the examples set by his mother and father, neither of whom had got a shoo-in to the business. With unvarnished pride, Kiefer declared: 'I've had some amazing people in my life. Look at my father. He came from a small fishing village of 500 people and at 6'4" with giant ears and a very odd expression, thought he could be a movie star. That he had the effrontery to go to London and pursue that dream? That's the amazing thing!' Kiefer adored Toronto, but his horizons were limitless. He revealed: 'I wanted to be out in the world making a big bang out of life.' His start was just around the corner.

CHAPTER 3

THE DIE IS CAST

DETERMINED TO INCREASE his chances of success, 16-year-old Kiefer enrolled at theatre school – but it wasn't for him. 'I found it really pushy and very self-indulgent,' he recalled. 'They say to you that the way to become a really good actor is to tell them everything about yourself, tell them all your fears and insecurities.' The premise was: lay yourself open to being hurt and see how you cope with it, something Kiefer was terse about. 'That kind of evil theatre crap is really offensive,' he declared. Needless to say, he walked.

Although Kiefer had got his way with his parents, and was free to attempt the tough task of breaking into acting, life was hardly a bed of roses. At Howland and Bloor in Toronto, he rented a one-room basement apartment with an exposed toilet, screened only by a makeshift curtain. In his entire living space there was scarcely room to swing a cat. Every day he would bound out of this apartment, either to his agent or to an audition. Frequently, by the end of the day he would return, sapped of his youthful enthusiasm. Over the next two years Kiefer endured dozens of fruitless auditions, themselves not even easy to secure, and he encountered an extra obstacle in having such a famous father in the business.

He explained: 'Everyone thinks it opened a lot of doors for me, and that's bull. It didn't help. Some producers would think it was too gimmicky, casting someone with a famous last name. Then there was the dimension of me looking like my father and that would tend to intrude. So in a way, being a Sutherland was a curse.'

This was not the beginning of Kiefer developing a chip on his shoulder. He is immensely proud of his family. It was also actively useful to have an inside track on how bruising a world acting is. He was less prone to be left shattered. In a sense, the size of the challenge was more likely to light him up. Speaking of the upside of having famous parents, he declared: 'The main benefit was that I learned early that it is hard to accomplish anything unless you believe in what you're going for. I learned that through my father on a very intimate level.' Kiefer never lacked intrinsic self-belief. He did lack money, however, and to keep the wolf from the door he got himself a day job, which, though hardly stimulating, had its perks. 'I was a short order cook in a restaurant,' he revealed. 'The guy I worked with was really good looking so at lunchtime the line up of girls was gigantic. I loved working with him.'

Kiefer's own looks meant that he wasn't relying on any second-hand attention from his friend's cast-offs, but with his vibrant personality he was also ripe for more than larking around with girls. One of the reasons he was later so convincing in certain screen roles, was that he hadn't had a pampered, silver-spoon-in-the-mouth upbringing. First in Los Angeles and now Toronto, he was rapidly learning the ropes at street level, even if he was still naive in some respects. Talking of the first time he was tempted to sample drugs, he admitted: 'I was with a guy. We were sixteen and in downtown Toronto trying to buy pot – unsuccessfully.' Kiefer knew his biggest buzz would be landing his first screen appearance, an excitement that was just around the corner, courtesy of his father. Since his 1964 screen debut, Donald

Sutherland had by now appeared in over 50 films. Well respected and well liked in the film industry, when he was making his latest movie, the 1983 Neil Simon-written sentimental comedy, *Max Dugan Returns*, Donald managed to get Kiefer a very small walk-on part, playing a character called Bill. *Leonard Maltin's Film Guide* described *Max Dugan Returns* as 'acted with verve and sincerity by a perfect cast.' Kiefer's part in it may have been minuscule but it still nourished him and had him firing on all cylinders again.

Kiefer had already learned that in acting it is possible to tell if you are trying to squeeze too much out of a scene. Likewise, that it is impossible to feel it if you are not wholly engaged with what's going on. Whether his father proffered any advice on acting seems to be unclear. Kiefer has recalled: 'He's never given me specifics. He's never said, this is something you should do or watch out for but I've learned a great deal from watching his work.' Donald himself recently maintained: 'The only piece of advice I ever gave Kiefer, and even then I wondered whether I should be giving it to him, was: The joy of this business is to look for the truth of the character, or the film, or whatever the director is looking to achieve, to see if you can find truthful information that will help him clarify that.'

Donald's reluctance to weigh in with pearls of wisdom lay not in any lack of interest in his eldest son's career, as Kiefer knew. He said of his father: 'He was so respectful of me when I first started. He really wanted to give me a clear gate to work out of and I'm very grateful, and yet I always knew he was there for support if I needed it.' Kiefer's view on nepotism is that it can only take a person to the point of being offered a shot at seeing what they are made of, that cronyism will never get someone a job, and that was true of his own experience. Donald had used goodwill to secure Kiefer his screen debut in *Max Dugan Returns*, but it was down to Kiefer alone that he beat off all competition to be cast in his first lead role in a feature film at just 16 years old. The film was *The Bay Boy*. Written and directed by Daniel Petrie, and set in a Nova Scotia mining town during the mid-1930s Depression, it was partly autobiographical. The lead role was that of Donald Campbell, a Roman Catholic teenager who, already conflicted over plans to go into the priesthood (a vocation favoured for him by his doting mother), witnesses the brutal murder of an elderly couple by a police sergeant who happens to be the father of his girlfriend. Liv Ullmann, Peter Donat and Alan Scarfe formed the core of the older cast. The lead part of 16-year-old Campbell was an attractive opportunity for any young actor in Canada, and Kiefer badly wanted this coming-of-age role.

Following on his initial audition, Kiefer was recalled a further three times before the final decision was made to offer him the lead in *The Bay Boy*. Director Daniel Petrie later reflected: 'Kiefer read for the part and won it. I had misgivings that night, thinking maybe there's just this wonderful dark side to him and he won't be able to play the comic lines. So I brought him back in and gave him all the funny lines and he was delicious. The kid had a haunting quality.'

Kiefer could not contain his joy at the news that he had landed the role. He was so thrilled, he was metaphorically bouncing off the walls inside his cramped basement apartment, so he bolted out up to street level where he literally jumped up and down with delight, too happy to care about the odd looks he drew from passing pedestrians. His excitement had not abated when he joined the cast and crew at the film's shooting location in Glace Bay, Nova Scotia. 'I'll never forget checking into the Holiday Inn,' he recalled. 'I was sixteen, unpacking my stuff and I caught myself walking by the mirror and I went: "I've done it!"'

That first evening the cast ate out at a Chinese restaurant, and fortune cookies were presented at the end of the meal. When Kiefer opened his, the printed message read: 'Go home'. To the superstitious, it might have seemed a depressingly mystic sign. Kiefer ignored it, and geared himself up for the task before him. With only a brief walk-on film role under his belt, it was a big ask to step seamlessly into the main lead in a feature movie, and reality hit Kiefer quickly. He admitted: 'The second day I had a long church confession scene that we had to do twenty-three times. That's when you start to sweat and you can't sit still. I wanted to cry.' Kiefer would acquire a reputation for possessing a strong work ethic, and that dedication started to show itself during this first lead role. Swiftly quelling such weakness, he had extra rehearsal periods added on to his already 12 hours a day work schedule.

Kiefer would never be a method actor, and from the outset held definite views on his chosen craft. 'I'm not that complicated as an actor,' he maintained. 'I have a formula in which I work, yeah, but I don't believe you can ever be someone else. You manifest different levels of your own personality to come up with a character.' His acting experience to date had been on stage, projecting to a live audience. Film work was entirely different, full of interruptions that broke the creative flow. As far as craft goes, on film and television some actors maintain that they do not always have to actually act; that it is enough to concentrate really hard on what they are thinking about and the camera will pick it up. Kiefer's approach, even so early, was to psych himself into truly believing in what he was doing on set and committing to it, even if it felt vaguely uncomfortable, and the result was that the camera could interrogate him severely with safety. There would be no chinks.

Fears of being weighted down by an expectation that he measure up to his parents' professional abilities didn't materialise on this film set. Daniel Petrie said of his young leading man: 'From the start, Kiefer asserted his personality. He is his own man as an actor.' Kiefer also proved popular with his fellow cast members. Liv Ullmann had been prepared to mother the new kid fresh off the bus, but found that off set Kiefer had a curiously indefinable air that gave him a surprising maturity beyond his years. That he was never late on set, never complained, and appeared indefatigable, also delighted the crew who, half way through the shoot, invited Donald Sutherland to visit the location to see his son in action. Donald politely declined the offer. Said Kiefer: 'He thought, this was my turn. I'd earned the spot, so I should have the light.'

When *The Bay Boy* was released in autumn 1984, it was not a commercial success. 'It was good stuff, a great cast,' recalled Kiefer. 'Nobody really saw it, but the reviews were raves and people in the movie industry were impressed.' So impressed were they, that *The Bay Boy* received nominations in 11 categories of the Genie Awards – Canada's equivalent of America's Academy Awards – and won six trophies. For his first major movie role, Kiefer received a nomination for Best Performance by an Actor in a Leading Role. This accolade lay a bit further down the track. For Kiefer, once filming wrapped in 1983, the most immediate boost was financial. For the lead role in *The Bay Boy* he had picked up a pay cheque for 30,000 Canadian dollars, which worked out at around US$22,000. He had never seen that kind of money before in his life, and quipped that he could retire on it. In fact, it lasted him one year.

Soon after filming *The Bay Boy*, Kiefer decided to spread his wings and leave his beloved Toronto, which he would forever consider to be home. He went to live in New York, where he would suffer his share of shadows. Twenty years later he was blunt: 'New York is the loneliest place I've ever been. I've shot a lot of films there and I am yet to make a single friend in NYC, not even one that's not a bartender! It's the hardest city to get along in for me and I want to love it.' He rented a less than desirable apartment in a tough neighbourhood, and immediately found life hard going. There was one bonus, in that he got to spend some time with his father who, in stark contrast, had a swish apartment in a luxury tower block in Manhattan.

Kiefer's relationship with his father grew ever more

complex, throwing up moments of emotional confusion. 'It was the first time we'd lived in the same city since I was a kid,' he said. 'When I got to know him after I left home, I regretted not having certain things from him on an emotional level when I was growing up, but it's nothing that hasn't worked itself out.' Concentrating on his future, there was no time to be maudlin, and Kiefer bent his mind to making up his resume to send out to New York theatres. He has happily admitted to having been somewhat creative when presenting himself and his capabilities. 'Half of it was bullshit,' he conceded. 'I think lying on your resume is a rite of passage for an actor under twenty.' However, he consciously gave a wide berth to a common pitfall, and did not claim in his c.v. that he had experience of performing in musicals. 'When you start lying about a talent you don't have, you can get yourself in a lot of shit,' he declared.

Despite beefing up reasons why casting directors ought to be snapping up his services, it quickly became apparent that it was even more difficult to find acting work in New York than it had been back home. 'I couldn't get a job to save my life,' said Kiefer, and in 1984 one demoralising experience after another unfolded. Constant disappointment fuelled frustration, which mutated unhelpfully at times, and before arriving at some auditions he would be in a latently explosive mood, especially if it was a day when he went endlessly from one audition straight to another. He revealed: 'By the time I got from point A to point B, I was so hostile. I thought I would have my composure come together in time for the meeting but I guess sometimes I didn't and I got sick of it.' Only years later did he admit that this bruising process went deeper than mere disappointment: 'When I was younger my whole sense of self-worth was based on whether or not I was working, which was awful.'

For a time during his high-school years, his parents had feared that Kiefer could go completely off the rails. Let loose as a young adult in New York, the scope for him to take the wrong path in an uncertain world filled with an as yet unattainable dream, was widened considerably. At 17, there was a noticeably coiled, restless energy about Kiefer that seemed only just contained, giving him a tangible aura of riskiness. He had been a smoker already for a couple of years, and now he acquired a taste for malt whisky. He enjoyed shooting pool in smoky snooker halls, where he still had a propensity to get into fistfights on occasions. He had no inclination to try to hang out in genteel company, but at the other end of the scale he had a habit of frequenting fringes of a nervy, deadly city that were a little too frayed for most people.

He was also a lot more sensitive than he was prepared to show, and one incident that occurred around now left him feeling deeply embarrassed about gaps in his education. He was dating a girl who was a few years his senior, and who often spoke about Truman Capote, the incisive American writer famous for the novel, *Breakfast at Tiffany's*, from which the celebrated 1961 movie was made. Having never heard of Truman Capote, Kiefer assumed the man taught at his girlfriend's college, and said something to that effect one evening at dinner with a group of her friends. Everyone round the table openly laughed at him. Kiefer managed to pass off the moment, but he was acutely aware of his literary ignorance, and within days he got in touch with the English professor he had liked at St Andrew's College in Aurora, Ontario, asking him to suggest a required reading list. Kiefer may have disliked the conformity of school, but he had enjoyed the stimulus of reading – a pastime he would always make space for.

Kiefer also kept in close contact with his mother, who was leading an increasingly hectic life. In addition to racking up roles in theatre, film and television, Shirley's activism continued, and she was a prominent supporter of movements such as Performing Artists for Nuclear Disarmament. Her strong socialist influence had remained ingrained in Kiefer.

When he talked of believing in the principle of people sharing their wealth, he had not been spouting a hollow sentiment, and in 1984 he put his money where his mouth was. That 30,000 Canadian dollars pay day for *The Bay Boy* had helped to keep a roof over his head in New York, but he had also shared his diminishing nest egg. 'It helped me get my girlfriend into the Circle in The Square theatre school,' he said. Making ends meet was a constant trial and so, in addition to working in restaurants, Kiefer put himself forward for certain types of modelling work, and duly landed a Levi jeans advert, the fee for which allowed him to buy a 1966 Mustang car he called 'Lucy', after which he was left with a cashier's cheque for $2,700.

Despite the stream of rejections he had suffered at auditions, his heart was still set on becoming an actor, but as the year drew to a close he came to the conclusion that it was not going to happen for him in New York. It didn't take him long to make up his mind in which direction he had to head. Los Angeles was familiar to him, since he had lived there until he was ten, but it was also obviously where most movies were made. Where hard-bitten New York had been unrelentingly inhospitable, perhaps laidback west coast America might be friendlier. Packing his vintage Mustang with their few possessions, Kiefer and his girlfriend drove across America in search of success and some sustainable cheer. It had been a frugal year dampened by dejection, and anything had to be an improvement on that. Or so he optimistically imagined. He didn't know that on arrival in sunny California, in a land of reputedly boundless opportunity, he would, for the first quarter of the New Year, be rendered utterly destitute.

CHAPTER 4

LOOKING FOR THAT RUSH

KIEFER HAD TRIED IN VAIN to love New York. Los Angeles, at least, was not an unknown quantity to him, but he had only known it as a young child. The kind of quarters he would explore as an 18-year-old would see him straying into far dodgier realms. His first port of call, however, on arriving with his girlfriend in the sprawling city, wearied from a monotonous overnight driving stint, was the tame environ of the College Grill, an old-fashioned cafe with worn-cushioned seating booths, framed prints of Elvis Presley on the painted walls, and ceiling fans that whirred arthritically all day long. 'I never figured out where the college came into it,' remarked Kiefer but, comfortable in the basic surroundings, he would make the College Grill one of his regular haunts over the next few years.

Any warm sense of satisfaction gained from being fed and watered that first day soon evaporated when Kiefer discovered that the $2,700 cashier's cheque he had left over from his Levi jeans advert fee had gone walkabout somewhere between New York and the west coast. 'My girlfriend had lost it,' he recalled, 'so we had no money.' Where he might have been understandably angry at this and daunted by the predicament it put them in, he chose resiliently to view it instead as an exciting adventure. How much his girlfriend shared this enthusiasm may be debatable, but the pair drove from the cafe to the seafront. Said Kiefer: 'I lived in my car for the first three months in Los Angeles. My girlfriend and I slept in the backseat of this '66 Mustang and we stayed down at the beach because they have public showers.' There was a public convenience block in addition to the outdoor showers. 'It was a cold shower but you could run through it, dry off and change.'

Even with eating sparingly, Kiefer's cash soon ran out, and he hustled a buck wherever he could, to avoid them both starving. If it seemed a grim existence, Kiefer has declared that 'it really wasn't that bad.' Excepting those people who were actually raised in Los Angeles, he maintained: 'I don't know an actor who hasn't spent a few nights on the beach. It was a good time. We used to party and have fun.' When this episode in his life later came to light there was intense curiosity as to how the rich and famous Donald Sutherland, or Shirley Douglas, could have stood back and allowed their son to live rough. Kiefer gave the succinct answer to this wave of criticism – his parents did not know that he was in such dire straits, because he didn't tell them. He knew well that one phone call would have brought money winging its way to him, but he was headstrong. He was determined to stand on his own two feet, and that didn't entail just scraping by. He had come to LA to make it as an actor, so from his lowly standpoint at this time he had a fair sized mountain before him. He was adamant, however: 'I had made a conscious decision that whatever I was hoping to do, I was going to do on my own. If anyone was going to end up proud of me, they were going to be proud of me for legitimate reasons.'

From a sheer practical perspective, Kiefer was scarcely well placed to get his acting career off the ground. He was living out of a car, and perennially too broke to afford to travel across Los Angeles to auditions, even if he could secure an agent to get him any. Appearance-wise, he did extremely well to conceal the fact that he was sleeping rough. By spring 1985, the novelty of this existence was wearing thin, and not just for Kiefer, with his dreams. Speaking of how he and his girlfriend would cosy up in the car, kept clean courtesy of the Pacific Ocean, and lived hand-to-mouth, Kiefer once called it 'like living in a Rod Stewart song.' His girlfriend found it increasingly difficult to survive on romanticism, however, and the young couple eventually went their separate ways.

As temperatures rose and the LA beachfront gradually became busier from earlier in the day, Kiefer decided the time had come to stop sleeping in his car. Finding casual work in restaurants, for a spell he rented a succession of rooms in rundown hotels. Other times, he could occasionally be persuaded to accept invitations to stay with friends of his parents. These mini oasis periods of comfort and normal living helped to recharge him and keep him afloat. He still managed to keep it secret from his folks that he was struggling. It was while he was enjoying the hospitality of a staunch friend of the Sutherland family that Kiefer came to a crossroads with regards to his father. 'I wasn't aware of what he'd done,' Kiefer confessed. 'When friends told me he was one of the greatest actors, I'd go: "Yeah, yeah."' There was a VCR at this house, and between what his host had in his personal video collection and renting films, Kiefer went on a two-day binge of watching just some of his father's many movies. Back-to-back he sat glued through *M*A*S*H*, *Klute*, *Kelly's Heroes*, *Don't Look Now*, *The Eagle Has Landed*, *Fellini's Casanova*, *Start the Revolution Without Me*, *The Dirty Dozen*, *Eye of the Needle* and *Ordinary People*. He exclaimed: 'It blew me away!'

It went a lot deeper than simple astonishment. Poignantly, Kiefer owned up: 'Seeing my father on screen made me feel closer to him.' He was bombarded by myriad destabilising emotions. He now felt acutely embarrassed that he had been oblivious of his father's acting talent. It also saddened him intensely to face up to the fact that he really didn't know his own father that well, though this was scarcely his fault. Kiefer revealed: 'I telephoned him to apologise for not realising how truly brilliant he is. He laughed and said: "That's really sweet."'

Kiefer had drunk in every nuance of Donald's acting, especially absorbing the layered subtlety laced into his portrayals of some of the quiet, intense characters he had played to enviable screen effect. Kiefer was reading a lot of Chekhov at the time and, by his own admission, he was going through a very idealistic, highly sensitive phase. That said, watching *Ordinary People* made a profound impact on him, which has remained throughout his life. Adapted by Alvin Sargent from the novel by Judith Guest, *Ordinary People*, released in 1980, depicted the emotional fall-out on a wealthy American family from the sudden death of the elder son. The highly charged tale of reflection and painful recrimination is portrayed mainly from the standpoint of the remaining, guilt-ridden younger son; at the helm, Robert Redford had made his directorial debut. *New Yorker* said of the Oscar-winning film: 'This is an academic exercise in catharsis. It is earnest. It means to improve people and it lasts a lifetime.'

Redford had approached *Ordinary People* feeling an intense affinity with the emotional problems the film dealt with when it came to handling communication between family members. He said: 'I was raised with the Irish-Scots ethic where you dealt with words like grace and honour, and you were measured by how strong you were both physically and your ability not to complain. So, of course, there was built-in restraint to your life. You didn't discuss problems. Therefore, how did anyone know how to deal with them?' Portraying this overwrought, troubled family were Donald Sutherland as the father, Mary Tyler Moore as his screen wife and Timothy Hutton as the suicidal teenage son struggling to come to terms with his brother's death. Donald once said: 'I have played about a hundred guys and I have a huge affection for all of them. So much of myself is invested in them and in the end they ended up liking or hating themselves.' Donald's dramatic performance as Calvin Jarrett earned him a Best Actor Golden Globe nomination. Kiefer was floored by what he saw.

He admitted the extent of the effect Donald's performance had on him. 'I was incredibly moved. To see my father portraying such sensitivity and hurt was inspiring to me. I wanted to phone him up and say: "I realise it's only a film, but I wanted you to know that everything with us is all right and I love you more than anything."' This nakedly personal reaction was brought on by one especially emotive scene between Donald and Timothy Hutton. Said Kiefer: 'They're talking on the porch and it was so beautiful. I remember thinking, I'd like to have a conversation like that one day with my dad. It made me think, I guess I'm partially responsible. I have to instigate conversations too. That film broke my heart.' Over the years, Kiefer has constantly held fast to the memory of that father-son soul-baring session, and although he and Donald have developed a uniquely close relationship, he only recently divulged about the Timothy Hutton role: 'I think to some degree I've always wished that was me.'

The other offshoot of overdosing on Donald Sutherland films was that, in waking up to how skilled an actor his father was, Kiefer had to ask himself if it spooked him at all. He seems to have ambivalent feelings about this. To the question, should he try to measure up to Donald's reputation, his response was, why bother? He has maintained that if he had tried to, he would have been finished. He has massive respect for his father's abilities, but he did not want to model himself on his father or to attempt consciously to emulate him professionally. He has made no secret of the fact, all the same, that he wanted to strive to be as good as his father.

Once over his initial emotional reaction to discovering his dad's screen talent, Kiefer quickly realised that in the past couple of years since his open admission that he wanted to become an actor, being in blissful ignorance of the size of Donald's shadow had actually been a bonus. 'I might have said: "Oh fuck, I could never get close,"' admitted Kiefer. Yet just a few years later he maintained: 'I was probably intimidated by him at first but when I realised that I had talent I saw no reason to think that I could never be as good.'

Come early summer 1985, Kiefer had a sudden spring in his step. Life was taking more of a shape for him in Los Angeles. He was able to sustain a roof over his head, albeit not a highly salubrious one, but he had got himself on to an agent's client list and was eager to be put up for parts. He was so hyped up about one particular audition that on impulse he went calling on his father, who was temporarily in town. Donald would move from Los Angeles to New York, and in time from there to Paris, but for now, rarely, he and Kiefer were in the same city at the same time. Donald recalled: 'Kiefer came to me one night, stood at the end of the bed and said: "Can I do my audition for you?" I was: "Oh dear, oh okay," and he did it and it was brilliant. I was so relieved.' Kiefer went on to say that while that was the way he was expected to perform the set piece, he had other ideas. Donald continued: 'Kiefer asked: "Can I show you how I want to do it?" So, he did it again, completely different. My hair stood up and I knew then he would be okay. He was wonderful!'

Leaving his father's house that night, Kiefer was keyed up, anticipating that his career breakthrough was just around the corner. Already he wanted to set some parameters. He did not want to go the route of some actors – doing commercials, hoping to be spotted – and he wasn't keen on getting his feet wet in television as a stepping-stone to movie work. In the mid-1980s, daytime TV was where a plethora of young, faceless actors ended up, grateful for the regular pay cheque. With the attitude, aim for the top, there's plenty of room, Kiefer had wider horizons, but he had to rethink his take on TV when he was offered the chance to make his US television debut with a role in *Amazing Stories*, a new NBC series created, produced and occasionally to be directed by Steven Spielberg. Since *Jaws*, ten years earlier, practically every major movie Spielberg had helmed had been a colossal success. So his temporary shift to television was a much-heralded affair.

Kiefer was offered one of the lead roles in the episode of *Amazing Stories* titled *The Mission*. He would portray Static, a radio operator on a World War II bomber plane that has been forced to attempt a dramatic emergency landing. Its fate appears to be doomed, short of a miracle. Setting aside his prejudice regarding TV work, Kiefer jumped at the chance, and filmed the extended episode that aired across America on 3 November 1985. Not only did *Amazing Stories: The Mission* give Kiefer his first acting job in Los Angeles, but the benefits he would glean from this role became clear even before the episode aired. As the summer months rolled out and auditions came his way, the moment he could say that he had just filmed a Steven Spielberg project, casting directors visibly sat up and took closer notice of him. This heightened interest translated into work, and soon Kiefer was on a roll, but he still had enough downtime on his hands to get into mischief of one kind or another.

Irrepressibly, Kiefer spoke of being an 18-year-old free agent, loose in Los Angeles. 'I lived on Harvard, just south of Sunset, and I had the greatest time.' Once again, left to his own devices, he prowled the far from glitzy side of Tinseltown. One of his favourite hangouts was Hollywood Billiards, a dingy, cavernous, poorly lit club that was open 24 hours a day. Kiefer was as much attracted by the pool of characters he encountered there, as by playing the tables. He said: 'It was full of all these great old hustlers, guys with names like Drummer and Rags, characters you'd only ever read about or heard about in songs. You could get lost in there, playing pool for ten hours.' When he wasn't cocooned away in this club, Kiefer was up for a lark – innocently and not so innocently. Partying on the beach still appealed to him, even though actually sleeping on the golden sands held its perils, as was proved when a couple of his friends came a near fatal cropper. Kiefer recalled: 'One morning they were fast asleep on the beach when a tractor drove along to rake up the sand and it drove right over them, pressing their heads about three feet into the sand! The guy said it didn't do either of them any serious damage, but they had really bad headaches afterwards.'

What happened to his friends was an accident, but Kiefer courted danger deliberately when he revived a dormant interest in drug taking. After his abortive attempt to buy pot as a 16-year-old in Toronto, he had made another attempt a year later in New York, an episode that had a darker outcome. Kiefer and another teenager had attempted to buy cannabis from an older guy in a shopping mall precinct. Kiefer was inexperienced, but his friend sampled the purchase and decided it wasn't the real deal, that it was catnip. Affronted at blatantly being taken for mugs, Kiefer rejected the stuff and boldly demanded his money back. Kiefer recalled: 'The guy said: "Fuck off, kid!" So I pulled out this switchblade that a friend of mine had given to me, flicked it open and said: "Don't fuck with me. Give me my money back!" – and it worked.'

Well, it would have worked, but never having done anything like this before, Kiefer had had a few drinks prior to attempting the purchase, and instead of keeping grimly quiet, he rambled on aggressively and began to slur his words. That he was both tipsy and nervous showed, and proved to be his and his friend's undoing. As the guy reached into his pocket, Kiefer never saw the power packed punch coming. The next thing he was aware of was waking up on the concrete to find that his friend had been stabbed in the leg. Blood poured from the wound, saturating the guy's jeans. With a rapidly bruising swollen eye, and in agony from the vicious kicking he had taken while lying unconscious, Kiefer helped his limping friend to the subway, where they were terribly self-conscious of their walking wounded appearance. Once at his flat, Kiefer used a ladies' sanitary towel and some hockey tape to bind up his companion's leg. They had been royally beaten up, yet all Kiefer could think of was that he just *had* to learn to punch like that dope dealer. He later excused this unorthodox response by confessing: 'I've always had a very different reaction to such situations.'

Cannabis and Kiefer never proved to be a winning combination. While still in New York, he had made a third and this time successful attempt to get his hands on marijuana. It happened when one evening a girl he had at his flat told him that making love while being high on pot really enhanced the performance. Willing to take her word for it, Kiefer duly hared out of his basement flat to Central Park where, as he put it, he 'picked up a dime bag'. Back at his apartment, he breathlessly rolled a joint, which they shared, and he promptly got completely stoned. He and his girl were on a lumpy settee watching television. Sure enough, in no time at all, Kiefer was passionately kissing and caressing the girl and they rather rapidly got down to it. Despite being stoned, Kiefer would have excruciating recall of how this steamy clinch ended up as not quite the earth-moving experience promised.

For a start, the cannabis made him so unfocused that his mind strayed off in the most mundane of directions. He found himself thinking of anything except having sex. Then something made him suddenly concentrate. He recalled: 'I was moving very quickly and I thought, Oh my god! I'm going to kill this girl. I'd better come, and I did.' Mentally it had all been disjointed and jumbled, but, feeling fabulous now, Kiefer decided that the girl had been right – dope had made it a fantastic experience – until he rolled over and discovered that the TV advert that had commenced when he had got hot and heavy was now just ending. His fantastic experience had lasted all of two minutes! Unsurprisingly, Kiefer vowed that that was it – pot was *not* for him!

Less humorous was the drug Kiefer got into in Los Angeles. This would be his only period taking drugs, and he has frankly admitted to it, telling *Playboy* magazine in 2004: 'I did drugs when I was 18. I liked the ceremony, the ritual of preparing cocaine, as much as doing it. I did it for a year, loved it and then stopped.' Kiefer left all drug taking strictly behind him after that year, but he went on to gain a reputation as a Hollywood wild child, though some of the stories attributed to him were not true. 'I've been said to have been loaded and abusive at parties, when I was actually filming thousands of miles away at the time,' he has pointed out. Kiefer does not deny that he could be boisterous, particularly when he had been drinking, but he was, after all, just a teenager. His penchant for pool halls, bars and nightclubs helped fuel a spicy reputation. He has defended himself: 'Every once in a while I go crazy. So what? It is only once in a while. I'm not like people say I am. I do a lot of stuff just like everyone else, but I'm no crazy guy.'

When Kiefer was living a life that involved rousing drinking sessions, peppered by taking drugs, he made sure that his parents were oblivious of it. What his mother did not know could not upset her, and although Donald would also have worried, he had made it clear to his son that he would be on hand if ever he were needed. Kiefer appreciated the non-intervention. He said: 'I don't like it when people interfere in each others' lives, and my father stayed clear of that.' Kiefer's relationship with the father he was professionally more aware of now continued to be poignant and complex. They both found that not having had a great deal of time together was deeply frustrating, to say the least, and they did make conscious efforts to catch up with each other. Kiefer has commented, though, that even when chances did crop up, for one reason or another they spent much of this precious time meeting in rather impersonal airport lounges.

Going about the business of finding acting work in Los Angeles, Kiefer also had to combat the old chestnut that people imagined that his famous father's name made doors open effortlessly for him. In 1988, Kiefer told *Rolling Stone*: 'All I know is, yes I do have a famous father but I *still* only get projects through a reading. I don't get phoned and asked: "Would you like to do this?"' Working in television was still a path Kiefer wanted to resist. His big-screen career would commence soon, and he would make a series of films back-to-back. Two of those films, though, were TV movies, one of which was *Brotherhood of Justice*. This drama, written by Jeffrey Bloom and Noah Jubelirer, and directed by Charles Braverman, centred on a secret band of teenage vigilantes whose own code of conduct disintegrates. Kiefer had second billing to Keanu Reeves, and the film was said to be inspired by real events that occurred in 1985 at a high school in Fort Worth, Texas, where a gang calling itself the Legion of Doom dispensed its own summary justice. Names and locations had obviously been altered for *Brotherhood of Justice*, but it was dubbed a 'violence for violence's sake' movie. Kiefer appreciated landing the work, and gave the role his best on set, but personally he was not too thrilled with the film. What did please him was that during shooting he made friends with a fellow cast member, Billy Zane.

In 1985, this distinctive looking, Chicago-born, 19-year-old actor made his movie debut in *Back to the Future*, and he too was feeling his way forward in the business. When Kiefer and Billy got back to Los Angeles after filming for *Brotherhood of Justice* wrapped, they kept in such close contact that Kiefer started hanging out at the flat Zane shared with three other young actors in upmarket Beachwood Canyon. These flatmates were Tom O'Brien, Ohio-born 20-year-old actress Sarah Jessica Parker, future star of the 1990s TV series *Sex and the City*, and Robert Downey Jr. Also 20, and hailing from Greenwich Village, New York, Downey had been acting since he was five years old. Robert and Kiefer became close friends, especially when Kiefer officially moved into the spacious five-bedroom apartment located above Charlie Chaplin's coach house.

It was a lively time in Kiefer's life, and the comings and goings at the flat were like Piccadilly Circus as they each worked hard at carving their individual careers. Sarah Jessica Parker and Billy Zane were flat out seeking movie roles, while Robert Downey Jr augmented his flourishing film career by making several appearances between 1985 and 1986 on the top rated TV show, *Saturday Night Live*. As Kiefer's career took off, over the next two and a half years he was away filming on location so often that he would come to view the apartment more as somewhere to keep his belongings. When the friends could get together, however, with an average age of 19 they knew how to enjoy themselves, all doing, as Kiefer put it 'stuff people told us we would never be able to do'. In Robert Downey Jr's case, some of that stuff brought him desperate problems with drugs, and it would sadden Kiefer to see the path his friend had taken. Kiefer maintains that he has met many an actor who has been interested at times in dabbling with the darker side of life. To an extent, he believes, that attraction is inherent in being an actor, certainly in living an actor's uncertain and itinerant lifestyle. Still he revealed: 'My best friend Robert Downey Jr succumbed to drugs. That was like a warning to me. He was so talented, witty and intelligent – a great buddy. He knew the dangers but he took the risks all the same, and paid the price.'

The mid-1980s saw a new generation of actors flourish. Kiefer's circle of friends over the next few years would expand to include Emilio Estevez and Charlie Sheen, both New York-born sons of actor Martin Sheen. In summer 1985 the emergence of this band of Young Turks in Hollywood led a writer of a feature article for *New York* magazine to coin the term 'Brat Pack' to describe them, a term that Kiefer instantly loathed. Kiefer's understanding of how this came about is that a magazine feature writer interviewed Emilio Estevez on his burgeoning career, and because the session seemed to go so well, Emilio invited the guy to join him and some friends for dinner at a restaurant later that night. This was intended to be off-duty relaxation time. Kiefer has maintained that the journalist secretly tape recorded everything with a handset held beneath the dinner table, then proceeded to write a feature which, Kiefer has claimed, 'nailed Emilio and coined the "Brat Pack" in the process, making every actor under thirty look like an arrogant upstart.'

The term 'Brat Pack' quickly caught on with the media, and over time it mutated until it assumed a negative connotation in some quarters. 'At one point,' Kiefer declared, 'if you were in the "Brat Pack", it felt like it was instant death.' Regardless of anyone's passionate disgust at the catchy label, it did not dent career prospects. On the contrary, in Kiefer's case he was just beginning, and in the coming months he was gratifyingly busy. Years later he revealed: 'When I was young, I spent my time waiting for life to start.' Finished forever with drug taking, as he turned 19 in December 1985 that wait was now over.

CHAPTER 5

A LIFE-
CHANGING
TIME

FOR KIEFER, 1986 got off to a bleak personal start with the death on 24 February in Ottawa, Ontario, of his grandfather, Tommy Douglas, who was 81 years old. Tommy had remained an MP up until 1979, by which time he had long since made an indelible imprint on the lives of his adoptive people of Canada. It was a two-way love affair. Few people, let alone politicians, ever earn the level of respect accorded to Tommy Douglas, and honours were heaped upon him before and after his death. In 1984, he became a member of the Queen's Privy Council for Canada. The following year, he was awarded the Saskatchewan Order of Merit to add to the Companion of the Order of Canada previously bestowed on him in 1981. His face would feature on a 45-cent limited edition Canadian postage stamp, and in 1998 he was post-humously inducted into the Canadian Medical Hall of Fame.

Among Tommy Douglas' pioneering innovations during his reign in political office had been bringing in legislation outlawing discrimination based on gender and race, which had predated by several months the adoption in 1948 by the United Nations of the Universal Declaration of Human Rights. He was the kind of man whose passing leaves an unfillable void in the lives of people closest to him; his activist daughter Shirley has been passionately dedicated to the preservation of Medicare. Tommy was also a hugely inspirational figure to Kiefer, who has firm views on his country's health care policy, but does not as yet have any leanings to enter the political arena himself. He holds clearly defined political beliefs, adheres to his own framework of values and morality, but when asked if he would ever be interested in impinging those beliefs on others, he replied: 'No, not by a large degree.'

In 2005, however, talk did surface of Kiefer possibly portraying his remarkable grandfather in a film of his life, the executive producer of which would be Shirley Douglas, but Kiefer's hectic work schedule on *24* appeared to set the project on the back burner. Back in the mid-1980s, Kiefer's career was due to ignite, and in terms of movie releases 1986 would be one of his busiest years. His second TV movie, this time a drama for CBS, was *Trapped In Silence*. Directed by Michael Tuchner and written by Torey Hayden and Vickie Patik, it told the story of Kevin Richter, a troubled teenager who, having been abused as a child, becomes an elective mute after witnessing the brutal murder of his sister by their stepfather. A dedicated psychologist takes on the task of coaxing him to speak again. Marsha Mason played the psychologist; she had starred in *Max Dugan's Return*, where Kiefer made his debut screen appearance. Kiefer portrayed Richter. John Mahoney, Stephen Pearlman, Frances Foster and Ron Silver co-starred, but it was Kiefer's moving, very internal performance in the main lead that lit up the touching tale. Plaudits rained down on Kiefer, but his sights were firmly trained on appearing on the big screen, and he was paying close attention to the new strain of younger leading men now breaking through.

Among his peers, Kiefer still particularly rated his friend Robert Downey Jr. He talked of Downey as having a uniquely childlike quality that was part of his ethereal magic as an artiste – not a term Kiefer will use lightly, or would ever apply to himself. Timothy Hutton had caught his eye when he'd played the role Kiefer wished had been his own in *Ordinary People*, and the third actor to register on Kiefer's radar was Sean Penn. Born in Santa Monica, California, Sean Penn had starred in a violent 1981 movie called *Taps*, which Kiefer considers opened doors for his generation of actors to play leading men. Kiefer had watched Penn deliver a totally different but equally captivating performance a year later in the teen comedy, *Fast Times at Ridgemont High*, and was struck by Penn's versatility. 'I specifically related to Sean,' said Kiefer. 'I wanted to be as good.'

Kiefer was elated when he was hired to play a small part in the Sean Penn movie, *At Close Range*. Crafted by Nicholas Kazan and Elliott Lewitt, the James Foley-directed crime melodrama set in Pennsylvania was so relentlessly brutal that *Variety* dubbed it 'a very tough picture which runs the risk of being an audience turn off.' With Penn, Christopher Walken and Mary Stuart Masterson heading the bill, Kiefer made a good fist of holding his own as gang member Tim. It was a step out of television, exactly what Kiefer craved, but arguably he got most satisfaction from watching Sean Penn around the film set. Penn was very approachable. He enjoyed the camaraderie among actors on film locations, and he and Kiefer often hung out together off camera. Kiefer noticed though that, as filming progressed, there were days when Sean would quietly withdraw from the exuberant melee. Curious, Kiefer later asked his friend why the change of behaviour, only to learn a lesson that he took to heart. Penn had discovered that to deliver his best work on camera during particularly exacting scenes, he had to conserve all his energy, which meant having to shut himself away off set in his own world. 'I thought that was smart,' confessed Kiefer.

While Kiefer was keen to enhance his understanding of his craft, his existing talent had already caught the eye of film director Rob Reiner, who was about to helm a movie called *Stand By Me*, which had been adapted by Raynold Gideon and Bruce A. Evans from the 1982 Stephen King novella, *The Body*. Set in small town America in summer 1959, it deals with a group of bored adolescents who go on a mission to find the body of a missing local 12-year-old boy. A couple of the boys are linked to the dead body, which more than one gang is trying to be the first to locate. The hunt itself exposes various aspects of the individual boys' lives, and leads to a showdown to see who can claim credit for the macabre discovery.

The standout role was that of gang leader Ace Merrill, a nasty piece of work with an acerbic tongue. At one point, he advises his delinquent mates that if they want to get laid, their best bet is to find a Protestant girl. Rob Reiner had caught Kiefer's performance in *Amazing Stories: The Mission*, and felt that he had the strong screen presence required to pull off the menacing character that is the linchpin of *Stand By Me*. His faith was fully confirmed when Kiefer turned in a blistering screen test for Ace Merrill that won him the part. It was the break Kiefer was looking for. It also came along for Kiefer at a crucial time. 'I did that film because I really needed the money,' he admitted. As soon as he had read the script, though, he knew it was a juicy role for someone his age. Sporting a spiky blond hairstyle and exuding a distinctly feral air, with his quiet, gravelly voice and his alluringly attractive bad-boy grin, Kiefer was perfect to play a rough-edged, diabolical delinquent who held the fascination of a snake.

Wil Wheaton, River Phoenix, Corey Feldman and Jerry O'Connell co-starred with energy and enthusiasm, but their characters paled in comparison to Merrill's menace. Kiefer thoroughly relished the challenge of portraying the movie's most hateable figure. Ace Merrill was pure evil, with not one single redeeming feature. Perhaps this made him a straightforward character to inhabit, but Kiefer created an indefinable extra dimension which brought Ace electrifyingly to life, as the director later commended. Rob Reiner recalled: 'Kiefer was great, and considering the fact that he is very soft spoken and is a sweet guy, a very intelligent person, it's fun for him to get to play those parts.'

Kiefer's mercurial, scene-stealing screen presence as the matchstick-chewing Ace Merrill was the start of him making a name for himself, and filming the role had a unique effect on him in two ways. For a non-method actor, he still inhabited the part when the cameras had stopped rolling. It was such a vivid role, it perhaps required that level of continuous concentration, that detachment from reality, but it made a lasting impression on his fellow cast members. Jerry O'Connell is from New York, and prided himself in not being easily intimidated, yet he has said of Kiefer as Ace Merrill: 'Kiefer Sutherland scared me! He really made himself very menacing to the four of us. Looking back, he was doing it to be in character, to make sure we were scared of him, and man, it worked! I was scared of that dude!' As for Kiefer, a part of him could not quite let go, and he was strangely unable to switch off. Ace Merrill stayed with him subconsciously in a way that no other character ever had; he found this faintly spooky. He knew that Ace was the worst screen persona he had yet portrayed but, in a sense, he took on a life of his own. Kiefer later revealed: 'I actually dreamed the character was shot in prison after the whole story was over. I think that's what he really deserved.'

Although Kiefer had accrued valuable experience making *Stand By Me*, he had no idea that the movie, released in 1986, would do so well. It went down a treat with the critics, who predicted that this film would be a springboard for Kiefer. They were correct, for it was a factor in his securing one of his most distinctive early roles, as a vicious, charismatic vampire in *The Lost Boys*, but he had no tangible awareness when shooting ended on *Stand By Me* that it would be so significant. Years later, Kiefer was candid: 'I was always a little late in realising what was happening at what time. When I was making films from the age of 19 to 28, I think I was pretty arrogant.' If that is true, he was also humbly grateful to be constantly working; the sheer exhilaration that comes from physically being on a movie set, acting out a scene for the cameras, is something that has never deserted him.

Kiefer currently rides the crest of a wave portraying a bona-fide 24-carat good guy as Jack Bauer in *24*, the epitome of the screen heart-throb action hero, but that is something of a turnaround. In the mid-1990s, ten clear years after making his mark as the vile Ace Merrill in *Stand By Me*, Kiefer reflected: 'I would say that at least fifty per cent of the characters I play are villains. One of the things that has always excited me about acting is that you do try to stretch and play characters that are estranged from yourself.' Kiefer was well aware that there is a responsibility inherent in providing the cruel or callous dimension to a piece, and to truly plumb the dangerous depths of certain chilling characters requires a very strong commitment to the art of acting – it does not work, when blurring those lines, if an actor is too conscious of how he will be perceived because of it afterwards. 'A lot of actors just won't play those characters,' Kiefer pointed out, 'but they are often the best written characters, who are better developed than the wishy-washy good guy roles.'

As Kiefer's career crystallised satisfyingly, he was leading a riotous off-screen existence. Still making his home base at the Beachwood Canyon apartment in Los Angeles, he was an unattached, roguish 19-year-old, living in the moment. 'I had a blast – more fun than anyone,' he has owned up. 'There were a few too many parties, girls, and I drank a lot, but I was never late for a day's work. I'd had a brief moment with drugs and had stopped, but not really because I couldn't handle them.' Kiefer always could keep to the line that separated his off-duty rumbustiousness from his responsibility to hold on to the reins of his career. He was ever conscious not to screw up where it counted on that score, which was just as well, as more and more film work flowed his way, including the main lead role in the off-beat love story, *Crazy Moon*.

The Tom Berry and Stefan Wodoslawsky-penned romantic drama, directed by Allan Eastman, took Kiefer home to Canada to shoot the role of Brooks, a rich, clever young man who falls in love with a mettlesome young deaf girl who works in a shop. The film had its darker shadows, but primarily it was a quirky, enchanting tale of special friendship and discovery. Peter Spence, Ken Pogue and Sean McCann co-starred, while Kiefer's leading lady was Vanessa Vaughan.

Sure enough, in contrast, in late 1986 Kiefer then reverted to the mantle of a sick psychopath in the low budget thriller, *The Killing Time*, written by Don Bohlinger, James Nathan and Bruce Franklin Singer. Rick King directed the movie, rated R for violence, whose cast was headed by Beau Bridges. Joining Kiefer were Wayne Rogers, Joe Don Baker, Camelia Kath and Janet Carroll. The film was set in a sleepy seaside town that, while respectable on the surface, was really a cesspool of intrigue, infidelity, corruption and greed. In this morally bankrupt town the local sheriff conspires with his lover to murder her businessman husband and pin the blame on the police precinct's new deputy sheriff. Unknown to these conspirators, the station's latest recruit is not who they think. On his way to take up his post, the real deputy sheriff has been murdered by a psychotic drifter, who then assumes the policeman's identity. Kiefer played the drifter, who is cast only as the stranger, and who in this tangled web of deceit has his own unholy agenda, which sets off a disastrous chain of events. As tension-filled murder thrillers went, *The Killing Time* struggled to rise above the ordinary. The nation's video rental shop shelves were already groaning under the weight of such formulaic movies, played out by stereotypical characters. For Kiefer, however, it had turned out to be much more than just another film role.

Laura Winslow, the character who wants her ruthless screen husband bumped off, was played by Camelia Kath, with whom Kiefer got along particularly well during filming.

Indeed, such was their personal rapport that Camelia would visit Kiefer four months later while he was on location in Utah for his next movie, *Promised Land*, and at that point their friendship turned romantic. Actors meeting on set and falling in love seems almost to be a given – Kiefer's own parents had found each other that way. What was different here was that Camelia Kath was so much older than Kiefer. In December 1986, he had newly turned 20. Twelve years his senior, Camelia was a widow with a 10-year-old child.

Born on 10 December 1954 in Puerto Rico, Camelia was named Camillia Emily Ortiz. In 1974, the dark-haired, petite and beautiful actress married Terry Kath, lead guitarist with the pop group Chicago, who had their biggest hit with the international chart-topping single, 'If You Leave Me Now', in 1976. That same year, Terry and Camelia had a daughter, whom they named Michelle. Publicly, Terry Kath was a highly respected lead guitarist. Privately, he was also an avid gun collector. On the evening of 23 January 1978, one week shy of his 32nd birthday, at a party at a friend's house in Woodland Hills, west Los Angeles, Terry startled the other guests by producing one of his revolvers and proceeding to clean it. Larking about, at one point he suddenly put the gun to his temple, cheerfully reassuring his aghast audience: 'Don't worry, it's not loaded.' Tragically, these were famous last words, for when he pulled the trigger it transpired that the revolver *had* been loaded. Terry Kath died instantly. The gruesome accident completely traumatised everyone present. It left a talented young musician unintentionally dead by his own hand and Camelia Kath, just three years into her marriage, widowed with a child under two.

Nine years on from that tragedy, by early 1987, Kiefer was in love with the late musician's widow and soon he, Camelia and 11-year-old Michelle were living together. It was obvious that this was no casual dalliance with an older woman, but the relationship must have been a source of some concern to Kiefer's family and close friends. Kiefer was a gregarious 20-

year-old who liked to party, and as a free agent had by his own admission been thoroughly enjoying sowing his wild oats with a succession of pretty girls. He liked to drink, sometimes to excess, to prowl bars, not minding if he occasionally got into a scrap or two. On screen, when he wasn't displaying an unfolding gift for encapsulating feral, edgy, scary figures, he was making a name for himself by poignantly portraying sensitive characters in coming-of-age roles. Yet suddenly he seemed to crave the cloak of maturity, becoming involved with a mother in her thirties, while Michelle could have passed for his much younger sister.

At least one of Kiefer's earlier steady girlfriends had been a few years older than him, and Camelia Kath would not be the only woman with children to become special in his life. Then again, perhaps this attraction to older women, although genuine, was part of a bigger picture. While growing up, Kiefer had always wanted to be perceived by others as older than he was. He has acknowledged this, calling it 'an issue of mine', and because of that, from a fairly tender age Kiefer has been a fascinating blend – on the one hand a vivid, red-blooded live wire, up for a lark, yet at the same time someone who emanates an intriguing wisdom and depth that no doubt explains why older women are, in turn, especially drawn to him.

According to Kiefer, Camelia was apparently unaware that he was 19, going on 20, when they had first met on *The Killing Time*. Kiefer is adamant that she felt 'terrible' for a long time after discovering his true age. He said that by the time he revealed his real age to her 'it was a little late for her to do much about it.' If others around him had imagined that it was a passing infatuation, Kiefer clearly thought that he wanted the sobriety of a settled family life, for before 1987 was out he and Camelia Kath would be married. Being an instant stepfather to the late Terry Kath's daughter was not likely to faze him either. With four half-brothers of his own, Kiefer was long accustomed to the stepfamily set-up.

Down the track, Kiefer would have to concede that he was not very good at being a husband. He and Camelia did not stay married for that long, but then among the pressures that would be upon them – apart from the 12-year age gap – was that Kiefer could not really be expected to be anything other than what he intrinsically was – a talented young actor on the rise. Show business is a notoriously tough environment for relationships to survive unscathed, particularly when a star is on the way up and one of Kiefer's most memorable film roles was just about to land in his lap – and this role would send his stock soaring.

Kiefer, aged three, with his father, Donald Sutherland.

With his father at the premiere of *The Bay Boy* at the 1984 Toronto International Film Festival.

With his first wife,
actress Camelia Kath.

Kiefer stepping out
with his second
wife, former model
Kelly Winn.

Kiefer gives away his stepdaughter, Michelle Kath, at her wedding in 2004.

With his daughter Sarah at the 9th Annual Screen Actors Guild Awards, 2003.

Kiefer and his mother, Shirley Douglas, in 2005.

An avid ice hockey player, as shown here in 1994, Kiefer is always in demand to play in celebrity charity matches.

CHAPTER 6

A NEW DAY DAWNS

KIEFER'S UNKEMPT CHARISMA caught the eye of those casting for the 1987 modern-day horror movie, *The Lost Boys*, a film that became a cult classic mainly on the strength of Kiefer's riveting portrayal of the softly spoken, mercurial leader of a vicious gang of teenage vampires who ride about raucously by night on motorcycles and live in an underground cavern dominated by a poster of the late Doors frontman, Jim Morrison. With his striking, blond, punk hairstyle, menacing grin and dangerous eyes, Kiefer made a vivid visual impact; he would assume iconic status for an entire new generation of filmgoers. In addition to gaining him a sudden legion of fans, *The Lost Boys* began his move into big budget films.

The screenplay by Janice Fischer, James Jeremias and Jeffrey Boam told the tale of a woman and her two sons who, having left Phoenix, move in with her eccentric father in the fictitious coastal town of Santa Carla, only to learn that it is the murder capital of the world, and that an alarming number of people are steadily posted as missing. The elder son, Michael, lured by a foxy young lady, is quickly drawn into a local group of hell-raisers, who turn out to be a lot more than noisy hoodlums. Kiefer's co-stars included Jason Patric,

Corey Haim, Dianne Wiest, Barnard Hughes, Edward Herrmann and Jami Gertz, while Joel Schumacher directed.

The ghoulish character of head vampire, David, stands as Kiefer's signature role, and his attraction to the part was uniquely strong. The challenge of portraying someone who has died and come back to life was, in Kiefer's words, 'a great little gift'. As he was keen to point out, just how was anyone going to be in a position either to tell him how to play David, or to tell him that he had got it all wrong? His blunt response would be to enquire, just when did they last rise up from the dead? This lack of artistic restriction gave him a valuable freedom when approaching the part. Of course, it was another villainous character, and the danger of being typecast already threatened to emerge. At the time, Kiefer combated: 'Evil roles *aren't* my trademark, but they just don't have a whole lot of parts for really nice guys.' It was easier for him to play bad guy roles at an early age, and years later he reflected: 'When you're a young actor, you like to go for characters with a bit of flair. So in many films I ended up playing the weirdo but I'm not a psycho, criminal or a bully.'

Joel Schumacher would go on to work with Kiefer on a further three films, and he found him an extraordinary actor to direct. He said: 'Kiefer doesn't need to be a hero. He's not afraid of looking ugly, of looking tired, of being a villain. He's afraid of being mediocre. He doesn't need the approval of an audience the way some stars do, and I admire that. When we did *The Lost Boys*, he was certainly one of the beautiful young actors around but he always had something else – this much older soul in him.' To Schumacher, this peculiarly poignant and unusual element made Kiefer capable of playing character roles convincingly even then. Almost ten years on from directing Kiefer in the vampire thriller, he declared: 'Kiefer has that fabulous elastic quality that all the great character actors have, and when you are a character actor time serves you, whereas if you're an ingénue it's your enemy.'

The role of David in *The Lost Boys* saw Kiefer in the film's opening minutes nail that sexy yet sinister smirk, the unholy glint in his eyes, as he exudes a placid menace and while possessing the most wickedly wonderful dirty laugh in acting, he quickly becomes the frighteningly ferocious snarling creature of the night. Yet Kiefer felt a clear sympathy for the character. He maintained: 'You have very similar motives in someone as charismatic as David, as you do in the mute lad I played in *Trapped in Silence*. An extremely aggressive person may suffer the same internal anguish as an extremely defensive person.' Kiefer went further, though, and saw the wild, vicious killer as having a sympathetic soul. 'To me, David is not the villain, only the antagonist,' he insisted. 'What I liked about David is that he has some kind of conscience, some kind of style and strength, and a manipulative quality that I found very attractive.' Kiefer was always eager for the chance to play characters that have lived long enough to suffer a degree of torment. If acting was to be an honest reflection of life, he believed, roles had to embody both joy and pain.

A different, self-induced kind of pain for Kiefer during the making of *The Lost Boys* must have been turning up on set with a head banging from having overdone it the night before. Reports later leaked out of excessive partying, yet Kiefer never once allowed an alcoholic haze to affect his work. He credits his parents with having instilled in him an indelible sense of responsibility towards work, and an ingrained gratitude that he was getting roles at all, considering that at any given time by far and away the highest percentage of actors are unemployed and waiting by the phone. Joel Schumacher said of this film shoot: 'Kiefer's always been very mature. If he was out all night partying until 5.00 a.m., he would arrange to be driven to the Warner Brothers studio, then sleep in his car parked next to the security guard's gate, having asked the guard to wake him up at six for a 7.00 a.m. make-up call.'

In the circumstances, Schumacher was amazed at how his young lead villain would march confidently on set each day, switched on and raring to go. It wasn't just the resilience of youth as far as the 47-year-old New Yorker was concerned. Said Joel: 'When I talk to Kiefer, I don't ever feel like I'm talking to someone that much younger than I am, although I'm old enough to be his father.' It was a curious coexistence of dependability by day and recklessness by night. Helping Kiefer to enjoy the high life at this time was the film's leading good guy, Jason Patric, who plays Michael, half turned vampire before fighting back against David's evil influence. The two actors became friends off set.

In 1987, though *The Lost Boys* was a bizarre blend of gory, blood-spurting horror and curious comedy, with the cast's youngest members cracking one-liner gags virtually throughout, it was a huge success. Jason Patric may have been the all-American good looking hero, but it was the blond, menacing, piercing-eyed Kiefer Sutherland who skewered the audiences' rapt attention. He even dominated the movie's poster material. Again, Kiefer had an unusual take on why the film was so successful. He firmly believed that many people were able to relate to someone like David. 'He may seem wild and way out,' he reflected, 'but people's inner feelings are not all that different.'

The movie produced some weird offshoots. Some time after its release, a series of killings in America was sensationally dubbed by sections of the media, 'The Lost Boys Murders' – a film title like that was a convenient hook for the press. The film that catapulted Kiefer's career did, however, prompt some adolescents around the country to re-name their existing street gangs – something Kiefer very quickly encountered personally. He was browsing in a Hollywood DIY shop one morning when a Mexican youth plucked up the nerve to buttonhole him. By now, Kiefer knew that the role of David had made him a fantasy anti-hero to a certain breed of teenager, but here the lines blurred when the excited youth proudly informed Kiefer that he had loved the movie so much, he had named his street gang in David's honour. Not quite knowing how best to respond, Kiefer quietly said: 'Thank you.' He watched dazedly as the happy fan walked away, revealing that he had 'Lost Boys' emblazoned on the back of his jacket. Kiefer knew that these gangs would have formed anyway, that it was not the movie's fault, but that kind of attention made him uneasy.

Kiefer grew accustomed to having guys come up to him to say that they adored David's most vicious antics, but he was unwilling to swallow it when the role made him a sex symbol. 'Are you serious?' he laughingly demanded, maintaining that he never received fan mail from girls calling him sexy, and when asked which term – style icon, sex symbol or cult figure – would most apply to him, with a straight face he countered: 'I would like to thank anyone who has ever called me by any of those terms very, very much.' Modestly, he did not associate personally with any of those labels, but *The Lost Boys* unarguably made Kiefer a cult figure and put him firmly on the map.

He made an impact with many he worked alongside. In 1987 he also shot the gritty romantic drama, *Promised Land*, for writer/director Michael Hoffman, co-starring with Jason Gedrick and Meg Ryan. In this film, two former high-school friends meet years later when they are on opposite sides of the law. Needless to say, in this atmospheric, downbeat depiction of unfulfilled hopes amid rural northwest America, Kiefer is cast as Danny, the criminal. *Promised Land* was developed and produced at Robert Redford's Sundance Institute, and was filmed in Utah. Meg Ryan remembered Kiefer most for his professionalism. She said: 'Two seconds before the camera rolls the guy just clicks in faster than anyone I've ever seen. He fleshes things out brilliantly and he is one of the best listening actors I've worked with.' She also described him as having a sweet face and, unwittingly echoing director Joel Schumacher, commented: 'Kiefer has a very old soul.'

Promised Land was steeped in moody disillusionment, and
although film critics considered that Kiefer rose convincingly
above a poorly written role, off set life had brightened for the
burgeoning star, courtesy of Camelia Kath's visits to the set
and the steady development of their personal relationship.
This was a serious romance, and to *Promised Land*'s director
Michael Hoffman, Kiefer and the much older Camelia were
not such an unlikely pairing. He revealed: 'Kiefer wouldn't
want to be a sophomore in college with a girlfriend who is a
member of a sorority. For him, domesticity has a kind of
flamboyance.' By the time *Promised Land* was released in
1988, Kiefer had long since married Camelia. It appears that
the 12-year age gap between them continued to cause concern
among those closest to Kiefer, but it was difficult for people
to express any well-meaning disquiet they may have
harboured. Donald Sutherland clearly did not have a clue
what to say when his eldest son came calling on him, nervous
about marrying, and seeking some advice. Considering that
Donald's first two marriages had been fairly short-lived, and
that he would take roughly 25 years to persuade Francine
Racette to wed him, perhaps the droll, laconic Sutherland
senior was not the ideal person to be looking to for guidance
on matters matrimonial.

Kiefer can look back now with gentle amusement and deep
affection on that day in summer 1987 when he went strolling
with his dad through verdant fields on Donald's fabulous farm
in Quebec. Kiefer asked his father what he thought of his
intention to wed. Kiefer would not be 21 for months, yet had
a clearly flourishing career beckoning in an unstable,
itinerant business. Donald was in a spot. He didn't know
what to say to his excited son, so he blurted out that Kiefer
should go into marriage as if he were Camelia's butler, that he
should take pleasure in the likes of putting toothpaste on her
toothbrush for her. It was such an odd response that Kiefer
stopped dead, stared at his father and demanded: 'What the
fuck are you talking about?' It was four years later, by which

time the marriage had foundered and ended in divorce, that Kiefer found out from a friend of his father's how foolish Donald had felt issuing such advice, but he hadn't wanted to deflate his in-love son. 'I loved my dad for that,' said Kiefer, who would learn in the coming years that it was sometimes hard being a parent.

Disregarding Donald's dubious pearl of wisdom, Kiefer married Camelia Kath on 12 September 1987, the low-key ceremony taking place in a friend's back garden. Neither Donald Sutherland nor Kiefer's mother, Shirley Douglas, attended. In his early twenties, Kiefer would become famous for fast living, and his pleasure in drinking with the lads until all hours did not vanish just because he got married and became a ready-made stepdad. The marriage then would become rocky. Kiefer had gone into marriage in good faith, but was too young, and there were times when his need to behave older than his years broke through. By the end of 1987, newly 21, he was married, Camelia was now pregnant, he had a stepdaughter and had moved up in the world materially. His home was a big, chic new house in Santa Monica, California, with lavish arched windows and a splendid concrete fountain in the grounds. If it seemed a little ostentatious to him at times, that was offset by his thrill at having his first real home since he was 15. When he wasn't enjoying a tipple of Scotch whisky, he drove a sleek Saab; now that he was viewed as a golden boy in Hollywood, film offers were flowing in.

'My mind works in a very simple fashion,' he maintained at this time. 'There are certain things I have wanted to acquire in my life that I've had in focus since I was ten.' He also maintained that balance was the key to almost everything, and that he tried to find equilibrium in his life. He was certainly seizing hold of life with both hands. By early 1988, he and Camelia already knew that the baby she carried was a girl, and they had decided to name her Sarah. Kiefer told journalists: 'Camelia, Michelle and the new baby are all part

of balancing the work. That's really what my life consists of
– family and work.'

In 1988, Kiefer had three film releases, one of which was
Bright Lights, Big City. Jay McInerney had written the
screenplay from his 1986 novel, and the drama, directed by
James Bridges, co-starred Canadians Michael J Fox and Kiefer,
with Phoebe Cates, Jason Robards and Dianne Wiest included
in the core cast. Kiefer was in charge of yet another colourful
character, New York advertising executive Tad Aligash, a
seductive, cocaine-snorting charmer. When Kiefer went to
New York for the shoot, at his first meeting with Michael J
Fox the pair ended up jamming on guitars. Having previously
read the book, Kiefer was well acquainted with the story of
how an aspiring young writer (played by Fox), swaps sedate
life in America's breadbasket for the wild club scene in
Manhattan, where the dizzy, hedonistic lifestyle of drink,
drugs and partying ends up taking a heavy toll.

Although the movie drew criticism over a lack of audience
empathy with the protagonist's plight, and that the novel
hadn't translated to screen as well as it might have, some
reviewers singled out individual performances. Michael J
Fox's personality was praised for compensating for some
perceived script deficiencies, while Kiefer, as Fox's on-screen
druggie friend, was applauded as having been miraculous as
the scene-stealing, smarmy slimeball Tad Aligash. Said
Kiefer: 'I guess I play the troublemaker. I liked the book a lot.
There was a point in my life which was quite similar.' Kiefer
had stopped taking drugs a long time ago, but he had certainly
not lost the ability to party, even though he was back in a city
where in the past he had found it hard to find friends. He was
among mates with the cast, and some of them had their eyes
prised open as to just exactly how gregarious Kiefer
Sutherland could be off duty. Michael J Fox was amazed.
Speaking metaphorically, he said: 'Kiefer has that three
degrees off morphine thing happening for him. It's this bizarre
energy and at the same time he has an elegance. He can do

great, undignified things, with a great deal of dignity. When
you see his crazy side, you go: "Wow!" but he carries himself
in a very adult way and surrounds himself with very adult
concerns. It's a weird juxtaposition of attitudes which makes
him really interesting.'

As well as making new friends on film locations, Kiefer
enjoyed it when the chance arose to work with long standing
buddies, and he and Robert Downey Jr teamed up for the 1988
movie, *1969*, in which they played draftees in the Vietnam
War era drama from writer/director Ernest Thompson. Other
cast members included Bruce Dern, Winona Ryder, Joanna
Cassidy and Mariette Hartley. As a gentle hippie, Kiefer
exuded a stylish screen presence, and as a light-hearted drama
1969 was a sharp change of pace for him, but his motivation
was to make movies he thought he would enjoy and stand a
chance of being proud of when they were finished. He refused
to pick roles designed merely to raise him up the ladder. To
some critics, *1969* was a missed opportunity. *TV Times Film
Guide* said of it: 'A whole crew of good actors is shipwrecked
in a sea of precious dialogue in this look at 1969, flower
power, Vietnam protests and all that. Kiefer Sutherland looks
good even when speaking these lines, while Robert Downey
Jr has to tackle yet another bag-eyed loner pressing the self-
destruct button.'

Kiefer's biggest 1988 film release by far, and one that
marked another milestone in his career, was the big budget
Western, *Young Guns*. Principal photography began in early
1988 and spread over three months on location in Santa Fe,
New Mexico. In Hollywood this genre of film had been on the
wane for some time, so it was risky when screenwriter John
Fusco wrote the story of a British ranch owner in New
Mexico in 1878 who befriends six youths ripe for going off the
rails, takes them in, educates them and attempts to give them
a new start in life, the pay-off being that as 'regulators' they
protect his ranch in a lawless land. When this dignified
philanthropist is brutally murdered, 'his boys' set out for

revenge. In the hands of director Christopher Cain, *Young Guns'* cast balanced the age and experience of Terence Stamp and Jack Palance with the fiery young blood of Emilio Estevez, Kiefer, Lou Diamond Phillips, Charlie Sheen, Dermot Mulroney and Casey Siemaszko. There was scarcely a young actor who wouldn't love to act out his childhood passion for playing cowboys, and Kiefer, cast as Josiah Gordon 'Doc' Scurlock, was fired up from the outset. The preparation for this role was a bigger task than he had yet experienced. Along with his co-stars, Kiefer faced six weeks of tuition in horse riding, spending up to eight hours a day, every day, in the saddle. The six would-be screen cowboys had to learn to ride in groups and separately. Real-life cowboys were brought in to teach the actors how to handle guns properly.

For Kiefer, learning to look deadly with a rifle was a lot easier than coping with horses. In time, he would come to adore horses, and would become a champion rodeo rider, but in 1988 they were an unknown quantity. Not a day into training, and he was rather saddle sore. 'I wore padded bicycle shorts under my trousers,' he confessed, 'and I had to wear bandages on my knees because of the indentations made by the saddle. They'd tell me I was hanging on too tight. Truth is, I was scared to death!' An understanding between man and beast took time to evolve, and Kiefer tried hard to have patience with this new challenge, but as he pointed out later: 'There's nothing more frustrating than sitting on the back of a horse that point blank refuses to cooperate.' It didn't improve his confidence when his horse went down twice while filming a fast flowing scene when the outlaws, fleeing from capture, ride hell for leather along a stream. The churning riverbed clearly disoriented Kiefer's mount and caused it to fall. Kiefer declared: 'No amount of expert preparation can help you to keep your cool when a 500lb horse goes down on you. You forget everything you've been taught in a flash.'

These scary moments aside, Kiefer knew he was going to

have a ball making this movie, and felt close to his fellow cast members. It was now that he first met Emilio Estevez's younger brother, Charlie Sheen, although he was well aware of his work. Speaking of a film called *Lucas*, in which Sheen played a high-school football star, Kiefer said: 'Charlie couldn't have been more than 19 when he made that movie and yet I saw a very young actor with a great deal of skill.' In the previous two years, Charlie Sheen's star had shot up on the back of striking performances in such box office hits as *Platoon* and *Wall Street* but with stellar success had come the temptations. Acquiring a taste for cocaine and Jack Daniels, coupled with a trigger temper on occasions, for a time Sheen became Hollywood's number one bad boy. He was also an articulate, kind and thoughtful guy, but that side of him was not so juicily newsworthy. Kiefer recalled: 'Box office-wise, Charlie was one of the country's top actors right then. He was incredibly courteous to the other actors and he also knew what he was doing as an actor. He approached that very seriously but when that wasn't going on, he was fun to be around. He created a really wonderful atmosphere on set.'

It was an exhilarating shoot all round, and a bunch of such live wires inevitably got up to mischief. Kiefer owned up to a couple of pranks they indulged in. He revealed: 'Emilio and I cellophaned the director's doorway one day, so when he walked out he wrapped himself up. Another time, Emilio bizarrely put a goat in a dress and a bonnet and stuck it in Lou Diamond Phillips's trailer.' The plan was that Emilio would hide in a closet, camera at the ready to capture Lou's startled puzzlement when he walked in. Only the off-the-wall joke went wrong. Said Kiefer: 'Lou didn't come in early enough, so the goat shit all over his trailer and ate half his bed!' The shoot would not be all fun and games, and for Kiefer, making this blockbuster coincided with the next personal milestone in his life – the arrival of his only child. The birth caught everyone on the hop. Kiefer recalled: 'I was out in the middle of nowhere, filming, sitting on this horse when the news came through that Camelia had gone into labour. I had to get a plane to come and pick me up, just land in this field, to get me to the hospital. That was crazy.'

Kiefer classes it the best 24 hours in his life when his 33-year-old wife presented him with a blonde baby girl whom they named, as planned, Sarah Jude Sutherland. Sarah has grown into a stunningly beautiful young woman who has a uniquely special bond with her father. Kiefer and Camelia separated and divorced before Sarah started school, and over the years Kiefer would often confess that for too long he was not the perfect father. With a refreshing candour in this day and age that has made gods of children, Kiefer has spoken of his very human frustration sometimes on days out with his little girl, at moments when he felt driven up the wall. He once commented colourfully that he felt he would die if he had to 'go sit in a park sandbox one more fucking time!'

On another occasion, picking Sarah up from school, wrapped up in his own thoughts momentarily, behind the wheel of his car he cursed aloud, calling himself an 'asshole' only to see in the rear view mirror the shocked face of his daughter perched in the back seat. Instantly apologising to Sarah, Kiefer tenderly tried to explain that sometimes he swore. With blind devotion, Sarah assured him that he could never be that bad, promptly and innocently deepening Kiefer's guilt tenfold. As the years unfolded Sarah would have an unearthly knack for getting through to her father, of understanding him, just as Kiefer would later work hard at making up for lost time with his flesh and blood. He has said that in a strange way, the pair almost raised each other.

In spring 1988, Kiefer's filming commitments meant that soon after the actual birth he had to rejoin the set of *Young Guns*, where he did a lot more than raise a glass to 'wet the baby's head'. Along with some of the film's cast and crew, he had some really raucous times out in Santa Fe. This wild partying would contribute to undermining his marriage. One of the actresses in *Young Guns* later remarked: 'It was a macho set, all those guys, lots of drinking. Kiefer is very intense. Camelia was at home being healthy with the baby.' Kiefer's reputation for letting his hair down leaked out into the press and must have made uncomfortable reading for Camelia. For Kiefer, this release of exuberance went deeper than merely getting smashed for the hell of it. He had been inhabiting the role of an outlaw in lawless days when people like his character, 'Doc', were always a whisker from death; absorbing this day in, day out had heightened his awareness of life and youth. Working on *Young Guns* truly made him think deeply about his own life. His screen character's struggle merely to end the day alive encouraged Kiefer to the conclusion that there was more to life, as he put it in 1988, 'than just getting your tax done on time.' His friends often marvelled at his ability to be both mature and reckless by turns. Right now, maturity and increasing responsibility were weights he wanted to throw off for a while. At the end of the three-month shoot he was tired but exhilarated. He'd also come a long way on the riding issue, even having found an understanding with the particular horse he rode throughout the movie. Said Kiefer: 'I got so attached to my horse, I bought him and started looking for some land to buy to give him a nice home.'

On its release, Kiefer said of *Young Guns*: 'We tried to add depth to a genre of film that has not been that successful in the last five years.' While Emilio Estevez riotously stole the show as Billy the Kid, as 'Doc', Kiefer was the thinking woman's favourite outlaw, just as deadly with guns, but sensitive, vulnerable and capable of showing a natural fear without sacrificing his masculinity. The whole cast had enjoyed the experience. Emilio Estevez called it 'a real ensemble feeling. Everyone was there to support everyone else,' and the film proved a massive hit with a wide age range, but especially its target younger audience. Adding *Young Guns* to his resume meant that in the late 1980s Kiefer was now earning over $2 million a movie. Both a golden boy and tabloid fodder, he was widening his repertoire, clearly capable of handling showy lead roles as well as giving depth and nuance to character parts. Along with his higher earning power, he was developing a businesslike approach to some aspects of his craft, and he set up his own production company at 20th Century Fox in Los Angeles. 'I started Stillwater Productions to develop films, to find great writers and scripts and to try to get new projects off the ground,' he explained.

As Kiefer approached his 22nd birthday, he had developed into a handsome young man with an eye to sartorial style. 'I love wearing suits,' he said, 'everything from Armani to Hugo Boss to Comme des Garcons.' He had also never lost his penchant for wearing the kilt, and with nothing beneath it. He stated, 'You have a sporran which lies over your crotch area, so if a wind picks up or you were to be excited, everything is weighted and your dignity is safe.'

With his trademark honesty, Kiefer does not deny the feisty side of his nature. He has acknowledged that he is not a calm person, that he can be irrational on occasions, and that he has a temper. In typically blunt fashion he confessed: 'I'm not a radical pacifist. If somebody tries to mug me, I'm going to break his fuckin' neck.' Naturally, he meant that metaphorically, but it would take a brave or foolish hoodlum to tackle Kiefer Sutherland. That self-contained ability to look after himself that he had learned at school and at street level would never abandon him, no matter how sleek he scrubbed up in svelte suits, and it contributes to his distinctly attractive aura of capability.

Emotionally, Kiefer had his issues to contend with. An obvious offshoot of his increased profile was that Hollywood watchers began comparing him with his father, some suggesting that the two should make a film, with Kiefer playing Donald's character at a younger age. For now, Kiefer fended off questions about teaming up on screen like this. The personal relationship between father and son also inevitably came under closer scrutiny now, to which Kiefer invariably replied that he and his dad had very busy careers to handle. If people were looking for negativity, Kiefer didn't give them any. He was proud to say: 'When we get together it's great. We're like old friends. I don't have many regrets. I'm not bitter, or anything like that.'

Kiefer's hardest task was fending off questions about life closer to home. His marriage was in serious trouble, a separation was not too far down the track, but he had no intention of letting that out to the press. It was a difficult enough situation to confront as it was. He turned his focus on his career prospects, and spent a lot of time sifting through scripts. *The Lost Boys* and *Young Guns* had been very well received, but other films had suffered attack from the critics. Pauline Kael for *New Yorker* had derided *Bright Lights, Big City*: 'The banality comes down on you like drizzle.' Kiefer wasn't the first actor in his family to displease this particular critic. Speaking of the 1975 film, *The Day of the Locust*, Donald said: 'Pauline Kael reviewed it: "There's nothing specifically wrong with Donald Sutherland's performance. It's just awful."' In his inimitably quiet way, Donald didn't mince his words: 'That was the most stupid piece of criticism I've ever received. I stopped reading reviews after that.'

Ploughing through the parts offered to him, Kiefer tried to find films that both audiences and critics would enjoy. That said, like his father, he would not select roles with an eye to pandering to fickle critics. Looking back, he blamed his own youth and a degree of vanity for some early career mishaps. He said: 'You look at a lot of scripts and sometimes there are inherent problems and your ego will go: "I can fix that. I can play that to make it work," but you're just lying to yourself.' Another thing that Kiefer shared with his father was that when it came down to it neither was exactly a career planner. It was certainly useless asking Donald for advice on rectifying the problem of taking wrong turns. Said Kiefer: 'When I tried to talk to him about my bad choices, he was like: "Ah fuck, I do the same thing." He wasn't too much help there!'

By the end of 1988 Kiefer had established himself as an unusually powerful young actor with gravitas. Film directors such as Joel Schumacher praised his screen ability to become anyone he wanted to and Kiefer's widening circle of acquaintances was struck by the intriguing dual aspects of his personality, some intuitively picking up on his innately 'old' soul. Privately, however, Kiefer's personal life was falling apart at the seams. His marriage was splintering, and divorce seemed inevitable. He had been and would continue to be a good stepfather to Michelle, but when it comes to parenting his own child he has been excruciatingly candid in criticising himself. He has acknowledged that he had been unprepared for fatherhood; speaking specifically of Sarah, he conceded: 'I missed a lot that I know I am never going to make up. I used the justification that I had to work. I'd say: "She'll want to go to college," but I worked because I wanted to. I was very selfish at times.'

CHAPTER 7

REGRETS BEST LEFT BEHIND

COME FEBRUARY 1989, Kiefer spent his free time at his opulent Santa Monica home, redecorating his baby daughter's nursery. Although he and Camelia would have preferred to stay together for the sake of Michelle and Sarah, both knew by now that there was no way of papering over the cracks in their 18-month marriage, and they soon separated. Camelia and the girls moved into a luxury condo in Century Hill, west Los Angeles. Some of Kiefer's acquaintances were quick to say that his penchant for living it up with friends had helped drive the couple apart, and despite those colleagues who admiringly thought of the actor as 22 going on 40, Kiefer candidly confessed: 'I wasn't mature enough to take on a family. I tried and I was not successful. Maybe I'm difficult to live with. I think 99% of all marriages go through a rough patch, yet they don't all end in divorce. Everyone copes as best they can. I didn't.'

Kiefer and Camelia filed for divorce, which came through in 1990, but they would always have Sarah in common. Years later, Kiefer spoke frankly about having married, not so much too young as with the wrong motivation. He stressed that he *had* loved Camelia, but owned up: 'I had an incredible desire at a very young age to want to be older than I was, and a way you can accomplish that is to say: "I'm married. I have kids," but those aren't the right reasons to do that, as we found out. Our marriage didn't last long, but we have a beautiful daughter and I'm very fortunate that Camelia and I have ended up remaining friends.' Kiefer also continued to be very much a loving stepfather to Michelle, and did not shirk his responsibilities. Most of his money, he said, went straight into the bank for his children's education and for those rainy days all too frequent in an actor's life.

Left alone in his chic Santa Monica home, Kiefer recalibrated his life as a single young man. He visited familiar haunts like the Hollywood Billiards club, and enjoyed largely solitary pursuits, such as skiing and camping. Michelle had loved listening to rap music, which drove him to distraction. 'Christ, that shit is the pits, noise pollution,' declared the forthright man, whose musical taste remained rooted in early 1970s progressive rock. Kiefer had hardly melted into a semi-hermit existence, however. He had several movies in the pipeline, and his face graced magazine front covers that spring when in interviews, in his measured, articulate way, he tried to distance himself from some of the more way-out tags attached to him by friends and acquaintances. He did not have a precious thin skin, could take a laugh, and knew that some over-the-top descriptions of his nature stemmed from affection and youthful joviality, but he defended: 'People say I'm eccentric and off-centre but I disagree.' He didn't deny that there were still times when he could erupt. 'Every so often, I go a bit crazy and hit a wall or go out and start drinking.'

Although he did not seek bad press, whatever he did drew attention. It was par for the course in Hollywood that stories with a kernel of truth would quickly mushroom into something far bigger, such as when Kiefer pleaded no contest to a reckless driving charge, an incident which mutated into a juicier tale when it emerged that there had been a gun in the car. It made the television news, which poured petrol on the fire. Kiefer doused the more hysterical reactions to this: 'It was no big deal. If I had been blasted out of my head and been carrying a pistol, I'd be in jail. These kinds of things get blown way out of proportion. It wasn't my car, it was late at night, it was up in the mountains where there are a lot of bears so people carry guns. That's it.'

While gossipmongers watched his every public move, and kept a kind of obsessive tally as to how many times per week Kiefer Sutherland dined out in Hollywood's fashionable restaurants, he concentrated on work. He commanded deep respect from directors, movie moguls and fellow stars, which flattered and pleased him – he valued their good opinion of him – but with the Sutherland trait of being bottom liners, Kiefer could come out with remarks like: 'I take acting as seriously as it needs to be taken. I mean, it isn't a cure for cancer or anything.' Nor had he let success with *The Lost Boys* and *Young Guns* go to his head. In the first quarter of 1989 he was talking earnestly of acting as something he could potentially end up being very good at. He was prepared to work hard to nurture his talent. He also knew what he liked and disliked in a role. He looked for a certain clarity and purpose. Intricately complex, as he put it, 'tricky-dicky' movies or characters didn't do it for him right then. Instead, he professed a preference for something straightforward, virtually black and white.

For the first time in years he had a notion for theatre work, which coincided with a definite yearning for his Canada home, and although some Toronto theatre productions appealed to him, he stayed focused on film work. Over the next two years he would rack up a string of films, most of which had something to do with law and order, starting with *Renegades*, which reteamed him with *Young Guns* co-star, Lou Diamond Phillips. Written by David Rich and directed by Jack Sholder, *Renegades* might have sounded like another Western. Indeed, it features a Native American on the hunt for a stolen sacred lance, but it was a modern-day action thriller in which Kiefer was cast in the lead role as undercover cop, Buster McHenry. Hollywood had for a long time churned out a surfeit of buddy movies, featuring violent explosive action and tediously long and noisy car chases, but *Renegades* tried to give a fresh dimension to this tired genre. Other actors drafted in to this tale of a maverick cop with an impassive sidekick on a unique mission, included Robert Knepper and Jami Gertz. On its release in 1989, reviewers were tepid in their reaction, but suggested that audiences should suspend disbelief and just enjoy.

One of Kiefer's main attractions to *Renegades* was that it came across on paper as a high-energy, exciting piece – just what he had been looking for after some of the smaller films he had been doing. 'It's a very aggressive film,' he said. 'It has a very aggressive attitude and a very aggressive pace.' He described the difference between some film roles as the vivid contrast between rock music and jazz. 'You burn from the first bar and that's what we intended to do with this film.' According to *Renegades'* producer, David Madden, Donald Sutherland visited the film set a handful of times to see how his son was doing. Madden found it hard to read Sutherland senior. 'Donald is a formidable man,' he declared. Kiefer appreciated his father's moral support, and it was a huge plus point to be working alongside Lou Diamond Phillips again. The two actors had become good friends, and Phillips spoke of his immense respect for Kiefer as an actor, and for his attitude towards the acting business. Lou Diamond Phillips went on to carve a busy career, and he and Kiefer would share the big screen again. Twelve years later, Phillips appeared in two episodes of *24*. Also featured in that 2001 ground-breaking first series of the hit TV show, in a far larger role, was the veteran actor Dennis Hopper, with whom Kiefer first worked in the 1990 film, *Flashback*.

Although a strong and versatile actor, Dennis Hopper is still best remembered for his hippie role in the 1969 movie, *Easy Rider*. In *Flashback*, Hopper's character of Huey Walker is an infamous 1960s counter-culture radical hero who, having been a fugitive from the law for 20 years, has finally been caught, and is being escorted to jail by repressed young FBI agent, John Buckner, played by Kiefer. The action comedy from the pen of David Loughery was directed by yet another director new to Kiefer – Franco Amurri. Handling the supporting roles were Carol Kane, Paul Dooley, Cliff de Young and Richard Masur. Although *Flashback* proved a misfire in Kiefer's resume, some found the flawed film underrated. The first half radiated some snappily entertaining comic exchanges between the two main leads when Hopper and Kiefer sparked off one another, and while the older actor tapped into his own screen image, Kiefer was singled out as having been in especially sharp form. It appears that it was the plot rather than the actors' performances that in the end let the film down.

Flashback was Kiefer's 15th film, but he was regularly approached with offers to work in other media. He continued to run shy of television roles, but began to pick up work lending his distinctive voice to animated movies. In 1990 came the family adventure, *The Nutcracker Prince*, based on ETA Hoffman's book, *The Nutcracker and the Mouse King*. Patricia Watson adapted Hoffmann's classic children's tale, and Paul Schibli directed. A host of actors voiced the various parts, including Peter O'Toole and Phyllis Diller. Kiefer provided the voice of the Nutcracker Prince.

In 1990, Kiefer crossed the Atlantic for a potentially fascinating lead role in the British film, *Chicago Joe and the Showgirl*, described as Bonnie and Clyde transferred to World War II Britain. It dealt with a real life murder case, which had resulted in Karl Gustav Hulten going down in history as the only American soldier to be executed in Britain during World War II. Writer David Yallop originally wrote the screenplay for *Chicago Joe and the Showgirl* in 1975, but it was only now making it to the big screen, 15 years later. Kiefer took on the responsibility of portraying Karl Hulten, and Emily Lloyd acted opposite him as Betty Jones. Other cast members included Patsy Kensit, Liz Fraser and Keith Allen; director Bernard Rose was at the helm.

Bernard Rose had made his feature film directorial debut with the 1988 fantasy, *Paperhouse,* and in *Chicago Joe and the Showgirl* he was once again dealing with a sense of the surreal. He had become aware of the project some time back, and found it hard to understand why the Hulten/Jones story had never been told on screen before. Now in charge of bringing these criminals to celluloid life, he made a close study of the pair and came to the conclusion: 'I saw them as victims of their own imagination. They'd become so divorced from reality, their whole life had become a film.' The hook for Kiefer to take on the role of Karl Hulten was that the central couple had created their own totally make-believe world. He said: 'All acting is obviously fantasy, just continuous manipulation, but this was complete fantasy, once removed.'

To the director, it was wrong to link *Chicago Joe and the Showgirl* with Bonnie and Clyde, as Karl Hulten and Betty Jones had preyed on defenceless people. It was by no stretch of the imagination a pleasant story, and actors were needed for the leading pair who could bring certain qualities to the screen. Studio executives were prepared to cast a wide net in order to find the man to fill the Hulten role, but when Bernard Rose met Kiefer, the director was instantly convinced that no other actor could fill those shoes. Rose also studied some of Kiefer's films, and was struck by his ability to convey vulnerability while being a rather nasty piece of work. He said: 'The role that really made me think Kiefer could handle Hulten was *The Lost Boys*. He had some good looks for hell in that movie.' To the director, Kiefer had the necessary screen substance to carry the film, and Bernard Rose believed that it had to rest on Kiefer's shoulders to carry *Chicago Joe and the Showgirl,* since it was his character that had to somehow engender audience sympathy – a very tall order, given the character and story involved. 'The thing I found most impressive about Kiefer,' said Rose, 'is that with a character like Hulten who is essentially a liar, who responds differently to different people in the movie all the way down the line, it means his character has an incredibly complicated through-line in terms of who he is at any given point, but Kiefer kept that consistency so well.' Kiefer always maintained that his job required an exceptional degree of focus, and although the film was shot completely out of sequence, he had a firm grip of the overall picture. He has also said that more often than not there is a bit of himself in each of his screen characters, but in portraying Karl Hulten he had to draw extensively on his creative imagination.

Chicago Joe and the Showgirl drew a mixed reception, but again Kiefer's individual performance stood outside the negative criticism. One reviewer wrote that the film 'could have worked, but severe script problems and a rare dud performance from Emily Lloyd are damaging minus factors. Lloyd's impish portrayal of the showgirl never captures the vicious unbalanced nature you expect. Kiefer Sutherland is convincing, by comparison.' *The Face* magazine's film critic decided that 'Kiefer holds your attention wherever he goes. He doesn't do this by simply distorting himself, but by a thorough definition of character. Apart from natural ability, Kiefer has what most actors would die for, that is the ability to pull you towards him whenever he is on screen. He's the luckiest kind of actor – a celluloid magnet.'

Despite this glowing praise, in spring 1990 Kiefer could not envisage becoming so famous that he would have difficulty walking down the street. Speaking of those Hollywood idols who attain that rarefied status, he concluded that it comes from working hard to maintain a very structured formula – something that would never appeal to him. He didn't feel suited to the kind of movies that had to be blockbuster success after success. 'I'm more all over the place,' he confessed. He looked rather to stars such as his father, whose films were so varied it made it hard to develop a consistently guaranteed audience. Kiefer may not have had a rigid game plan, but from the moment he'd decided that acting was for him, he had had confidence that he would get to his current place on the totem pole. Now 23 years old, he stated: 'I know I can go further but only in a very specific way. I know I can be an actor all my life but I don't know if I can be a star.' With four film releases in 1990, Kiefer was conscious of a need to slow down. He feared that by working too hard his performance levels might suffer. He also wanted to take time to step back and actually see some of his work on screen. He had hunches about a couple of his recent roles, and was curious to see if he was right.

Acting itself, although something he loves, is an unusual way of life. Kiefer has called it 'an addictive little world', and aspects of the cocoon he found himself in did not sit well with his independent spirit. For instance, at his level now it was commonplace for a film studio to have someone call personally at his house of a morning to wake him up. He didn't have to buy in much food and cook for himself – all that was catered for on set. He was presented, as were all his fellow actors, with money once a week for expenses, which cut out trips to the bank, and each day he didn't even have to bother picking what to wear, since there would be a wardrobe set aside for him. Kiefer rasped drily: 'I'd be as well going to work in fuckin' pyjamas!' It wasn't a case of complaining for the sake of it. Kiefer disliked those elements that isolated actors from real life. There was enough make-believe before the camera. His concern was that in making too many films in a row, living in that bubble continuously, it would be hard to remember what reality is, and tougher still to portray that convincingly on screen. Of his four 1990 film releases, two would be hugely successful, and one of those continued this cops and robbers phase when he pulled back on his battered dusty hat and reloaded his six guns to reprise the role of Josiah Gordon 'Doc' Scurlock in the sequel to *Young Guns*.

Like the original, *Young Guns II* was written by John Fusco.

Alongside Kiefer, the lead cast again featured Emilio Estevez and Lou Diamond Phillips, with newcomers to the story, Christian Slater, William L Petersen and James Coburn. The director was New Zealander Geoff Murphy, and this sequel was intended to be darker than its predecessor. Kiefer had an aversion to sequels *per se*, and inevitably, with few exceptions, they do tend to be let-downs, but he agreed to return as the soft-centred outlaw because, for as much as he and the cast had had riotous fun making the first box office hit, he personally felt that they had ultimately not quite managed to make the truly great Western he had envisaged back in 1988.

By December 1990, Kiefer had three films showing concurrently in US cinemas – *Chicago Joe and the Showgirl*, *Young Guns II* and a movie he had made prior to the Western sequel – a film that would change his personal life and bounce him into a bright, and eventually cruel, spotlight.

CHAPTER 8

THOUGH
PROMISES
WERE MADE

KIEFER RECKONS THAT mankind's fear of death has been the biggest single motivator of our time, and that the public at large has an intrinsic fascination with the question of whether there is an afterlife. These beliefs appeared to be founded when, on its release in autumn 1990, *Flatliners* – a film all about medical students audaciously experimenting with journeying beyond death's door – became one of the five top grossing movies in America. This unique story, written by Peter Filardi and directed by Joel Schumacher, was brought alive on screen by Kiefer along with Kevin Bacon, Oliver Platt, Julia Roberts and William Baldwin.

This second chance to work with *The Lost Boys* director very much appealed to Kiefer, as did the script for *Flatliners*. He found it intriguing and imagined that it would be a medical version of the 1973 legal drama, *The Paper Chase*. Buoyed up then, in October 1989, he joined his co-stars in a rehearsal room at Columbia Studios in Los Angeles. They would learn to look like budding doctors with the help of two medical advisors, who showed the actors routine procedures such as how to give injections. When they had mastered the art of stabbing oranges with hypodermic needles, filming began. The cast and crew would later bail out of California for location shooting in Chicago, but before that fears quickly kicked in for Kiefer.

He recalled: 'I found myself on a soundstage at Columbia Studios, running by the Statue of Liberty's head and I thought, Oh my God! I can't do this! I looked at Joel and said: "None of this makes sense! We're trying to revive a guy over a wind grate. The air is so unsterile. No doctor would ever do this!"' Joel Schumacher told his young star to take a deep breath and trust him. He assured Kiefer that he was fully aware that his career was in his hands. 'You'll be fine,' the director promised, and Kiefer believed him. 'I didn't have a lot of trust when I was younger,' admitted Kiefer, 'but I would always work for Joel. I trust him.'

Flatliners was not just another film role to Kiefer. He had particularly high hopes that his performance would somehow set him apart. He was determined to pull together all the acting experience he had garnered over the last five years to hone his portrayal of his character, Nelson, into the very best he was capable of. Filming wrapped in early 1990, and when *Flatliners* opened across America, it earned a great deal of attention; for many, Kiefer was the undoubted draw. *Saturday Night* magazine declared: 'Kiefer Sutherland has to be singled out for his edgy presence, the measured pace of his performance. He is straddling the gap between screen youth and adulthood, waiting patiently for more complex roles, waiting for his screen life to mature.'

In the meantime, Kiefer's personal life had hit a spectacular new high, courtesy of co-star Julia Roberts. Speaking of the first day of rehearsal for *Flatliners* at Columbia Studios, Joel Schumacher recalled how the male cast had all assembled an hour since, when 'the doors flew open and this redhead flew in. It would be accurate to say, there were sparks everywhere.' The spark between Julia and Kiefer took hold and quickly kindled into a flame that survived the end of filming. Kiefer and Camelia had separated back in spring 1989 and were heading for divorce. Kiefer then was free, and perhaps even ripe for romance. He had met his first wife on a film set. It looked suspiciously like the same thing was happening again. Unlike Camelia Kath, Julia Roberts, born in Georgia on 28 October 1967, was ten months younger than Kiefer. While for some film buffs she is a Hollywood princess, others see simply an image of long legs, long hair and a wide letterbox smile. Since 1988 she had appeared in six feature films and one TV movie, and was better known towards the end of 1989 as the sister of actor Eric Roberts, but her last two films, *Steel Magnolias* and *Pretty Woman*, were set to change that.

Julia Roberts would go on to have a volatile love life, and already by 22 she had been romantically involved with her leading men. At 19, she moved in to live with Liam Neeson, with whom she made the 1988 teen drama, *Satisfaction*. Subsequently, she became briefly engaged to Dylan McDermott, her screen husband in the 1989 women's weepy, *Steel Magnolias*. With Kiefer it was the third time that on-screen chemistry flowed over into off-set romance. Ultimately, it would not be a case of third time lucky, but at the time who knew? Julia Roberts was certainly not shy of singing Kiefer's praises in all departments. 'I think he's a wonderful actor, I always have for many years,' she declared. 'I really respect what he does.' In several interviews she would later tell millions of TV viewers of how she fell for Kiefer while shooting some of the more testing and gory scenes in the medical thriller, and she was not the first person to pick up on Kiefer's 'old soul'. 'It seemed to me that he was a thousand years older and yet he's only a year older than me. Kiefer has totally captivated me,' she insisted, maintaining that they had become *so* close that when they were apart sometimes she missed him so much, she wept.

They weren't apart that often. Once the romance clearly survived the end of filming *Flatliners* in spring 1990, Kiefer made the major decision to move out of his opulent Santa Monica home and move in to Julia Roberts' million-dollar home in Benedict Canyon, in the Hollywood Hills. By now, Kiefer owned a 300-acre ranch in Whitefish, Montana, and he had instructed work to begin there on building a 19th-century-style log home at the foot of a mountain. Back in the plush Hollywood Hills, the romance continued to smoulder privately. According to Julia Roberts, she and Kiefer liked cosy nights in alone. She would deftly ply an embroidery needle, while he loved to read. This contented, low-key domesticity, however, would soon be upended when she racked up her first major acting achievement.

Her role in *Steel Magnolias*, alongside Sally Field, Dolly Parton, Shirley MacLaine, Daryl Hannah and Olympia Dukakis, earned her an Oscar nomination for Best Supporting Actress, and won her a Golden Globe in the same category. When she took to the stage to accept the Golden Globe, clutching the coveted trophy, she announced to the worldwide television audience: 'I want to thank my blue-eyed, green-eyed boy who supports me through everything.' In a town lusting for the latest celebrity gossip the floodgates flew wide open, and Julia was happy to wax lyrical about Kiefer. 'We're together all the time, we're in love with each other. That's a life, you can't ask for more,' she maintained.

The paparazzi set their sights firmly on the pair – she, the elfin-faced, open-hearted redhead, he the blond, mercurial star. Kiefer already had an intriguing hinterland and, though no less in love, was naturally less effusive in public. His comments were more along the lines: 'We first met before *Steel Magnolias* came out. I didn't know who she was. I thought I had discovered this great talent. ... I think Julia is one of the best actors I've worked with and she said that to me too, which was great. It made me feel better than anything in the world.'

In March 1990, *Pretty Woman* was released, with Richard Gere as the classy businessman falling in love with a hooker, played by Julia Roberts. With Kiefer's girlfriend's star in the ascendancy, their profile as a couple rocketed sky-high. That summer Julia began filming the thriller, *Sleeping with the Enemy*, in South Carolina, and Kiefer frequently visited her on set. The movie's director, Joseph Ruben, said of the lovebirds: 'They make each other laugh. What can you say? It's chemistry.'

Kiefer and Camelia's divorce had by this time come through and approaching one year since they had met, Kiefer gave Julia an expensive diamond ring. It was said to be a friendship ring and, in trendy Hollywood-speak, Julia Roberts would only tell reporters that the ring had been given to her 'without questions and without response', the implication to the avid media being that the ring came with no strings attached. If anyone, however, was looking for chinks in this celebrity romance, this was deflected when, around her 23rd birthday in October 1990, Julia went with Kiefer to Sunset Tattoo and had a tattoo of a red heart inside a black Chinese symbol etched over her left shoulder blade. The Chinese symbol was meant to stand for strength of heart. In what was becoming a familiarly effusive way, Julia declared that her love for Kiefer would 'last as long as this tattoo'. Not surprisingly, even without an engagement announcement, Kiefer Sutherland and Julia Roberts were now Hollywood's reigning couple.

While Julia was understandably keen to keep on a professional roll, Kiefer, having made 18 movies, had promised himself a well-earned break. He was receiving film offers daily, and his fee per film continued to run into seven figures, but the star of two hugely successful Westerns stuck to his guns. He needed to step back a while. Insecurity had made him make four films back-to-back, taking up an entire year, and though that unsettling sense never completely leaves an actor, he was strong enough to act on his instinct. He said: 'I realised that my life had been very one-dimensional and I had to do something about that. I get very nervous about not having a clear purpose.'

Kiefer was also still awake to the dangers of losing touch with street-level life. Though he was prominent among Tinseltown's glitterati, often photographed in designer suits, perfectly groomed and carrying himself with innate dignity and humour, he could just as easily melt into those parts of Los Angeles definitely not frequented by feted film stars. Kiefer never lost the buzz of going to these hangouts, and still relished playing pool at the Hollywood Billiards club, where long ago he had been taught to shoot pool one-handed by a one-armed man nicknamed 'Vulture'. In the vast, dimly-lit basement pool hall, Kiefer played for $5 a game, often double or quits; he was often a reckless player, but always good to watch. Here, no one treated him like the movie star they knew he was. He was genuinely just one of the guys in a macho environment. Women were allowed into the place, but if a girl did arrive, she stood out like the proverbial sore thumb. Kiefer once remarked of a dainty, timid lass shooting pool with her boyfriend: 'It's funny to see a girl like that in here, wearing that flowered dress. She looks so vulnerable.'

The only girl to interest Kiefer was Julia Roberts, and early in 1991, one evening over hamburgers he proposed. She said yes and the frenzy began. Julia's publicly voiced devotion to Kiefer reached new heights. She spoke to reporters and television talk show hosts about how she and Kiefer would be together forever, that she counted herself immensely blessed to have found someone who wasn't only her closest friend but with whom she was wildly in love. When the doyenne of American TV interviewers, Barbara Walters, asked Julia about Kiefer, several million viewers sighed soft-heartedly to hear the sparkly-eyed actress admit: 'Forever love. I believe in that and I believe this is it. We live together, we're in love with each other. Isn't that what being married is? He is the love of my life. He is the person I love, admire and respect most in the world. Kiefer is probably the most wonderful, understanding person I have ever met.' Excitement deepened. This was one of those showbiz mergers that would be sure to provide the eye-popping wedding of the decade.

In spring 1991 the ante was upped when Julia received her second Oscar nomination, this time for Best Actress for *Pretty Woman*. She told Britain's *Sunday Express*: 'The success you achieve on a professional level can have nothing and everything to do with your personal life.' Proudly watching his fiancée's career flourish, Kiefer told Julia: 'I don't think you could get any hotter or you would spontaneously combust.'

Whether it was the strain of stardom or the relentless media spotlight, sharpened by their high-profile engagement, pressure *was* actually building up behind the scenes. Privately, Kiefer and Julia tried to keep a cap on it. By having so loudly trumpeted their undying mutual devotion they had set themselves up as targets, together and individually. Glowing publicity is great but totally unmanageable, and nothing will stop the knives coming out, even the tip of a blade trying ever so slightly to winkle out a potential source of trouble. Kiefer's pool hall associates were not the only vultures in Los Angeles, and no sooner had Julia Roberts' name appeared among the nominees for the Best Actress Oscar than the Hollywood rumour mill began to grind out speculation that the Sutherland/Roberts romance would now end. In a city awash with sources that speak anonymously to its mighty press machine, someone now claimed: 'There is definitely a problem and the problem is work related. Kiefer is not getting offers for roles and Julia's phone is ringing every two minutes, but she is madly in love with him and wants the relationship to work.'

In fact, Kiefer was continuing to turn down work. Not for the first time, these unnamed sources feeding Hollywood's media had got it wrong. However, something did happen around now which the couple would not talk about, but which resulted in Kiefer moving out of Julia's house. Kiefer has said: 'Occasionally, I will go do something that will give me a different view on life.' This touchstone time saw him move into the downmarket St Francis Hotel, situated across from the Hollywood Billiards club. In this haunt, Kiefer felt among a whole different set of friends and acquaintances. One of those acquaintances was a pretty 24-year-old named Amanda Rice. She would be variously described in the press as a dancer who went by the stage name of Raven, and who worked at the Crazy Girls club in Hollywood. To Kiefer, she was an aspiring actress. He said: 'I know people always use that term, but it is true.' She hung out at the pool hall. Kiefer classed her as a friend. He would later have to address the subject of this friend to the press, but for now the interest became intense when he was spotted in her company in public. Kiefer was photographed leaving a Sunset Boulevard burger joint in step with Amanda, and staff at the Crazy Girls club came out of the woodwork to tell journalists that Kiefer had a couple of times turned up at closing time and left the club with the dancer. One of the other dancers believed that Kiefer and Amanda had once taken Amanda's young child on a trip to Disneyland.

This 'slumming it' at the St Francis Hotel did not last long, and within a fortnight Kiefer moved back in with Julia. Not long after, through their respective publicists, they announced their wedding date – 14 June 1991, just six weeks away. With an explosion of head-spinning activity, the period that followed rushed by and was not without its hiccups when, in May, newspaper allegations duly surfaced linking Kiefer to Amanda Rice. Amanda was said to have told journalists that Kiefer had spoken about Julia Roberts to her, and had once said his fiancée had become an 'ice princess' since *Pretty Woman*. Kiefer's publicist, Annett Wolf, vehemently denied on his behalf any allegation that he and Amanda Rice had had an affair, or that he had been in any way uncomplimentary about Julia Roberts. Wolf was adamant: 'Kiefer has never denied that he met her [Rice], because he likes to play pool. He is denying that he had a relationship with her.'

Forty-eight hours later, according to LA newspaper reports, Julia checked into Cedars Sinai Medical Center with the flu, where she stayed for a few days. Kiefer visited her there daily. A spokesman for the hospital was happy to tell the media that Kiefer was a big hit with all the staff working on that floor. This mini scandal seemed to die down for now, and did not affect plans for the wedding.

Joe Roth, head of 20th Century Fox, wanted to give the glamorous couple their wedding, and the extravaganza quickly came in at a cost of around $500,000. It would take place at Soundstage 14 of Fox Film Studios in Los Angeles, which would be transformed into a vast faux garden paradise. Gourmet food company, Marcondas Meats, would handle the catering, local liquor merchants would supply the fine champagne, and there would be a spectacular four-tier wedding cake. Freshly cut roses would adorn each table, the cutlery and crockery would be exquisite, and fabulous ice sculptures were commissioned. The guest list ran into hundreds, and included celebrities – Emilio Estevez, Lou Diamond Phillips, Michael J Fox, Charlie Sheen, Bruce Willis, Joel Schumacher and Richard Gere. Four of Julia Roberts' *Steel Magnolias* co-stars – Sally Field, Daryl Hannah, Dolly Parton and Shirley MacLaine, along with Demi Moore – were among others invited, and top-flight security had been hired to keep the paparazzi at bay.

Julia was to have four attendants – agents Elaine Goldsmith and Risa Shapiro, make-up artist Lucienne Zammit, and actress Deborah Porter. Their sea-foam green silk gowns were to come from Fred Hayman's boutique on Rodeo Drive, with matching Manolo Blahnik shoes. Julia's custom-made wedding dress would be the work of designer Richard Tyler, whose Tyler Trafficante salon stood on Melrose Avenue in west Hollywood. There was no word of what the groom would be wearing. Virtually the only thing known was that Kiefer's bachelor party would be held on 11 June at Dominick's restaurant in LA. That wasn't so unusual, as weddings tend to be 'a girls' thing'. Julia had a final fitting date scheduled with Richard Tyler just prior to the big day, and by now the wedding of Kiefer Sutherland and Julia Roberts had assumed the characteristics of a media juggernaut ready to mow down all in its wake – the hysteria surrounding the nuptials was quite staggering.

In early June, Julia's agent and bridesmaid, Elaine Goldsmith, threw a private party for the bride-to-be at which Julia was showered with gifts of lots of designer lingerie. Her mother, Betty, was among the two dozen guests. With the wedding about a week away, Kiefer flew to his ranch in Whitefish, Montana, to oversee arrangements there. He planned to whisk his new wife to this lovely ranch for part of their honeymoon, and he wanted everything to be right. Julia and some friends meantime headed for the Canyon Ranch Spa in Tucson, Arizona for a weekend stay on 8/9 June; it was at this point that things began to unravel. The sequence of events later became excruciatingly public knowledge.

On Julia's return to Los Angeles on Monday 10 June, she and Kiefer had a telephone conversation. That evening, Julia and her mother went to stay at Elaine Goldsmith's home. Betty later said: 'I took Julia to her agent's house where we thought we'd be safe.' She meant from the press pack they knew would be descending. The next day, on the morning of Kiefer's planned bachelor party, he received a phone call from a friend of the couple, telling him that the wedding, so publicly planned and now just three days hence, was off. To say that he was shocked is an understatement. He tried for hours to contact Julia, without success. Later that day, 11 June 1991, their respective publicists issued a joint press release announcing: 'It has been mutually agreed upon that the wedding has been postponed.' For that, the media read 'sensationally called off', and the shit hit the fan.

The news that this glitzy wedding of two supposedly gilded lovebirds was off made television news and front page headlines the world over. Los Angeles' newshounds and photographers descended, plus a small army from out of state, and it was pure bedlam as they tried to corner Kiefer and/or Julia. The sky above Elaine Goldsmith's house filled up with news channel helicopters, and a swarm of rabid scandal seekers thronged around the property's perimeter. It was estimated that more than 100 photographers were present. Julia's mother described the scene that met their eyes as staggering. At one point, she ventured out to face the pack, which clearly was not keen to disperse, to say: 'C'mon, guys! All she did was break off the engagement.'

The issue of it being Julia who called the wedding off would naturally be a sensitive one for Kiefer. Shell-shocked, he still could not get through to her on the phone. Trying to go to her in person was a non-starter, since he was under siege every bit as much the media's quarry, and now he had to think of immediate matters, such as embarrassingly cancelling the bachelor party planned for that evening at the west Hollywood restaurant.

Kiefer's family, thoroughly shocked by this sudden development, was aching to help. Donald Sutherland had already arrived in Los Angeles for the wedding, and was later said to have been wonderful, comforting his bewildered son in the coming days. Never a man to betray a confidence, Donald would only comment years on: 'Kiefer's life is his life and I truly do not interfere with it at all. He is a very independent person who keeps his own counsel.' Kiefer's mother, Shirley Douglas, declared: 'That was a very, very hard time for Kiefer.'

Kiefer's friends were quick to leap in defensively when approached for comment. When asked how Kiefer was taking this stunning turn of events, one friend hurled back: 'Well, what would you think if someone who goes on every talk show and says how much she loves you, did something like this? He's shocked.' Another friend would only say that Kiefer was despondent. Kiefer himself kept a dignified silence. It was not until months later that he would insist: 'The decision to end the relationship was mutual. If it wasn't mutual on the specific day the wedding was cancelled, it was shortly afterwards.'

On Wednesday morning, as the garden paradise wedding set on Soundstage 14 was dismantled, the blame game had already begun, with Kiefer bearing the brunt of a tabloid frenzy that accused him of all sorts of offences – he still partied too much, he was jealous of Julia's success, etc. etc. The juiciest allegation naturally was infidelity, and Amanda Rice's name bounced big time into the spotlight. Amanda Rice publicly denied having a sexual relationship with Kiefer. She plainly stated that they had not had an affair, and made it clear that the newspaper feeding frenzy had blown out of proportion. Kiefer's friends revealed that this infidelity accusation was upsetting Kiefer enormously. 'This thing with Amanda Rice,' said one friend, 'there was nothing sexual.' Again, Kiefer would not speak about it at the time, but months later came out emphatically with: 'I did not have a relationship with Amanda Rice. We were friends. I play pool with a bunch of people all the time. She was one of them. There was no physical relationship. I've said this and Amanda has said this.'

In June 1991, however, events were unfolding by the hour. An unnamed friend of Julia's now came out swinging on her behalf, declaring: 'It was Julia who called the wedding off. She has wanted to do it for some time but didn't know if she could find the courage.' A Hollywood insider opined: 'The problem is not money or other women, but Julia. Every time she gets close, she shies away.' Julia later told *Entertainment Weekly*: 'I had made an enormous mistake in agreeing to get married. Then I made an even greater mistake by letting it all get so big. I thought: I'm not going to make the final mistake of actually getting married.' An extra dimension to events, however, would emerge.

On 13 June, the eve of what would have been her wedding, and in the eye of Tinseltown's biggest celebrity revel for years, Julia Roberts posed for scheduled publicity shots for her latest film, *Hook*. She was wearing a Notre Dame baseball cap. On the following day, the woman most hunted by America's media was seen at the Nowhere Cafe in Los Angeles in the company of actor Jason Patric, Kiefer's friend and co-star in *The Lost Boys*. Born in Queens, New York, in 1966, Patric is the son of Pulitzer Prize-winning playwright Jason Miller. It also emerged that Jason's favourite football team was Notre Dame. Suddenly, Jason Patric found himself named as the man in the middle. *People Weekly* quoted staff members at the Canyon Ranch Spa in Tucson, where Julia and her friends had their girlie weekend on 8/9 June, as claiming that on the Sunday night, Patric had shown up out of the blue at the resort. Someone even claimed to have seen Patric comforting a distressed Julia as she left the dining room. Speculation was now red hot. Was Jason Patric Julia Roberts' boyfriend, or just a male friend?

While all this could only have pained Kiefer more, by poignant contrast he spent what would have been his wedding day removing his belongings from Julia Roberts' Hollywood Hills house. That night he spent hours alone thwacking balls about with his custom-made pool cue in the basement of the Hollywood Billiards club. Understanding friends, unsure of what to say, and perhaps deterred by a dangerous air emanating from him, gave him a wide berth. Kiefer is said to have said privately that Julia had broken his heart, and of Jason Patric he believed the rumours and vowed: 'When I get hold of Patric, I'm going to tear him limb from limb.' Obviously, this was not a literal threat, but Kiefer's embarrassment continued. On Saturday, Julia Roberts flew out of America with Jason Patric, ultimately to Dublin in Ireland, where they took two rooms in the sumptuous Shelbourne Hotel. The newshounds, in even stronger cry, chased after them. Hotel staff were buttonholed for any minute detail; one waitress reported that Julia was not wearing her engagement ring and looked drawn. Though it was too early to tell at that stage, Jason Patric did become Julia's new boyfriend. Their relationship lasted until early 1993.

Kiefer's sense of betrayal must have been enormously deep. He had already been branded the bad guy. Now, he was called a cuckold in the press. Sunday 16 June 1991 was Father's Day, and while his runaway bride was in the Emerald Isle with Jason Patric, Kiefer spent the day privately with his daughter, Sarah. At three years old she was too young to feel for her saddened father, but Camelia tried to help simply by giving him a happy family day.

Many people felt deeply for Kiefer. Director Joel Schumacher said: 'Kiefer is in a situation where you either grow up very fast, or you die.' Joel was certain that Kiefer was made of stern stuff and would weather the heartbreak and the public humiliation. Michael J Fox pointed out that it was so easy to become the *National Enquirer*'s poster boy of the month, and so his advice to his friend was that although the cancelled wedding was a hugely public event, Kiefer should just focus on a very small number of people around him and cut himself some space.

Kiefer continued to conduct himself with dignity, in a way that made his mother proud. 'I admire Kiefer enormously, the way he handled it,' said Shirley Douglas. 'It's one of those things in life that does you in for good or not. You need to have a strong core to take that.' Kiefer, meantime, had moved into a small apartment on Sunset Boulevard, not hiding away but needing to slip off the media radar. Things were far too raw. For almost two years, Julia Roberts had mattered more to him than anyone else in the world, apart from his daughter Sarah, and a lot of what he read about himself in the reams of lurid newspaper coverage was deeply hurtful and puzzling to him. He later said: 'It was the most amazing thing to watch. It was out of control and there was nothing I could do about it. I've been accused of having a sadistic tattoo fetish. I even read that I'd branded Julia! It was a real private, wonderful moment at Sunset Tattoo. I mean, how do you make someone get a tattoo? Tie them down? It was ridiculous.' Julia Roberts subsequently had the tattoo of a red heart inside a black Chinese symbol removed from over her left shoulder blade.

When asked if he felt resentment at events Kiefer deflected the question, saying he'd felt hurt and sad, but added that he was not the easiest person to be with. What got to Kiefer was the fact that the enormous media circus which spun into action over the cancelled wedding managed, with lies and wild accusations, to despoil the happy, loving time he and Julia had had together before the balloon went up. He was candid about the fact that he and Julia had unwittingly asked for a media backlash. 'You can't court the media on the level we did about our plans to wed, then call it off days before and not expect a tidal wave to knock you on your ass,' he said. As to all the past effusive interviews in which Julia had poured out her adoration for him, Kiefer again shouldered part of the blame saying: 'Well, I was with her. I could have said: "Please don't do that."' As he pointed out, he was just 24 and she 23 at the time.

Media-wise, this momentous time in his life would dog him for years. Once Kiefer did break his silence, he stated that in hindsight it was absolutely the right thing that he and Julia had not married. It just had not made dealing with it very easy at the time. He vividly recalled his awareness from the moment he received the phone call that his wedding was off, that he was going to be tossed about as if by a twister. He said: 'You could see it coming and you go: "Hold your breath, this is gonna hurt!" Such a lot of nasty things were said [in the press] but I couldn't really afford to pay much attention because it was hard enough just breaking up. You could drive yourself insane if you took notice of the silly stuff in tabloids.'

Along with hurt and embarrassment, Kiefer's sense of self-worth took a direct hit. 'I'd been working for about seven years, but all that didn't seem to matter. Your life is reduced to this mistake and it does a number on your self-confidence, your sense of purpose,' he confessed. In the blinding glare of hysteria between the time when Kiefer and Julia's romance had first become public knowledge, through to the sensational cancellation of their wedding, it was easy to forget that the pair had only been together for 21 months, one month short of the total time Kiefer knew Camelia Kath. Just as he had loved Camelia, so he had truly loved his *Flatliners* co-star but, contrary to media suggestions, he would *not* forever pine for Julia Roberts. He would love again and marry a second time, and eventually he was able to put this failed relationship firmly behind him. Over the years, Kiefer was relentlessly quizzed about Julia. He preferred not to look back, but speaking of her sense of humour when they had first met he said: 'She was one of the funniest people I'd ever known, but I don't know her now. We don't talk.'

CHAPTER 9

TAKING TIME TO HEAL

IN SUMMER 1991, Kiefer wore a gold ring designed with the Norman version of the clan Sutherland crest. Inscribed inside the ring was *indurare*, the Latin word for 'endure', and resilient is what he fully intended to be, despite it being a time of great personal turmoil. He had, however, myriad and complex emotions to grapple with. He was also the talk of Hollywood, and it was clearly going to be more than a nine-day wonder. Although he remained resolutely silent in the immediate aftermath of the sensationally cancelled wedding, he was taking up more column inches in the press than ever, and it was time to bail out of Los Angeles. Kiefer headed for his ranch and beautiful log-built home in Montana, where he spent the lion's share of the next 18 months in self-imposed exile, at least from starring in films. It was a soul-searching time from which he would gain a lot of solace. 'That time off was the best thing for me,' he later said. 'It put things in perspective.' Kiefer also subscribed to the theory that life comes in cycles, that every seven years an important event occurs in your personal life. 'Either you deal with it, or you become one of the walking dead,' he declared, but his determination to cope would be tested.

A man who always has to keep busy, he skied a lot and

tried to interest himself in dozens of new hobbies, none of which held his long-term attention. He took pleasure in increasing his stock of horses – he had again bought the horse he had ridden while making *Young Guns II* – but by his own admission there were times when he did not handle things too well. 'I can get self-destructive,' he confessed. America's tabloid journalists still had Kiefer firmly in their jaws, and were happy to run stories about his excesses in the clubs and bars. Kiefer enjoys a drink. The problem was, where whisky normally makes him happy-go-lucky good company, that particular summer the alcohol percolated with the pernicious feelings that were festering inside him. Understandably, he harboured a grudge against the way things had gone in his personal life, and that could sometimes express itself violently. Years later, he was able to reflect on how wasteful that had been, but right then he was a hurt, humiliated and angry young firebrand, who was sensitive to the harsh spotlight focused on him.

It was difficult for Kiefer to read wild accounts in the press, in which he struggled to recognise himself. He talked of the garbage written about him, the lies and exaggerations that went on so relentlessly that one morning he balked at going to his nearest newsagent to buy cigarettes for fear of being confronted by yet another lurid headline painting him as the bad guy. He accepted that by having allowed his engagement to Julia Roberts to become such a public matter, the public would take an inordinate interest in its dramatic demise, but individual members of the public sometimes overstepped the mark, and would actually tackle him. Kiefer was blunt: 'I didn't want to get in a fight, but if someone said something really rude to me, then I knew I'd have to.' Not that scrapping in itself actually fazed Kiefer. 'When I was younger I thought getting in a fight meant I was cool,' he said.

For a while, Kiefer was sucked into a downward spiral; it only beefed up his bad-boy image, and he did not always come off best in these bar room brawls. In Montana one night, he became embroiled in a fistfight with two off-duty soldiers who were, together, getting the better of him. At one stage he and one of the soldiers were locked in battle, rolling about the bar floor which was strewn with broken glass. Bruised, bloodied and sore, Kiefer returned to his ranch that night to clean himself up. He wouldn't know for several years that a piece of beer bottle had cut him so deeply that glass had embedded itself inside one of this elbows.

Of course, Kiefer could socialise and *not* get into brawls, but there were other ways to trip up. On a trip to Los Angeles, one evening late that summer he met fellow London-born actor Gary Oldman, whose latest screen role was playing Lee Harvey Oswald in Oliver Stone's 1991 movie, *JFK*. Together they had been knocking back the booze in a trendy hangout called One. It was the first time the two actors had met. When once asked what they had had in common, Gary Oldman quickly quipped: 'Bourbon!' Later that evening Kiefer, drunk, accompanied Oldman to the bar car park, to try out the car's brand new sound system. Once behind the wheel, Oldman started the engine and attempted to drive away, when policemen suddenly loomed as if from nowhere and promptly arrested the actor for drunk driving. The paparazzi hanging around the chic bar hit pay dirt when Oldman was handcuffed by the cops in full view and led away to spend the night behind bars. Kiefer was merely the passenger and not in control of the car. He had not tried to drive the vehicle while drunk. Nevertheless, this incident tainted his name as well as Gary Oldman's.

Back in Montana, away from hysterical headlines, in the sober light of day Kiefer continued to work through the meaning of what was really happening in his life. There were encouraging signs. He had taken some of the hardest knocks yet and although they had made him waver, he now knew that he was far from being in danger of falling down, because he realised that work as an actor was his unwavering bedrock. 'My strength is that I really love what I do and that somehow nothing has really ever interfered with that,' he said. Kiefer's screen work came into focus towards the end of 1991 with the release of *Article 99*, a gritty hospital drama he had shot on location in Kansas City, Missouri, late the previous year. He plays a surgeon who has his eyes opened when he joins the staff at a Veterans' Administration (VA) Hospital. It was his first film since *Flatliners*, and he had been drawn to the movie by the message it conveyed. Health care is a burning issue with Kiefer. Speaking of his mother, he said: 'She brought me up with the perspective that wealthy people in our society should take their fair share of the bill for health care, that society has a responsibility to itself to make sure that the weaker and less fortunate get taken care of.'

In Canada, Shirley Douglas was a prominent activist for the protection of the publicly funded health care system from privatisation. She is instrumental in organising fundraising and media events, was deeply involved in the Toronto Health Coalition and Friends of Medicare, and lobbied both Federal and provincial government officials. Tommy Douglas's grandson is no less vocal. During the 1991 US Presidential election, Kiefer made his strong opinions on this issue clear when he stated: 'Something has to be done about the national health care structure. It has to be done with helping to get the money the private sector and the public sector have raised for the homeless. That money unfortunately vanishes somewhere amid the bureaucracy buying all its paper before it buys a can of soup.' On a separate occasion, in 1992, Kiefer blasted: '*Article 99* addressed the fact that health care in this country is a national disgrace. The US has the best health care in the world – if you can afford it. Many people cannot.' Invoking the name of his former Socialist premier grandfather, he went on: 'I know what I'm talking about here. Until Brian Mulroney started fucking around with it, Canada had a great health care system for everyone, not just the rich.'

Kiefer passionately hoped that *Article 99* would go some way to heightening public awareness of the true extent of the problems that exist in Veterans' Administration Hospitals, and in the health service across the board. As part of his preparation to play one of the film's lead characters, Dr Peter Morgan, he read a pile of poignant letters from veterans about their plight. 'These guys have an incredible frustration with the system that makes it so difficult for them to get into hospital, first of all, and then to get the care they need,' he recalled. Kiefer was also vocal about the failure of the US government to honour its promise to the people in the armed forces that they would receive the best health care that America could provide.

Article 99, written by Ron Cutler, was directed by Howard Deutch. Joining Kiefer to make up the cast were Ray Liotta, Forest Whitaker, Lea Thompson, John Mahoney, Keith David and Eli Wallach. Kiefer's character arrives at a VA hospital, viewing his internship as a stepping-stone to lucrative private practice. Shockingly, what he finds is a place strangled by red tape, and run by an administrator who puts profit before patients. Morgan teams up with a maverick surgeon, played by Ray Liotta, to break the rules and save lives. *Variety* called *Article 99* 'ultimately more successful in awakening the viewer to a desperate situation, than in providing a good time,' which in this instance pleased Kiefer no end. He had a good time making a movie with such a message, and he was also aware that as he grew older, he bore an ever increasing on-screen resemblance to his father. Some people saw a direct link between Kiefer in *Article 99* and Donald Sutherland in *M*A*S*H*, 21 years earlier. One Hollywood reporter maintained that 'in the closing shot – a freeze frame of Sutherland and Liotta, arriving late and unkempt to meet the new hospital administrator – the pair could easily pass for Donald Sutherland and Elliott Gould.' While Kiefer would not go so far as to concur with that, he did reveal: 'In the scene where I put on an old army hat, I *did* do that for my old man so he would say: "Geez! We really *do* look alike!"'

Apart from the release of *Article 99*, which had already

been in the can, Kiefer's career had hit a slump. An offshoot of the very public cancellation of his wedding was that in a town where perception is all, his professional profile had altered overnight. Kiefer had gone from being talked and written about as a respected, versatile and thrusting young actor, to the man Julia Roberts didn't marry. His bad-boy image of pub brawling, and even the Gary Oldman incident, all weighed against him in the scales. Of course, Kiefer had deliberately stepped back from making so many films in the period prior to his intended marriage, but because of events his planned one-year break had now entered a third year. That said, he was initially unaware of how out of favour he had become. 'I didn't realise I'd gone away until I started reading about it in the papers,' he said. 'I knew I hadn't made any major hits recently, but it's not like I'd died! This industry though is not forgiving of people who take an amount of time off. It busted me up worse than anything else I've ever done.'

Years later Kiefer could quip drily: 'You could say I was not on everybody's first list to do the bigger films,' but at the time it came as a shock to him. Because he had had a run of success with *The Lost Boys*, the *Young Guns* movies and *Flatliners*, he assumed that that was the way of his world. He imagined that, having reached a particular plateau, good film opportunities would continue to flow to his door. 'Then, somewhere around 25 years old, I got hit with a frying pan and realised it wasn't like that,' he recalled. He confessed that he simply had not been prepared for a situation where work offers abruptly dried up. 'I had a chip on my shoulder,' he revealed, 'and it was getting pretty heavy.' As Kiefer resisted this feeling worsening, he was helped by two factors. He'd been paid very well as an actor and so could afford the lean work spell. He also did not scoff at taking smaller roles. To him, it was not the be-all and end-all to play the flashy lead. A quality minor role would attract his eye, which is what happened when he was offered the supporting part of quirky FBI agent Sam Stanley in the David Lynch-directed movie,

Twin Peaks: Fire Walk With Me, the film prequel to the cult US television series, *Twin Peaks*. Already a fan of the TV show, Kiefer had also had an ambition to work with David Lynch, and was happy to join the cast, which included Sheryl Lee, Kyle MacLachlan, Ray Wise, Madchen Amick, Dana Ashbrook, Moira Kelly and David Bowie.

Co-written by Lynch and Robert Engels, the film handled events leading up to the murder of a local girl in the town of Twin Peaks, and had an audience largely comprising fans of the TV series. The critics were not kind. Britain's *Guardian* said: 'It looks like a very bad movie made by a very good director, tired of fooling around for a television audience.' The *TV Times Film Guide* queried the indulgent two and a quarter hours running time. 'The wanton Laura Palmer (Sheryl Lee) is bumped off by her possibly incestuous father (Ray Wise). Who cares? David Bowie appears and says nothing, while other stars appear and may wish they had said nothing.'

Kiefer had filmed his scenes for *Twin Peaks: Fire Walk With Me*, which was released in 1992, in the space of a few days. Back in LA, his main job as 1992 unfolded was reading film scripts at his Stillwater Productions office at 20th Century Fox. The smart office had an inspiring view of one of the studio's soundstages; donning collar and tie, he got into the way of going there every day. 'There are three of us in our office at Fox,' he said, 'and we're all scrambling for a good film.' This routine was not perhaps how Kiefer envisaged best spending his time, but he was determined to do whatever would give him more control over his life.

The notion that Kiefer Sutherland was completely forgotten by Hollywood's movers and shakers was wrong, as was proved when Rob Reiner – *Stand By Me*'s director – got in touch, asking Kiefer to consider taking a role in an upcoming feature film, *A Few Good Men*, written by Aaron Sorkin and starring Tom Cruise, Jack Nicholson, Demi Moore and Kevin Bacon. The powerful courtroom drama about two marines standing trial for the killing of a fellow marine handled complex issues of loyalty, duty and honour, and exposed a fictitious, sacred military code by which soldiers are ordered to carry out serious physical assault on any fellow soldier deemed to be weak. Kiefer's role was that of Lt Jonathan Kendrick, a brutal, overly religious marine involved in the murder. It was an intense and powerful part that Kiefer nearly did not take when the director came calling. Kiefer has admitted: 'I almost turned the movie down. Rob asked me to do it and said: "I want you to play Kendrick, but I don't have much money." That was the beginning of teaching me that it's what interests you as an actor that's important.' The role of the Bible-thumping military officer appealed to Kiefer, because he loves character parts. He also liked it that the movie was saying that elements exist within America's military machine that can get out of hand. Personally, he did not believe that the US military was as controlled as the nation liked to believe.

Kiefer filmed his scenes for *A Few Good Men* in a three-week period, and there was a freedom for him in the fact that the film was not riding on him. Kiefer had fifth billing, and was blown away watching veteran star Jack Nicholson in action. Till then, he had admired Nicholson, but felt that he was one of those actors who played himself in practically every role. After watching Nicholson shoot his courtroom scene, Kiefer swiftly revised that opinion. 'I watched how hard Jack Nicholson works to *be* Jack Nicholson,' he said. This impressed Kiefer, but his own turn before the camera drew deep praise. He is universally considered to have turned in a riveting performance as Lt Jonathan Kendrick, stealing virtually every scene he is in. Oozing his innate screen presence, Kiefer inhabited the unsympathetic character so completely that it was his co-stars' turn to blink and look again. Kevin Bacon said: 'Kiefer is *very* good at tapping into the darker side. He always has been. He enjoys it. He's one of those actors that I appreciate, in that he has no problem showing his ugly side.'

Released in 1992, *A Few Good Men* became a critically acclaimed box office smash hit. For Kiefer, it opened a new door, for it was a case of like father, like son. In 1991, Donald Sutherland's breathlessly electrifying few minutes of screen time in *JFK* as the shadowy character known only as X, made far and away the most memorable impact with audiences. Now Kiefer had just shown that he had that same gift to shoot in and out of a star-studded movie and imprint his individual presence on the mind. Inevitably, it increased calls for Kiefer and Donald to co-star in a film. Their respect for one another was not in doubt. Indeed, Kiefer said around this time that there were about three actors in the world he would sacrifice an arm to have the chance to work with, and his father was one of those.

Perhaps mindful of how Donald's career commitments had left great gaps in his own growing up, Kiefer strove to maintain quality time with four-year-old Sarah. Father and daughter and Sarah's dog spent a lot of time taking long walks in the park or along the beach he had slept rough at on reaching LA as a hungry, aspiring actor. Sarah would happily snuggle up to her daddy and watch old movies, or they would finger-paint together. Kiefer confessed that their work was not destined for any gallery showing, but he was proud to pin up a couple of Sarah's offerings on his office walls. Their time together was very precious.

By now, time had been a healer for Kiefer. He was calmer, able to put the traumatic events of 1991 behind him, and was philosophical about the quiet professional spell he had lived through. 'Things were changing, times were changing. People wanted to see something new,' he said, pointing out that many actors have busy periods interspersed with lulls. In his inimitable fashion he remarked baldly: 'It's important to give audiences a break from your mug.' In time he also reflected: 'One of the great things that came out of that mess is that I hadn't realised before how fortunate I was with how I feel about what I do.' Aiming to be fair about the press, which had severely scorched him in the past year, he was able to say: 'I've been working for ten years and only in the last twelve months have I had a lot of things blown out of proportion, misunderstood or flatly lied about.' While, as to his love life, he simply said: 'It's nice to be lonely.' He was ready personally and professionally to go forward and not look back. He stated emphatically: 'I make mistakes. I try my best to recover from those and I can go to sleep at night. I live my life how I see fit.'

CHAPTER 10

BACK IN THE SADDLE

WHEN KIEFER RETURNED to the limelight as a leading man in 1993, it was ironically in an American remake of a Dutch/French film called *The Vanishing*. Based on Tim Krabbe's novel, *The Golden Egg*, it is a psychological thriller about a young couple on holiday. The woman mysteriously disappears when they randomly pull in at a petrol station, plunging her distraught boyfriend into a dogged but nerve-racking three-year search to find out what happened to her. Todd Graff's screenplay for this tension-filled tale had been sent to Kiefer to see if it would entice him to end his absence from frontline movies. After his own period of intense personal turmoil, Kiefer found the boyfriend's plight appealing. The character of teacher Jeff Harriman is relentless in his quest for answers, however devastating these may prove to be, and he is prepared to risk his own life in the process of that discovery. Kiefer immediately tapped into that stubborn single-mindedness. 'I don't think that's obsessive,' he maintained of his character's determination. 'I think it's reactionary.'

George Sluizer had directed the original 1988 movie, and once again helmed this new version. The cast included Jeff Bridges, Nancy Travis, Lisa Eichhorn and Park Overall, while

Sandra Bullock played Diane, the girlfriend who is abducted without a trace. *The Vanishing* was filmed on location in Washington State, with the lakeside scenes shot at Camp Omache, near Monroe. As a young man unable to accept his girlfriend's sudden disappearance, Kiefer set out to turn in a highly charged performance. While it felt good to be back in harness in a lead role, he would remember *The Vanishing* as the film that gave him one mightily frightening experience. It happened when his character had to be put in a coffin and buried. Kiefer lay down in the wooden box and the lid was placed on top, a mere inch from his face. Stifling as it was, he was doing alright, expecting to hear the sounds of handfuls of earth being sprinkled on top and that would be that, end of scene. What he heard instead was an electric drill driving in eight screws all round the lid. A tractor then shovelled a load of earth with a heavy thump onto the coffin, and everything went terrifyingly black. Kiefer panicked.

In the movie, Nancy Travis has to claw frantically at the coffin lid and find Jeff Harriman dead. Kiefer later discovered that the actress had been stunned when director George Sluizer told her that Kiefer was actually buried, and that she would have to hurry up and dig him out. It was assumed that the director had kept this vital detail a surprise from Nancy in order to capture her genuinely panicked reaction on camera. What Kiefer could never fathom was why *he* had been similarly kept in the dark about the intention to literally bury him alive. In the scene when Jeff Harriman is unearthed and the coffin lid prised off, Kiefer admits that he looks very far from 'dead' for the cameras. His jugular vein was visibly pounding wildly, because his heart was absolutely hammering with the intense fright he had sustained. Kiefer later said that when the shot was in the can, he and the director 'had a conversation about communication. He understood where I was coming from.' Perhaps it was as civilised and as calm as that, but one cannot help wondering if this politely phrased piece about reaching a better professional understanding was a euphemism for an irate Kiefer going hotfoot after the director's blood for having unnecessarily scared him half to death!

Kiefer, however, put this shocking experience behind him and was looking forward to tackling his other feature film lead role that year in another remake, this time of the classic Alexandre Dumas swashbuckler, *The Three Musketeers*, which would re-team him with *Young Guns* co-star and friend Charlie Sheen. Friendship is very dear to Kiefer, and having gone through the mill in recent years, he had learned just who his true buddies were. Charlie Sheen and his brother, Emilio Estevez, had both been among the guests for the wedding that never was, and had empathised with Kiefer's acute hurt and embarrassment. In the early 1990s, Charlie Sheen was plunged into his own very different and hugely embarrassing situation.

Already a Hollywood bad boy because of his drug addiction, now Charlie was caught up in a juicy, headline-grabbing, real-life sex scandal when the notorious affair of glamorous Hollywood madam Heidi Fleiss made front-page news. Fleiss was being investigated by the police in connection with a call girl service for LA's rich and famous. She refused to hand over her client list, but the investigation revealed that Charlie Sheen was on her book of regular customers. The scandal had the newspaper presses red hot, the public salivating, and more than a few wealthy, well-known people in a nervous sweat for fear of exposure. Caught out, Charlie made a taped deposition in which he admitted ordering up call girls at least 27 times between December 1991 and 1993, and having paid Heidi Fleiss in excess of $50,000 in travellers' cheques. The handsome young star came in for some intense heat, but he weathered the media's blistering blast in his affable way. Kiefer felt for him. He said: 'I think, when you can't believe that you are in that kind of situation, Charlie's reaction is to tell a joke and protect whatever his emotions are, to keep those private.'

The strain and pressure brought about in the early 1990s was all a far cry from the boisterously playful antics Kiefer and Charlie Sheen had earlier indulged in when the chance arose in 1989 to get their own back on Emilio Estevez, who enjoys playing on-set practical jokes on people. Emilio had been directing and acting in *Men at Work*, which starred Charlie. Kiefer recalled that although both he and Charlie were actually deep down proud of Emilio for taking on the twin burden of director and actor, they did not give the lively young star a break. In *Men at Work* there was to be a shoot-out scene filmed on Hollywood Boulevard. Kiefer disrupted proceedings somewhat by arranging to have a 3,000-pound cow delivered to the film set. The consternation caused when the lumbering beast happily strolled in had everyone in stitches of laughter, especially when the placid cow had to be tethered to a parking meter to be looked after until it could be returned to its owner.

On the same shoot, Charlie Sheen chummed up two LAPD cop friends to come and supposedly arrest him on the set. Emilio was thrown into a tizzy, not least wondering which scenes he could possibly film now with the main lead in handcuffs! It was a good hour before Emilio learned that his colourful brother had not truly been arrested and was not languishing in jail. 'It was hilarious,' recalled Kiefer. He would soon find out what it was like to make his own directorial debut, but in early summer 1993 his sights were trained on donning the stylishly romantic garb of one of France's fabled musketeers.

There had already been several big screen adaptations of Alexandre Dumas' 19th-century novel about how three courageously loyal musketeers, Athos, Aramis and Porthos, plus D'Artagnan, a green but game would-be recruit to their elite ranks, save the King and Queen of France from the evil machinations of the powerful Cardinal Richelieu who, aided by the beautiful Milady De Winter, plans to overthrow the monarchy and place himself on the French throne. The colossal success of *Robin Hood: Prince of Thieves* in 1991 had sent Hollywood movie makers scrambling to repeat the triumph by bringing sword-wielding, rip-roaring adventure back to the cinema screens, and more than one film company had focused on this popular family story. Disney, however, beat all competitors by moving fast and getting under way with what would be one of its biggest budget movies.

Screenwriter David Loughery had handled the adaptation, and director Stephen Herek had been hired. The producers were Roger Birnbaum and Joe Roth, formerly head of 20th Century Fox, who had intended giving Kiefer and Julia Roberts their spectacular wedding in 1991. It was Joe Roth who approached Kiefer, saying that although no screenplay was yet to hand, Disney would like to offer him the role of the strong and brooding Athos. Kiefer trusted Roth's judgement and accepted immediately. With Kiefer committed, the filmmakers signed up the other cast members. Charlie Sheen would, not inappropriately, prove to be well cast in the role of ladies' man, Aramis, while Kiefer's *Flatliners* co-star, Oliver Platt, made for a larger than life comedic Porthos. Casting needed an actor for D'Artagnan who could pass for being appreciably younger than the three main musketeers, and 23-year-old Chris O'Donnell fitted the bill.

Hugh O'Conor, Gabrielle Anwar and Paul McGann played King Louis, Queen Anne and Girard, D'Artagnan's hometown pursuer, respectively. The performances of Tim Curry as a predatory Cardinal Richelieu, Michael Wincott as the sinister, gravel-voiced Rochefort, and Rebecca De Mornay as the sensual but lethal Lady Sabine De Winter, provided an extra richness to the film's tapestry. *The Three Musketeers* was mainly filmed on location at Perchtoldsdorf in Austria, with the film's sword fighting climax shot inside the magnificent throne room of the Hofburg Palace in Vienna. Disney wanted to stay true to Alexandre Dumas' characters and have the musketeers in their twenties; 26-year-old Kiefer would carry off the charismatic but complex Athos with aplomb. As ever, his deep, velvety voice was a decided asset, and the sense he projected of carrying a secret inner hurt shone subtly through on screen. In this adaptation there was an added twist, in that after the audience discovers that Athos had once led a very different life as a wealthy count who had renounced his name, title and lands after a bitter betrayal by his wife, it emerges that Lady Sabine De Winter had been *that* wife.

To Kiefer, *The Three Musketeers* represented a classical way of men sticking to their principles of honour, loyalty and duty, no matter what. There was a lot to enjoy in making this film, and by the end of the shooting schedule he felt he had truly learned the art of horse riding. Tim Curry commented about the enduring appeal of swashbuckling adventure films, that swordplay was very sexy; putting the young bloods through their paces with the rapier was Bob Anderson, the veteran fencing coach who, at the outset of his long career, had taught the legendary star of swashbuckling, Errol Flynn. The character Athos had always been a fierce swordsman, and Bob Anderson called Kiefer's Athos 'a rugged, hard fighter'. Said Kiefer: 'Charlie's a much more elegant fencer than I.' Despite the relentless high energy scenes to enact in a pacy movie, once off duty Kiefer, Charlie Sheen and some others still had more than enough stamina to revel in late night partying in Vienna. The younger Chris O'Donnell was frankly amazed at how Kiefer and Charlie were ever ready to hit the high spots. That these live wires loved a good time was obvious but the filmmakers had no complaints, for everyone without fail showed up on time, sober and eager to work the following day.

In the movie, D'Artagnan's closest affinity is with Athos, but it was Charlie Sheen who remarked on how fresh-faced and youthful Chris O'Donnell was, a young actor still with the eye of the tiger. Like Kiefer, Charlie was in his tenth year of making movies. He said affectionately that the older cast members were there to break the young lad in slowly. *The*

Three Musketeers was an ensemble piece, aimed specifically at bringing a younger generation into the cinemas in their droves when it was released countrywide in America in November 1993. Some critics lambasted the beautifully filmed, all-action romp as being *Young Guns* with swords, but the man and woman in the street loved it right to its blatantly feel-good ending.

In complete contrast, the third lead film role Kiefer undertook in 1993 was as Denver Bayliss, a cold-blooded killer awaiting execution on death row; this was in *Last Light*, a made-for-television movie that saw Kiefer making his directorial debut. The grim prison drama was written by Robert Eisele, who also played Bayliss's lawyer. Under Kiefer's direction was Forest Whitaker, with whom he had worked in *Article 99*, and who in *Last Light* acts opposite him as the prison guard who ends up befriending Bayliss. Other cast members included Clancy Brown and Tony T Johnson. Such is the fast turnaround in television that the shooting schedule was a mere five weeks, but Kiefer managed to fulfil his obligations with even a little time in hand, and it stunned his cast to see, on a daily basis, how he was able to inhabit the skin of the dark, deadly killer so completely in front of the camera, and then switch off to become Kiefer Sutherland, picking up the director's reins for the first time.

In the film, the unusual communication that evolves between two men on opposite sides of the prison bars, and the repercussions of that developing friendship, gave a poignant and intelligent dimension to a genre of film that all too often depends simply on violence and naked brutality for its appeal. *Last Light* debuted on America's Showtime in autumn 1993. In trying his hand at directing, Kiefer had wanted to see if he could forge inroads into making a bigger impact within the acting industry, and this hard-hitting drama brought him high critical acclaim. In addition to drawing some of the best reviews received by any cable production at that point, *Last*

Light earned several Cable Ace Award nominations, which was a source of immense pride to Kiefer.

However, it could not be said that deep down he was especially satisfied by his return to the acting world. In 1994 he made an uncredited appearance as a roadblock officer in *Teresa's Tattoo*, and took a lead role in a big-screen comedy, but the ever unpredictable path of his life as a result of the latter film would take an astonishing turn.

CHAPTER 11

CALL OF THE WILD

CHOOSING A FILM ROLE was never, in itself, a piece of Kiefer's overall grand design, although his participation in certain movies *had* ultimately altered the path of his life. When he signed up to play one of the two lead roles in *The Cowboy Way*, he had no idea of the radical direction in which it would steer him, nor of the exhilarating new horizons it would open up.

Based on a story by Robert C Thompson and William D Wittliff, the buddy action comedy directed by Gregg Champion seemed a harmless piece of froth about two rodeo champions who ride from New Mexico to New York City in search of the kidnapped daughter of an old friend. It was replete with scenes such as rodeo riding, hicks from the sticks gallantly tipping their Stetsons to passing ladies, bar room bust ups, horse riding down New York avenues and catching up with a speeding commuter train on horseback, The cast included Ernie Hudson, Dylan McDermott and Cara Buono, with Woody Harrelson taking the other lead. As rodeo star Sonny Gilstrap, Kiefer was the more intensely serious of the main duo, and it was his real-life reputation for disquieting intensity that had drawn the filmmakers to him. At the same time, producer Brian Grazer was concerned that

Kiefer's sometimes menacing presence might prove too much of a contrast to the giddy goofiness to be portrayed by Woody Harrelson. Said Grazer: 'I said to Kiefer's agent: "I like Kiefer a lot as an actor, but I don't know him. *Is* he this dark, brooding, moody guy?"' Any unease on the producer's part was erased once filming got under way.

Brian Grazer was also surprised that Kiefer didn't simply show up on time, hit his mark and deliver the goods. Instead, he also showed interest in the movie's development. Perhaps it was the burgeoning director in Kiefer, but absorbing the whole project of *The Cowboy Way*, he had a central creative vision that extended beyond his role, and it was input that the producer genuinely appreciated. 'Kiefer is really smart,' declared Brian Grazer, 'but he's not pretentious. He was really helpful in establishing an overview of the movie's goal.' *The Cowboy Way*, however, could not rise above the average. Whether that became obvious to Kiefer, he was perfectly sanguine when he learned that the studio's marketing plan omitted him from some of the movie's pre-release print adverts. One such advert featured Woody Harrelson standing alone and naked, preserving his modesty courtesy of a strategically placed Stetson. One Hollywood wit commented: 'With an ad like that, an unsuccessful movie might be perceived as Woody Harrelson's failure, not Kiefer Sutherland's.'

When *The Cowboy Way* was released in 1994, critics were split on the performances of its two stars. *Halliwells* maintained: 'Smug and unlikeable lead performances sink this comedy from the start, although it would have sunk anyway whoever had played the roles.' *Film Review* weighed in with: 'The action sequences are lacklustre and the bickering and bonding between the likeable leads is drearily predictable.' After filming wrapped, Kiefer publicly professed to have high hopes for the comedy, but privately he was not laughing, and with a heavy mind he quit Los Angeles for his ranch in Whitefish, Montana. Dubbed 'Big Sky Country' because of its sparsely populated wide-open spaces to the east and its magnificent mountains in the west, Montana is home to the Glacier National Park, where some 2,000 crystal clear lakes nestle between glacially carved valleys and high alpine peaks. The National Park is also the protected home of black and grizzly bears, wolves and mountain lions. South of Glacier National Park, on the shore of Whitefish Lake, the lumber village of Whitefish is one of the coolest hangouts in the Rocky Mountains.

Lying in the shade of the Big Mountain Ski Resort, Whitefish bristles as a magnet for enthusiasts of hiking, climbing, mountain biking and skiing, while its quaint downtown area is alive with exquisite restaurants and bustling taverns with character. It is hardly surprising that Kiefer classed this place his bolt hole. He often spoke about how he worked in Los Angeles but his heart lay at home in Canada. Here, he'd found a halfway house, for his spectacularly lovely ranch was a mere 60 miles south of the Canadian border.

Ranching suited Kiefer. Rearing thoroughbred horses, he was very comfortable milling around the barns with his bare feet in clogs. In this environment he seemed to inhabit another peaceful sphere, which was always a panacea for him in troubled times. Here too, he had every opportunity to kick back and indulge his love of sport. As an avid skier, snow and ice draws him, and he spent hours on the Big Mountain, the second largest ski hill in Montana. A staunch Toronto Maple Leafs fan, Kiefer himself shows power and panache as an ice hockey player, which means he is much in demand to play in celebrity charity matches. Actor Denis Leary said that Kiefer is one of the very best actors to be on the ice with in a game. Certainly, Kiefer's enthusiasm never wanes. He said: 'I played in a beer league team in Los Angeles for eight years. It didn't matter what anybody was working on, you just never missed a game. Ninety per cent of the guys were Canadian and the camaraderie we shared was great. The bonds that are created in team sports are irreplaceable.' Kiefer also enjoys a close friendship with Ontario-born Wayne D Gretzky, the ice hockey legend universally known as 'The Great One'. Gretzky will occasionally join in amateur matches, and has said of Kiefer: 'He's very determined and serious, but the NHL is safe.'

Team pursuits and the lively socialising afterwards were all very well, but behind closed doors, alone in his Montana home, Kiefer was once again reflecting seriously on which path to take. In December 1993 he would turn 27, and he felt at the crossroads all actors face. 'Between the ages of 27 and 35 is very dangerous professionally,' he maintained. 'You're too old to play the high school student and too young to play a proper leading man. You're in a kind of no man's land.' It was much more than that, however. Kiefer was tired of Los Angeles and unhappy with his choice of film roles. The insecurity of never knowing when the parts will dry up had led him to justify undertaking work that he really, on hindsight, ought to have elbowed. 'It's a terrible thing to get into: well, you need to pay the bills, your kids have to go to school, horses cost money, etc., etc. I was doing really shitty work, which I only blame myself for. I needed to take time off to figure out what I was doing with my life,' he explained. He would not miss LA too much either. In autumn 1993 he confessed: 'I got really mean [minded], tired and cranky. I didn't have a lot left to put into films. It's embarrassing when you stay at the party a little too long. I certainly did.'

Of course, rattling about without any sense of purpose would not do either, so after long, solitary contemplation Kiefer came to the somewhat startling decision to make a complete change in his life, to put his acting career on hold for an unspecified spell and to see if he could become a professional cowboy. It's hard not to conclude that, of his generation of actors, only Kiefer Sutherland would do something so radical. Said Kiefer: 'I had been roping since *Young Guns* and I'd learned enough to be on the cusp of knowing that if I pushed it a little further, I could really do it.' Champion team roper John English, one of the technical advisors on the set of *The Cowboy Way*, had spotted that potential, and the two men became friends during the shoot. Said John English: 'Everybody else kind of tiptoed around Kiefer because he was a movie star, but we hit it off.'

Kiefer blossomed so pronouncedly under John's tutelage for the role of Sonny Gilstrap, that English invited him to his ranch in New Mexico, to train properly full time. Though there was some filming to be done in New York, Kiefer seemed keen. Yet English revealed: 'I thought well, that'll be the end of that but sure enough, Kiefer called.' Kiefer had decided to go the whole way and attempt to join the American rodeo circuit. He threw himself into it, planning to purchase the horses, the cattle, the tractors and other vehicles he would require, but first he hotfooted it to the small town of Belen in New Mexico, where he moved into accommodation at English's ranch.

He was eager to take on a new challenge. Roping was a lot harder than the professionals made it look. While making *The Cowboy Way*, he had started out by roping furniture. In his hotel room he had repeatedly tried to lasso the chair across at the desk. Then outdoors, on horseback, he had to learn to rope a dummy. It was a gradual process but, intrigued, he'd been keen to perfect his skills, and on downtime he would avidly seek something to practice on. This had unlooked-for consequences one day when, on impulse, he lassoed a young woman working on the film set. Lounging beside a telegraph pole, Kiefer had spotted the unsuspecting lady, clipboard in hand, walking spritely across an open space, and cheekily he couldn't resist it. He successfully roped both her feet, but before he knew it the knot had slipped home, bringing the startled woman crashing down. Appalled and contrite, he rushed to help her, but as he untied her and fussed over her, raising her up and dusting her off, she mercifully took it all in good part.

At John English's ranch, Kiefer restricted himself to learning how to rope steers. It was a fairly disciplined life there. Every day, he rose at dawn to practise solidly for hours before the sweltering heat became too much for the horses and the cattle. In the afternoons, teacher and pupil usually got stuck into games of baseball, when the competitive streak in both men brought an enlivening edge to the matches. Come sunset, Kiefer would be back in the dusty, dry corral for more practice, and would end the day quenching his worked-up thirst with some new friends in a local bar in town. For weeks on end, this formed the pattern of his days – film roles, Los Angeles, his 'other life' all ceased to exist. This complete opting out of the Hollywood scene shocked many of Kiefer's acquaintances, but those friends who knew him well were not surprised by this new enthusiasm. Years later, Lou Diamond Phillips said: 'Kiefer's always been serious about his acting but if he's got an urge to do something, he'll do it. He doesn't just stick his toe in, he goes all the way in. He became a real cowboy.'

It is perhaps more accurate to say that, initially, Kiefer became an apprentice cowboy. He went out on the road working for John English, accompanying the rodeo star to competitions. 'I worked as a groom basically, as well as cleaning up the horse shit and doing the driving,' said Kiefer. 'The other cowboys loved that – a movie star being a groom.' Kiefer loved this period when he, English and another guy, with the horse trailer hitched up to their truck, drove from town to town on the rodeo circuit. To Kiefer, it was the closest he would get to being on the road with a rock band. He most adored the companionships that evolved by dint of being cooped up together for prolonged periods. 'Those were my missing college years,' he claimed. 'We had to haul our horses, so we logged up 100,000 miles a season, easy. Generally, one person would sleep and two would sit up and talk. There's nothing like two o'clock in the morning on the highway.'

Another immensely pleasing aspect of this new world was that his celebrity cut no ice whatsoever. It was yet another touchstone experience of the kind Kiefer valued. He'd always known that the bizarre world that is planet Hollywood was totally unrepresentative of normal life, but now he felt: 'It's funny when you look back and think about how much time you've wasted trying to acquire something that really didn't fucking matter in the first place.' Kiefer worked his way through this phase in his life by acting on his gut instincts, and by early 1994, with relentless practising and rapidly learning the ropes behind the scenes on the championship rodeo circuit, his confidence had grown to the point where he decided to enter the rodeo competitions himself. At first he tried to do this low key, and would enter contests under various pseudonyms, usually drawing on his five middle names, but that did not last long. John English recalled: 'Everyone knew who Kiefer was anyway, so I told him, you might as well just enter under your own name.' He did so. 'There are two kinds of event in rodeo, and bull riding is one of the roughstock events. I was into immobilising cows myself,' explained Kiefer, which meant charging on horseback into an arena surrounded by baying spectators to rope steers, against the clock.

In spring 1994, at a San Antonio rodeo, Kiefer took part in a major team roping competition for the first time. Although tense, and concentrating hard on the task before him, as he backed his horse into the starting box, poised and ready, amid the noisy hyper expectant crowd who'd heard his name announced across the tinny tannoy, Kiefer heard some men behind him clearly laughing at him. It neither surprised nor offended him. He felt that they had every right to be amused. Most of these professional cowboys had been swinging ropes practically since they could walk, and here was some actor who had appeared as a cowboy in a movie, thinking for one tiny instant that he could do it for real. Seconds later the chute opened, and a raging, bucking steer thundered out.

Kiefer followed on horseback, and within seconds his rope flew through the air and roped the cow by its horns, exactly as he was supposed to. As the crowd erupted with delight, and deafening applause and whistles rang out, Kiefer was busy getting over his profound shock that he had actually pulled it off, and so impressively. 'It was the perfect combination of exhilaration and relief,' he later recalled.

That unforgettable buzz was not a one-off thrill. Emboldened by this flawless beginning, Kiefer embarked on the competitive rodeo circuit with great zest and determination. 'I drove all over the country and I felt like a tough guy, for a minute. It was a lot of fun,' he said. The unpredictability of the event also energised him. 'It's absolutely exhilarating because a horse and a cow will never react the same way twice. Every time out of the gate, it's a whole new experience.' It wasn't a painless experience. He revealed: 'I've broken every finger doing rodeos.' Any discomfort paled against what he got out of having thrown himself so wholeheartedly into this alternative lifestyle. 'By working with horses and roping, I got a better perspective on things,' he said. 'My sense of self-worth was not simply reliant on whether or not I was acting.'

Immersed in this testosterone-soaked macho world, as well as working hard at developing his rodeo and roping skills, sating his highly tuned competitive streak and enjoying the rough-and-ready male comradeship, Kiefer could also work off any inner aggression, frustration and tension, leaving him as a cheeky, footloose free agent happily pursuing the ladies. He wasn't looking right now for deep and meaningful connections; in the light of the way his love life had gone in recent years, this was perhaps just as well, or was maybe even something of a relief. Roguish, vibrant and a very earthy man with unconventional good looks, he had no shortage of pretty women keen for his company.

Kiefer likes the diversity within people, and prefers there to be a hint of mystery about a woman. He finds that far more appealing than to know every last detail. Revealing what he found sexy in a woman, he said: 'I think the most attractive thing is a sense of humour. If someone can make you laugh, you've gotten a lot out of the way.' As to whether he would find a woman making the first overtures off-putting, he admitted: 'I like a mutual flirtation and then we would have to meet halfway. I don't like a one-way street. It's not that interesting.' He has described the perfect date as being when the woman still cares for him the next day, and if she returns his call. Best of all, says Kiefer, would be a woman who rang *him* the day after a date, to say they had had a good time. Only, he states, he wouldn't be so bold as to expect that. He also knows that he has blown potential relationships because of his lax sense of timekeeping in his social life; he never wears a wristwatch, which doesn't help, and he is easily distracted. He's been known to arrange to meet a woman at a certain time, then some detour takes longer than he has bargained for and he loses all track of the hour. When that happens, he usually opts not to ring to say he is running late, since he fully expects to get a hard time from the irate lady who's been left waiting for him. He reasoned: 'I figure, do I want to get yelled at now on the phone or later, face-to-face?'

As yet he had been unlucky in love, in the sense of relationships standing the test of time. Ten years on, he would be in little better shape in that department. Yet he continues to believe that life is better with love in it, than without. He also counts himself among those men who find women enigmatic, hard to fathom – which he likes. He declared: 'The day you have figured out the difference between women and men is the day that you're no longer attracted to women. It's the difference that is so fantastic and frustrating, angering and really sexy.'

Never having had any great opinion of his looks, Kiefer had never envisaged encountering problems with stalkers, but one disturbing event occurred in the 1990s when a man somehow got hold of a personal phone book belonging to someone in the movie industry; the book contained the private phone numbers of several stars, including Kiefer's. It took a while to unfold, but it transpired that this guy was passing himself off as Kiefer in phone calls to various people in Hollywood. The potential to cause mischief this way was immense. Kiefer only discovered that something dodgy was going on when an actress in a popular television show rang him to ask why he had rudely stood her up the night before. Bewildered, Kiefer had to say that he had no idea what she was on about, that he had never met her and had certainly never arranged a date with her. The actress, doubtless feeling slightly foolish, knew by now that something was very wrong, because the man she had arranged to meet, who had called himself Kiefer Sutherland, did not have the distinctively deep, velvety voice she was hearing right then. Alerted to the fact that some impersonation was taking place, Kiefer got the authorities to investigate. In the end, it turned out that the guy who had come by this private phone book was by then a prisoner in a Californian jail. Ironically, although he had been violating Kiefer's privacy and probably that of other stars, his legal rights as an inmate protected his identity, which meant that Kiefer never found out who he was.

The rodeo lifestyle had not lost its lustre for Kiefer, and he would return to it at the end of the decade, but in early 1995 there were signs that his 'old life' was tugging on him when he began to edge back towards acting with involvement in two TV projects. He directed and starred in an episode of the Showtime film noir series, *Fallen Angels*. As Matt Cordell, he appeared in 'Love and Blood', about a boxer who is framed for murder; it aired in America on 8 October 1995. That same year, Kiefer also took on a supporting role in the Oscar-nominated short movie, *The Duke of Groove*, written by Adam Brooks and Griffin Dunne (who also directed) and starring Kate Capshaw, Chris Chavkin, Elliott Gould and Uma Thurman.

Despite the colour, excitement, challenge, peace and relief that competing on the rodeo circuit had given Kiefer, he had not at any stage viewed it as a permanent replacement for acting, and so after two years he was now happy to hang up his Stetson and mosey on back to Los Angeles, to pick up the reins of his Hollywood career – if not a new man, certainly an enriched one ready to face the task of re-entering this once familiar domain.

CHAPTER 12

TREASURED TIMES IN TORONTO

ANY NOTION THAT, after his sojourn away from Hollywood to re-evaluate his life, Kiefer would return to the screen to portray mellow, benign characters exploded over the course of his next five film roles, when he separately assumed the mantles of chilling psychopathic killers, a remorseless rapist and a brutal leader of the notoriously sinister Ku Klux Klan; the latter performance earnéd him a nomination as best screen villain. 'If I didn't play the bad guy, you couldn't have good guys,' he reasoned.

Perhaps the lowest key killer Kiefer portrayed was school counsellor Bob Wolverton in the film *Freeway*. Written and directed by Matthew Bright, the thriller told the story of a 15-year-old illiterate girl who, after her drug-addicted prostitute mother and stepfather are arrested, decides to seek out her grandmother rather than let herself be put back into foster care. En route, she falls in with Bob Wolverton, whom she learns to trust to the point where she confides in him about the systematic sexual abuse she'd suffered at the hands of her stepfather. The kind, mild, seemingly sympathetic counsellor is in fact the freeway serial killer whose heinous crimes are currently being plastered all over the media. Kiefer headed a cast including Reese Witherspoon, Wolfgang Bodison, Amanda Plummer, Dan Hedaya and Brooke Shields. *Freeway* aired on HBO in 1996.

That same year, audiences saw Kiefer switch from projecting an under-the-radar type of psycho to a truly frightening portrayal of a remorseless villain who rapes without compunction and kills without conscience in the John Schlesinger-directed feature, *Eye for an Eye*. Erika Holzer's powerful novel was adapted for the screen by Amanda Silver and Rick Jaffa, and tackled the thorny issues of loopholes in the law, and people taking the law into their own hands. In this case, lowlife Robert Doob breaks into the house of a middle class family and rapes and murders the pretty teenage daughter, who was alone at home. Doob is quickly arrested, but despite overwhelming evidence, when the case comes to trial he is released on a legal technicality. The distraught parents' shock and sense of injustice turn to something deeper when the dead girl's mother seeks to have her own revenge on the brutal killer. Bringing this disturbing story vividly to screen life, along with Kiefer as Robert Doob, were Sally Field, Ed Harris, Beverly D'Angelo, Charlaine Woodard, Joe Mantegna and Olivia Burnette.

This role was more than just another chance for Kiefer to inhabit a thoroughly despicable character. *Eye for an Eye*, he felt strongly, projected something about America in the mid-1990s. He said: 'This film was so indicative of the feeling at that time. People felt that crime was rampant, that violence wantonly permeated and frightened our society in a way that I don't think it ever had before. The news was responsible for taking individual crimes and making you feel you couldn't walk out of your house.' A strong believer in civil liberties, a person's right to privacy and proper due process of law, he yet declared: 'The law had handcuffed itself because of so many rules and regulations but there comes a point where you go: no, no the guy's blood matches – at what stage do you find him guilty?' Kiefer believes that *Eye for an Eye* is a film that could be buried deep in a sealed time capsule, and when unearthed a century later would provide a truly realistic snapshot of American society around 1996. It is important to him to invest in the whole concept of a movie, and while, in reality, films often fall short of his expectations, this one did not. In terms of acting, though, it proved a sometimes harrowing experience for him.

As Robert Doob, he had to embody a ruthless man without a shred of decency, and with a complete disregard for anything or anyone – the kind of killer beyond the comprehension of society. He was surprised to find it a tougher task than ever before to crawl inside this character's skin. Trying to get his head around such an evil person challenged him to the nth degree, and when he did find a way in, he said: 'It's a dirty feeling, very disturbing.' As part of the process of constructing Robert Doob for the screen he found himself imagining the most frightening figure that could ever threaten his girls, Sarah and Michelle, which was effective craft-wise, but was so upsetting it made him feel physically sick after some takes.

The trend in the mid-1990s was for filmmakers to push the female lead as the main focus. From that viewpoint the problem in this case was that as Robert Doob, Kiefer was *so* strong, so compellingly dangerous, that it was too much of a stretch to believe that an ordinary, normally law-abiding mother, however grief-stricken and bent on vengeance, could realistically go up against him. Accomplished though the other cast members were, Kiefer towered above everyone. Indeed, so vivid an impact did he make on the minds of the film's audience that some time after *Eye for an Eye*'s release, he encountered two women with children in an LA restaurant who visibly recoiled from him and hurriedly drew their children protectively towards themselves. Kiefer had only called in for a pizza! He later remarked: 'I thought, this is unbelievable! It's only acting.'

Kiefer provoked more off-screen reaction later that summer, when his third unsympathetic character came to celluloid life in the hit film, *A Time to Kill*. From the novel by John Grisham, Akiva Goldsman's screenplay told the tale of a young, idealistic white lawyer in a small Mississippi town who bravely takes on the task of defending a black man who killed the two white men arrested for the rape of his ten-year-old daughter. This tenacious lawyer quickly comes up against enormous intimidation from the still powerful Ku Klux Klan. His and his family's lives are put in serious danger, his home is torched, the local law firm he inherited the reins of from his legal mentor haemorrhages clients, pushing it towards bankruptcy, and his pretty young apprentice is abducted and physically assaulted, while he comes up against a completely biased white judge. This stirring courtroom drama was helmed by director Joel Schumacher; its impressive cast boasted Matthew McConaughey, Sandra Bullock, Samuel L Jackson, Kevin Spacey, Oliver Platt, Brenda Fricker, Ashley Judd and Patrick McGoohan. The two prominent supporting roles were held down by Kiefer as Ku Klux Klan leader, Freddie Lee Cobb, and Donald Sutherland as the idealistic lawyer's radical mentor, Lucien Wilbanks, who has withdrawn from practising law, having vowed never to set foot back inside a courtroom. Although liking a drink, Lucien still has a formidable legal brain, and Matthew McConaughey's lead character has need of him.

Donald had by now assumed legendary status as an actor. His role as a Russian colonel in the 1996 film, *Citizen X*, earned him a Golden Globe best supporting actor nomination, and it was reported that in *A Time to Kill* he had envisaged making his character pronouncedly more radical and alcoholic than planned, truer to the Lucien Wilbanks that Grisham drew in his novel. However, the director was concerned that nothing should dilute the dramatic tension. It was patently a wise decision, for although in terms of actual screen time Donald did not exactly hog the film, his gravitas and luminous screen presence ensured that his character later lingered longest in the mind. This was the first time since *Max Dugan Returns*, 13 years ago, that Kiefer and his father had appeared in the same movie, but in *A Time to Kill* they do not share a scene together. Of the pair ever actually acting opposite one another, Kiefer said: 'There have been a number of near misses, but we do intend to do it sometime.'

In this movie, Ku Klux Klan leader Freddie Lee Cobb is a malignant element who comes into his own when, along with other redneck thugs he forces Sandra Bullock's character off the road and into woods. Before the leering, salivating gang he viciously rips her clothes off, humiliatingly stripping her, then ties her up to a tree and threatens her to get her to stop helping the lawyer to defend the black man. The film was awash with Klan terror tactics, activist marches, riots and media frenzy, at the core of which is one stubborn man's quest to uphold the law and see that justice is served. The ugly issue of racism is, of course, the glaring central plank throughout. Kiefer pointed out that, abominable as his character is in *A Time to Kill*, the frightening fact is that there are Freddie Lee Cobbs everywhere in America. The provocative subject matter was one thing, but Kiefer's convincing depiction of a Klan member outraged African–Americans enough to make a few people collar Kiefer in the street to demand heatedly to his face how he could possibly have portrayed such a character. Kiefer's contrastingly calm response to such confrontational moments was to point out that if racism was not shown nakedly in films for the evil thing it is, then people would not fully appreciate what the other characters are determined to fight against.

However, people increasingly tended to blur the lines between an actor playing a part and being himself in real life, and just after the film's release in late summer 1996, Kiefer encountered a potentially hairy situation when he attended a hockey tournament in Las Vegas. There were several thousand black people in the venue, and Kiefer went to a kiosk to buy cigarettes, minding his own business. Some faint sense of unease percolated into his brain just before a stranger said softly into the back of his head: 'I bet *you're* scared now!' Hiding his nerves, Kiefer replied honestly: 'Kinda,' whereupon the guy laughed. When Kiefer turned round there was a sea of black faces before him and literally hundreds began to laugh too. 'It was a really nice moment,' recalled the mightily relieved actor. *A Time to Kill* pushed the buttons for a lot of people, for it became one of the financial big hitters of 1996, raking in approximately $109 million at the US box office. Kiefer received a nomination for best villain at the subsequent *MTV* movie awards.

Playing villainous characters so effectively did not mean that Kiefer was incapable of taking on contrastingly romantic lead roles, but he claimed: 'It's kind of what you have to do if you're not really good looking. You have to make your way with the parts they allow you to do.' The fear of being typecast had not so far bothered him either. 'I was very cocky through my teens and twenties,' he confessed. 'When people would say: "You'd better be careful," [of typecasting] I'd say: "Oh, screw off! I'm having fun playing these textured characters and look at how deep I can go into this realm."' As an actor, Kiefer likes actually being aware of working. Before stepping on to a film set, when he looks in a mirror he needs to see a change, proof however infinitesimal that he has somehow left Kiefer Sutherland back in the dressing room, and that before him is this other guy, who is going to give the film's audience the creeps! That said, by the time he had returned to the public eye, making *Freeway*, *Eye for an Eye* and *A Time to Kill*, Kiefer had a strong urge for a change of pace. 'If anyone would want me to play a nice man, I certainly would,' he said.

In stark contrast to these vile screen characters, away from acting Kiefer had by this time become the real life romantic leading man in one woman's world. She was Toronto-born Elizabeth Kelly Winn. Known as Kelly Winn, she was a former model, four years older than Kiefer, and had two young sons – Julian, born in 1990, and Timothy, born three years later. Kiefer met Kelly in 1995 at a Rod Stewart birthday bash, held in Los Angeles. Once he had spotted the beautiful young lady he could not tear his eyes off her as she sat some distance away from him. Impudently, he drew her attention by throwing a dinner roll at the man sitting next to her. He was a friend, who laughingly didn't mind a chunk of bread bouncing off his head. In contrast, the charged eye contact between Kiefer and Kelly at that moment ignited a spark, and Kiefer knew it. Excitedly, he later told a friend: 'This might sound really weird, but tonight I met the girl I'm going to marry!' His friend duly groaned at the corny claim.

Kiefer was not wrong, however, although bearing in mind his chequered love life to date, he wasn't exactly brimming with confidence initially when Kelly Winn agreed to go out with him. He felt the need to clear up certain misconceptions about him, and so as they got into the shallows of learning about one another, he found himself bringing up tabloid stories which had not been true, or owning up to some behaviour that he *had* been guilty of when he was much younger. Because he knew Kelly was going to be important to him, it was essential to put the record straight. This touching candour may have been unnecessary, for despite the miles of newspaper print expended on Kiefer over his dramatically cancelled wedding to Julia Roberts, his bad-boy antics and his on-screen successes, it seems that Kelly Winn had not read about Kiefer. Nevertheless, their romance gathered pace and they quickly became very close. If friends and family feared Kiefer getting burned again he, for all his streetwise savvy and screen strength, is something of a closet romantic, and he throws his heart genuinely into what he feels is going to be a deep relationship. In Kelly's case, he also had no problem connecting with her two little sons. Their momentum became unstoppable, and in 1996 Kiefer proposed. Kelly said yes, and marriage number two was on the agenda for summer time.

Simply living together, it appears, was not an option for Kiefer. He declared that Kelly Winn was the woman he wanted to be with, and that he wanted to buy into the whole happy wedding scene. He stressed that marriage had always represented to him an outward acknowledgement of a couple's commitment to one another in the face of their friends and family. 'It's a commitment to spend the rest of our lives together,' he said. 'You pick that one day to share the joy of that commitment with everybody else. It's also a wonderful excuse to get everybody together in one room and have a drink.' There were eerily familiar chimes of a past period in his life best forgotten – getting into such public declarations of devotion and commitment. Yet Kiefer also risked setting up a press conference in Toronto two days before the wedding. On 27 June, 29-year-old Kiefer and his 33-year-old bride-to-be faced a phalanx of journalists and photographers to introduce her to the media. Coming from Toronto, Kelly was viewed as a local girl, and it further pleased the press when she said that she and Kiefer hoped to make the city their home base.

Asked if he was a nervous groom-to-be, Kiefer told the assembled scribblers: 'At this point, I just hope the day goes smoothly and that everybody has a bit of fun. We're going to have a blast. We've got 200 people coming. Both of our families are rather large and we have the friends you accumulate over the years. You just have to hope that everyone has as nice a time as we're going to have.' The size of the guest list apart, no other wedding day details were given out. Kiefer kept the time and place of the ceremony private, and no names were released regarding the guests, but it got out that as well as Shirley Douglas, Donald would be there, as would Kiefer's eight-year-old daughter, Sarah, and Kelly's sons, six-year-old Julian and three-year-old Timothy.

Kiefer and Kelly Winn married on 29 June 1996 in a ceremony conducted on the campus of Kiefer's old school, St

Andrew's College in Aurora, near Toronto. The bride was radiant, but the male members of Kiefer's kin provided the spectacle. He recalled with pride: 'When I got married, I wore a kilt. My family is from Scotland – Douglas and Sutherland. Both sides had on kilts and black military turtlenecks. I felt really comfortable in that. There's something very masculine and defining about a kilt.' Buoyed up on a tide of joy, the happy newlyweds took off for a honeymoon in the Caribbean.

On their return, Kiefer settled into domesticity for a second time in his still-young life. He knew already that being a parent was not, as he put it, 'an overtly calming thing,' but with a family of four now ranging in age from three to 20, it was scarcely surprising that he found it stimulating. It amazed him most that no two consecutive days were ever alike. Kiefer readily acknowledged that as children grow, so parents' fears are amplified. A protective father to all four children, he was also conscious of worrying about his girls, and Michelle was already proving to have a strong independent streak. Kiefer continued to be a close stepdad to Camelia's daughter, and on some issues he and his first wife took a joint stand involving Michelle. These were minor teenage rebellions, and later Kiefer admitted that privately he had often been in a bit of a cleft stick. When Michelle had wanted to shave her head, he had joined with Camelia in saying a firm no. Putting their foot down merely resulted in Michelle coming up with a clever compromise and presenting her parents with a *fait accompli*. Headstrong himself, Kiefer confessed: 'I had to act like I was mad at her, but part of me was proud of her. She made it work for herself.'

This father-of-four mantle did not mean that Kiefer always took the ultra responsible approach to everything in his own life. He can still get involved in fistfights, though they have become fewer over the years. Indeed, what would be his last public scrap for a long time occurred not long after his second marriage, but it could be argued that he had been provoked in a way that would inflame most men. It happened one night in

Toronto when Kiefer and Kelly were out for a drink with some family and friends. While Kelly was sitting at the bar counter with one of Kiefer's stepbrothers, Kiefer was playing pool with a guy who subsequently went up to Kelly and, as Kiefer delicately phrased it, 'touched her in an inappropriate way.' Initially, Kiefer was prepared to allow that the guy had had a bit to drink, so he asked his erstwhile pool opponent simply to apologise to Kelly. The man refused. Kiefer asked him again, saying he should not have touched up his wife. The man, said Kiefer, threw back that Kelly had asked him to do so.

At that, Kiefer's temper snapped and he punched the man, who went down, but that was just the start. A full-scale fight between the two ensued, resulting in blood being spattered onto the pool table, which Kiefer later paid to have re-covered. Kiefer appears to have come off the victor in the fight, but he takes no pleasure in that. At home that night, tending to his skinned and bloodied knuckles, he felt abjectly sorry that the incident had flared into a fistfight. Kiefer can almost always be relied upon to have an unusual take on things, and interestingly, when it comes to the subject of punch-ups, he has never felt bad about the 180 or so stitches that he has had over time in his head from fights he has lost, but when he wins a fight he worries that he might have been fighting with a guy who was not his even match.

That explosive event apart, Kiefer and Kelly concentrated on family life and his work. Kelly had left her modelling days behind her to focus on raising her sons, and she wanted to help Kiefer in his professional life. Not an actress like Camelia Kath or Julia Roberts, Kelly was the first woman Kiefer was serious about who had no connection to his working world. Yet, for the first time, he was ready to let the woman in his life truly into that sphere. 'I used to be selfish with the work – this was *my* thing. I didn't want to allow anyone to watch what I did with it, but I have a whole life with Kelly and I bounce work ideas off her,' he revealed.

Conscious that she had no acting experience, Kelly would frequently remind her husband that, strictly speaking, she really didn't know what she was talking about as they sifted through film scripts together. Kiefer's view, however, was that she paid good money to see a film at the cinema and came away with an opinion, and that made her as qualified as the next person. He pointed out: 'People have reasons why they like or dislike a movie, what it is about a performance that moves them or doesn't.' Selecting roles meant Kiefer was likely to be away from home on location, but although he accepted that this aspect of acting had its downside personally (particularly from a partner and/or a child's point of view) he maintained that 'there are incredible benefits too.'

Come Christmas 1996 Kiefer had just turned 30. As a guy who had been in such a hurry to be older, he'd always focused on the milestone of 40 – not as an age to fret about losing his youth, but rather as an age when a wider range of terrific acting opportunities could open up. So he was adamant that being 30 only affected him inasmuch as it brought him closer to where he wanted to be. In a personal sense, although he smoked and liked a drink, he was in his best shape yet. Ever a high-energy guy, his horse riding had built up his body strength, and he was lean and fit. Not prone to self-analysis when life is treating him kindly, there was nevertheless something he could not help but acknowledge round about now. He said: 'I see my father in me every day. I see his looks and I see his acting style. I am my father's son.' Remarrying had heightened Kiefer's sense of family, all round. As at 1997, his twin sister Rachel Sutherland, having carved a career behind the scenes in television, was working on a children's series. Kiefer's older half brother, Tom Douglas, had given up acting and turned to academic study. His younger stepbrother, Rossif Sutherland, entered acting in the late 1990s and in time played Dr Lester Kertzenstein in the hit US TV medical drama, *ER*.

Donald Sutherland continued to star in major movies, and

throughout the decade Shirley Douglas had mixed film work with television roles. As at early 1997, she had newly completed a season of the CBC family drama, *Wind at My Back*, in which TV series she had the major role of May Bailey, a formidable matriarch figure who secretly has a soft heart. Despite reaching a wider audience, Shirley Douglas was still most renowned as a consummate stage actress, and in spring she and Kiefer were about to make a small piece of Canadian theatre history by co-starring in a stage production, playing fictitious mother and son roles in the Tennessee Williams play, *The Glass Menagerie*. It was an exciting prospect, and there was a lot of goodwill surrounding this unique pairing, for the Sutherland and Douglas names hold a strong appeal in Canada. The late Tommy Douglas remained widely revered. In addition to her acting fame, Shirley Douglas was synonymous with being a frontline fighter for good causes, a strong campaigner who is impossible to ignore, and Donald Sutherland is one of Canada's most famous sons. Hollywood maverick star Kiefer, married to a Canadian, never failed to declare his love for the country openly. Kiefer was now one of those actors whom people felt they had watched growing up on screen, and so felt close to.

Kiefer and Shirley had long wanted to work together, and had signed up to play Tom and Amanda Wingfield in a National Arts Centre, Ottawa, production of *The Glass Menagerie*, to be staged between March and May 1997. Other cast members included Kathryn Greenwood as Laura and David Storch as her gentleman caller. At the helm was director Neil Munro. The fact that a real-life mother and son were taking on this fictitious, angst-ridden mother–son duo attracted a lot of press attention, and so the pressure felt greater. Kiefer admits that it was a strange feeling. When rehearsals got under way in February, Shirley became two people. Said Kiefer: 'It was like being with someone I'd just met. We'd be two professionals working together but when they'd call lunch, she'd grab me by the ear and take me to the cafeteria. I was her son then. When lunch was over and the rehearsal resumed, she'd turn.'

Kiefer was happy to return to the stage. He had fond memories of his younger years in Toronto's theatre land. He hadn't ever specifically abandoned treading the boards, and had never envisaged it taking him so long to return. Now he felt reminded of a process that it was easy to lose a grip on when working in films, and both he and his mother were thrilled that this long-awaited professional pairing should be in this particular play. 'It's not only a beautiful classical play,' said Kiefer, 'but one of the few where we could actually have an equal shot at working together, with two well-balanced roles that suit our ages and allow us to take advantage of our history together.' Of the subject matter, Shirley Douglas said: 'When you're doing plays, you're often doing stories of people who are troubled. Those are the stories that are more interesting.' Both mother and son were moved by the play's evocative style of writing. Shirley considered Tennessee Williams and Arthur Miller to be the first playwrights to project characters in this harrowingly exposed way. Kiefer, who had the task of narrating the play, described the poetry in it as being akin to machine gun fire.

This new production of *The Glass Menagerie* opened on 25 March 1997 at the National Arts Centre in Ottawa, and then moved to the Royal Alexandra Theatre in Toronto. Opening night could not have been in a more natural venue, for the NAC was where Kiefer, aged 13, had been knocked out seeing his mother play Martha in *Who's Afraid of Virginia Woolf?* (coincidentally, under Neil Munro's direction too), the catalyst moment that had led him to become an actor. On stage before a live audience, Kiefer's adrenalin levels surged. He'd had no true idea what it would be like to act opposite his own accomplished mother, but in fact he learned a great deal from seeing her in action. Working before a live audience, to a different crowd each night, was obviously one of the biggest changes for Kiefer. Audiences have moods that the actors pick up on and respond to accordingly. Kiefer confessed: 'I go out there and I can hear people react to the play and I'm really interested to hear what's being said.'

The Glass Menagerie was a steep learning curve for Kiefer, but he was quick on the uptake. Shirley was delighted by his diligence. She was not surprised by it, just pleased to confirm with her own eyes her original belief that he had a natural stage presence. When Kiefer was asked if he had feared falling flat on his face as a theatre performer, he was typically forthright that if he thought along those lines he would not have tried half the things he'd already achieved in his life. He had clearly inherited this grab-life-with-both-hands attitude from his mother, for Shirley called fear 'a terribly wasteful emotion', declaring that to spend one's life in a state of fear and anxiety is not to live at all.

The Glass Menagerie ran at the Royal Alexandra Theatre, Toronto, until 3 May 1997, at the end of which time Kiefer classed Tom Wingfield as one of his toughest roles yet, because of the sheer intensity of the play. He had loved the challenge of him and his mother taking on these dramatic characters. 'We had an amazing time,' he said. 'I'm not sure how, if at all, it's affected us in the long haul. It's a heavy play for a mother and son to take on and as actors we would try not to take whatever our stuff is into the performances, but there were times I remember thinking that's not possible. I mean, she definitely yelled at me in some performances louder than she would in others.'

Overall, it was a critical success, but some reviewers did have their gripes. The *Toronto Sun* said of the opening night performance: 'What's missing in this production is nuance. Inexperienced on stage, Sutherland captures Tom's frustration and detachment but is crippled by moments of awkwardness. While the more experienced Douglas turns in a performance as the faded belle, Amanda, that is far more Melmac than heirloom china.' The *Ottawa Sun* decided: 'While Shirley

Douglas is a commanding presence on stage, she never portrays the really suffocating and destructive mother figure that Williams drew. Kiefer Sutherland is a strong narrator and is particularly convincing in the lighter segments of the play when he and Douglas banter back and forth but again when the play requires that seething tension, Sutherland appears awkward. Tom Wingfield is a man burning with repressed anger and resentment but that anger is not palpable.'

Whatever others said, Kiefer was thrilled to have shared a stage in Canada with his mother in a powerful play. In late spring he was also looking ahead to two new film releases in 1997, one of which was the film noir, *Last Days of Frankie the Fly*, in which he had one of the lead roles. Written by Dayton Callie and directed by Peter Markle, this movie revolved around a less than ruthless man trying to break away from working for the Hollywood mafia; to help him do so, he enlists the aid of a would-be film director. It was not a film destined for great things, but it did team Kiefer up for a second time with veteran star Dennis Hopper. Daryl Hannah and Michael Madsen co-starred, and Dayton Callie poached himself a part.

Kiefer's biggest film focus in 1997 was *Truth or Consequences, N.M.*, which he directed and starred in. It was his second directorial credit, but as *Last Light* was a TV movie, *Truth or Consequences, N.M.* marked his first time at the helm of a big screen feature film. Written by Brad Mirman, and shot on location in Utah, it is a violent thriller about a drug deal that goes wrong, sending four robbers on the run led by a psychotic killer. Along the way, with a stash of cocaine, they take hostage two people whose own story is far from straightforward. Described as a gritty tale of lost second chances, it follows the thieves to a small town in New Mexico, where police and the mob close in on them for an explosive showdown.

Kiefer plays psychotic killer, Curtis Freley. His cast included Vincent Gallo, Mykelti Williamson, Kevin Pollak,

Kim Dickens, Grace Phillips and James McDaniel, with stalwart stars Rod Steiger and Martin Sheen adding lustre to proceedings. What had attracted Kiefer to this thriller was that the lead characters were not life's winners. 'They are losers,' he stated, 'but if these characters had turned left instead of right, they might have been really special and there is something interesting and very tragic about that.'

As a director, Kiefer was aiming for a collage of the darkly moody elements epitomised in 1970s films such as *The Getaway* and *Dog Day Afternoon*, while adding another ingredient. 'I tried to incorporate my sense of humour,' he said. 'When people realistically react to being in a stupid position, it always makes me laugh.' Some in Hollywood thought Kiefer was having a laugh in thinking he could rope heavyweight actors into this movie, but he proved the doubters wrong. As ever, he was bluntly honest in revealing how he pulled off the coup. 'I phoned Rod Steiger and begged. With Martin Sheen, it was the same thing,' he revealed. Both Steiger and Sheen were happy to oblige.

Once again, Kiefer's screen character was a nasty, violent man. He described Curtis Freley as being like a lot of people – concerned purely with himself, someone who has no thought about another living soul. As director, he had his pick of the roles. So why choose Curtis? 'Curtis is the driving force of the violence,' explained Kiefer. 'He's what makes the film go forward, so he gave me the widest range of mobility as a character.' As to where he got the motivation from to portray Freley, Kiefer would only say that he drew on his imagination. He was equally economical about whether directing had been some lifelong dream of his, replying starkly: 'No.' Nor did he concur with recent remarks made by other actors-turned-directors which built the task up to being among one of the toughest jobs in the world. 'Directing is as hard as you choose to make it,' he declared, though adding: 'It becomes difficult somewhere during the process, when you realise that the entire piece is representative of all your sensibilities.'

Kiefer did not make a big deal of directing himself, finding it not that different an experience to acting for a director. He pointed out that he had a team of people to whom he could turn, if needed. He clearly has his own style of directing, and actors respond well to his sometimes unorthodox flamboyance. Said Grace Phillips: 'As a director, Kiefer is constantly aware of the performer's needs within a scene. He trusts your expressive skills, which is a very rare quality. He is part good old boy and part nurturing mother hen. That's a pretty inspiring combination.' Someone else who felt inspired while working on *Truth or Consequences, N.M.* was the movie's stunt coordinator, Chris Howell. He said: 'Kiefer is such a terrific athlete but he rides pretty close to the edge. My challenge with him was to watch him constantly because he has so much confidence in his own physical capabilities. I have to make sure he doesn't put himself in a situation where he could possibly hurt himself. He would do every stunt on his own, if he could.'

On its completion, leaving aside all his originally high aspirations, Kiefer was proud that *Truth or Consequences, N.M.* made sense, calling that the bottom line. The experience had further enhanced his directing skills, and his reputation as a good director to work for was spreading in the industry. His father says that he would love to be directed by Kiefer. Kiefer responded: 'That would be a sheer joy. We've talked about it, but our schedules are really hard to manage.'

Early critical reaction to previews called *Truth or Consequences, N.M.* 'a dazzling crime thriller conceived as a road movie. It blazes new trails through the genre, while mocking its own stylish excesses.' One film writer remarked: 'Kiefer both deftly jolts viewers' senses and, through a cinematic alter ego, catches audiences in the act of covert fascination with uninhibited evil.' The disappointment for Kiefer was that his film became a casualty of the fact that the company releasing it changed hands at the time. In the upheaval, the movie ended up running in fewer than ten theatres, which naturally strangled its chances of success at birth. However, in the late 1990s, the outlets for film had exploded beyond measure, and in early 1998 *Truth or Consequences, N.M.* became the number one independent movie on video. It would take legs; it just needed a bit longer than originally planned.

Meanwhile, mid-1997, 12 months into his new marriage, Kiefer declared: 'I've had a hell of a year. I'm going to take a break for a few months. It'll be nice to be at home.' However, upheaval lay ahead. He had thrown himself into five film projects since his return to the movie world, but as time passed he realised that he had not found what he was looking for professionally. Personally, too, there were ominous signs.

Hollywood watchers started to scent that all was not well in the Sutherland marriage, but Kiefer would not confirm that his second marriage was in jeopardy. Vultures latched on to it, however, when he confessed: 'I've been going away from home to make movies all my life. It's pretty hard to maintain a relationship.' Was the writing already on the wall? Donald had had two short-lived marriages, both ending in divorce by the time he was 35. Was it really, truly, deeply a case of like father, like son?

CHAPTER 13

THE VAGARIES OF LIFE

THE CRACKS THAT would appear in the Sutherland marriage had not yet begun to develop when Kelly and her two sons, Julian and Timothy, upsticked from Los Angeles and accompanied Kiefer to Australia, where he joined the cast of the 1998 Alex Proyas-directed supernatural thriller, *Dark City*. Though not a lover of science fiction, Kiefer found this film intriguing. Co-written by Proyas, Lem Dobbs and David S Goyer, it is an atmospheric tale of an amnesiac man who wakes up in a hotel room to discover that he is wanted for a spate of brutal murders in a nightmarish world where the sun never rises and an alien race is carrying out medical experiments on humans. Alongside Rufus Sewell, Jennifer Connelly, William Hurt, Richard O'Brien and Ian Richardson, Kiefer took on a lead role as Dr Daniel Schreber, the stooped, limping, disfigured and demented physician who is assisting the aliens.

It was a strange character to be drawn to, but Kiefer had spent so many years tackling the offbeat or unsympathetic roles, that playing a regular guy in a movie would be like taking on a character part. Dr Schreber was certainly no regular guy, and when this screenplay landed in Kiefer's lap an extra element struck him. 'When I read it, I thought: my father would be great in this,' he said. Kiefer joked that he would have to keep the chance of this role a secret from Donald, and indeed, 30 years earlier, audiences could well have expected to see Sutherland senior turn in an eerie portrayal of this accented, shuffling but fascinating figure. Donald appreciated his son's joke, saying recently: 'My presence has been like a thorn in his sense of originality.' Kiefer said of the story: 'What I like is something that deals with a conflict, deals with people I'm interested in and who have some sense of resolve. I like flexing my imagination and coming up with something intellectually, then being able physically to do it.' It also appealed to Kiefer that *Dark City* held echoes of the 1940s film noir movies. 'It's a great story. That's what hooked me.'

For all Kiefer's enthusiasm when he read the part of Dr Daniel Schreber, director Alex Proyas had his own specific ideas. Said Proyas: 'I saw Schreber as older, a combination of Peter Lorre and Ben Kingsley,' but he came up against Kiefer in highly persuasive mood. Kiefer strongly impressed on the Australian director how much more tragic the mad scientist would be if he were younger. He put his case relentlessly until Proyas opened up to the idea. Kiefer then prepared to throw himself wholeheartedly into the role as the hobbling, wheezing traitor. He said: 'My take on Dr Schreber's disfigurement was that if a person was betraying our entire race, the loneliness and the guilt would affect him. I wanted him to look like he'd been beaten.' Dr Daniel Schreber's facial disfigurement – one eye dragged lower than the other – meant Kiefer having to wear an elaborate prosthetic piece that was glued to his face for upwards of 14 hours a day. Long before he finished shooting the film, he made a mental note to elbow any such disfigurements in the future. That apart, making *Dark City* was an invigorating experience. Kiefer clowned around off camera, hamming it up with co-star William Hurt as a Bela Lugosi/Boris Karloff type screen monster, anything to lighten the darkness of the dense thriller.

Kiefer was also delighted to have his family with him. Normally, he would jet home from location every few weeks, but 18-hour flights from Australia would have been impractical. Julian and Timothy, at seven and four years old, were young enough to be disrupted from school without it harming their education, but it was still a major move for the family. When filming was over, Kiefer commented that they would likely not do it again. Still, it had been an experience for Kelly and the boys to live for a couple of months 'down under'. *Dark City* was given a special presentation at the 1998 Cannes Film Festival, and though *Variety* called it 'engaging mostly in the degree to which it creates and sustains a visually startling alternate universe,' it was critically acclaimed.

On leaving Australia, Kiefer and his family returned to the beautiful house that he had bought in 1992. Nestling in one of Los Angeles's elite enclaves, the two-storey Tudor-style house was built in 1919 – historic by Tinseltown's standards – and was redolent of old world charm, with hardwood flooring and imposing stone fireplaces. A unique feature was a hand-stamped tin ceiling in the kitchen. A sunroom looked out on to a spacious back yard boasting a glinting swimming pool and a quaint pool house, all shielded from public gaze by luscious, mature trees.

There wasn't a lot of kickback time there, however, for Kiefer had three further appearances to make in movies also to be released in 1998. One of these was a TV movie called *A Soldier's Sweetheart*, a war drama based on a short story by Tim O'Brien. Thomas Michael Donnelly wrote the teleplay and also directed the Showtime production. Kiefer played a US soldier, Rat Kiley, who narrates in a series of flashbacks the story of how a lonely army medic manages to bring his American girlfriend over to join him at a jungle base camp at the height of the Vietnam War. Fellow cast members included Skeet Ulrich, Georgina Cates and Daniel London. To some the film vaguely harked back to the collection of field medics portrayed in *M*A*S*H*. Kiefer commented: 'It broadens the scope of the war-is-hell issue, to include women. It also talks about how the war was only about survival for the soldiers who fought it.'

A Soldier's Sweetheart premiered as a gala screening at the 1998 Toronto International Film Festival, which Kiefer attended. The last time he had attended the festival he was 16 years old, promoting *The Bay Boy*, in which he had nailed his screen debut in a leading role. Happy as ever to be in his home city, Kiefer could also grab the chance to catch up with his busy father, who was at the festival to back his latest movie, *Without Limits*.

Kiefer then returned to the silver screen with two lead roles. One was in the Paul Marcus-directed thriller, *The Break Up*, in which he portrays a cop, John Box, starring opposite Bridget Fonda, Hart Bochner, Steven Weber and Tippi Hedren. The other was as a troubled air traffic controller, Jack Harris, in *Ground Control*, a tense action adventure co-written by Mark Shepherd, Robert Moreland and Talaat Captan, and directed by Richard Howard. Despite the diversity of these roles, come 1998 Kiefer was unsettled again. Working with director Alex Proyas on *Dark City* had brought back memories of a friend, Brandon Lee, who was killed four years earlier in a shooting accident while filming Proyas's *The Crow*. Kiefer had attended the funeral of actor Bruce Lee's son, and had really mixed feelings about watching the film, which was completed after the fatal shooting. Kiefer recalled: 'Brandon's fiancée was my secretary for three years. It was one of those very odd experiences and I had an emotional problem with it. Visually, *The Crow* was beautiful. Alex [Proyas] and I talked about that whole tragedy a lot.'

In late spring 1998, Kiefer feared he may, in different circumstances, be about to lose yet another young friend. Charlie Sheen, the twinkle-eyed Aramis to Kiefer's moody Athos in *The Three Musketeers*, had reached a desperate nadir in his battles with drugs and alcohol. Sheen's life in the fast lane had been catching up with him and, like Charlie's family, Kiefer was very worried about the actor's awful weight loss. One evening in May, the 32-year-old frighteningly lost all sensation from the waist down and collapsed at home. Somehow Charlie managed to call 911, and an ambulance rushed to his house. Kiefer grew very emotional watching along with millions of others on TV, when a white-faced, stricken Martin Sheen held a media conference to confirm that Charlie had overdosed on drugs and was in hospital. Years later, Kiefer said of his friend: 'Charlie's made his mistakes and was certainly dealing with demons that were larger than he was at times.' Charlie Sheen eventually entered rehab and worked hard to straighten out his life. 'Charlie is like a prize fighter,' declared Kiefer. 'He goes down and he gets right back up. There are a couple of times when Charlie got knocked down, I probably would have stayed on the canvas. He's got an awful lot of heart.'

Looking inward, 31-year-old Kiefer assessed his own world. 'Certainly with regards to work, I've matured,' he maintained. 'You can't go through this many years and not grow as a person.' Career-wise, he again reflected on the times he had taken film roles mainly for the money, thinking he was invulnerable, and he knew he was beyond that now. He had not, by a long way, sated his appetite for directing. He described it as an extension of his craft as an actor, and he set his own parameters. 'I couldn't direct a film like *Dark City*,' he confessed. 'I don't have the kind of vision that Alex has, that imaginative visual scope. People like Alex get on a computer and do weird shit. I can't even turn a computer on!' What attracted Kiefer to take a turn behind the camera were focused, character-based films. In spring 1998 he was yearning to direct a family drama to be shot in Montreal, starring Barbara Hershey and a friend of his father's, Christopher Plummer. He would, in time, embark on his third spin as actor/director but the experience would leave him disillusioned.

Something that *did* brighten him at this time was that the Saskatchewan government offered financial assistance to help make a much-anticipated biopic of his remarkable grandfather, the late Tommy Douglas. It was an understatement to call it a fascinating story, and naturally Kiefer had a goldmine of material to draw upon for such a project. All round, it was right up his alley. He had once stated: 'Canada, as a country, I find fascinating. I'm not a writer but if I got hold of a script that dealt with Canada specifically, I'd be very interested in being a part of it.' Part of it? If this biopic came to fruition Kiefer, it was said, would be portraying his own firebrand grandparent. Nothing got off the ground immediately, but this idea would resurface over the coming years.

Perhaps it was indicative that life changes loomed on Kiefer's horizon once more, when he had the yen to clap his cowboy hat back on and return to the rodeo scene. He had never severed his connection to that alternative way of life. He had long since sold his ranch in Montana, but in addition to his house in Los Angeles he now owned a huge ranch in the Santa Ynez Valley in central California, at which, with 500 head of cattle, roughly 450 calves would be born each year. When the urge struck to go back into team roping competitively, Kiefer linked up again with his friend John English, and this time they trained at Kiefer's ranch. Said Kiefer: 'I love reading a cow. You watch its withers, right in the shoulder blades. It's the initial hint of which way a cow is going to go.'

Kiefer, Kelly and the kids often spent time at the Santa Ynez ranch near Santa Barbara, just north of Los Angeles. Kiefer normally found it relaxing, but he was less comfortable when it was occasionally necessary as a cattle rancher to shoot wild boar. An episode at the ranch in 1998 upset him when, trying out a new rifle, he got a bird some distance away in his sights and instantly pulled the trigger, blowing the bird's head clean off. His emotional reaction to what he had just done was a barometer to deeper, more personal imbalances that were threatening his private life.

Closing off these undercurrents, Kiefer concentrated on getting back into sync with John English. Team roping requires a range of finely honed skills and Kiefer wasn't thinking small. He planned to compete on the US Team Roping Championship circuit. Both he and John English would ride after a steer, and while Kiefer's task was to rope the cow's horns, English would rope its back feet; together they would immobilise the animal and lay it down. According to Kiefer, a huge factor was having a horse that could match a stampeding cow's speed and maintain a constant parallel position with it; this would allow the rider to rope as if throwing while standing stationary. To perfect this tricky art, he and his partner practised relentlessly until they felt ready to take on the championship challenge.

Kiefer and John English entered themselves in rodeo competitions, and set out on the road. Said Kiefer: 'I found something invaluable – just friends experiencing time together. I wanted to ride around with these guys and exaggerate stories about how cool we all are.' Kiefer had no problem this time around in being taken seriously from the get-go. He said: 'As soon as they realised I wasn't doing it just so that *Entertainment Tonight* would come and film me, it was alright.' Kiefer's event was in team calf roping. In 1998, John English was ranked ninth in the world for calf roping, and not only did Kiefer have an enviable asset there, he was also conscious of how different it was for him, in the sense that he did not need the prize money. First cash prize in some competitions at that time ranged between $1,000 and $2,000, money that to some guys meant a great deal. Kiefer could compete purely for the achievement, and therefore was not so uptight.

As he and his partner competed, Kiefer felt his confidence building, and before long the Sutherland/English partnership began to hit gold. Together they won several competitions, winning rodeos in Phoenix and Albuquerque. 'I was as shocked as anyone when we won our first rodeo,' said Kiefer. 'I'm a competitive person – I wanted that buckle – but that wasn't the driving force of why I did it. I just really enjoyed the whole process, the discipline and the whole experience.' After winning their event at the Arizona Championships in Scottsdale, Kiefer and John English took first place in the 1998 US Team Roping Championships, an accolade they would earn twice before the end of the decade. 'I was never *the* champ,' Kiefer said modestly, 'but I won the US TRC twice in Phoenix and I won in New Mexico.'

Kiefer was putting his all into this, working himself bone-weary in testing conditions. Between June and August, daytime temperatures in Phoenix average highs of over 100 degrees Fahrenheit, making it the hottest city outside the Middle East. Even in winter, temperatures hover around 65 degrees, but Kiefer was almost driven. He was not actively making hard and fast decisions about his life, but there were times when the prospect of never returning to acting fleetingly crossed his mind, and it didn't particularly worry him. He was rightly proud of the trophies he was accumulating, and he never considered the cost too high. Of the prize belt buckles themselves he said: 'I've got some great ones from Gallup, New Mexico. There were a couple from Phoenix that were really nice. The buckles have either a ruby or a diamond in them. I remember the first time I won one, I figured what I'd spent on horses, a ranch etc. – it was well over a million, to get this little buckle.'

Whatever sense of achievement Kiefer got from this involvement in the rodeo world, it could not compensate for the sadness that was setting in over the fact that his second marriage was on the rocks. He and Kelly had married with such high hopes in summer 1996, but two years on the picture had changed. Kiefer said: 'Unfortunately, our marriage failed and I take the larger part of that responsibility. I spent

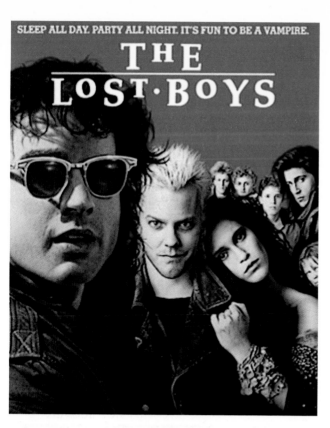

Kiefer assumed iconic status with his portrayal of David, the charismatic but vicious head vampire, in the 1987 cult movie *The Lost Boys*.

With Julia Roberts. In June 1991, Julia dramatically cancelled their wedding at the last minute.

Emilio Estevez, Kiefer, Charlie Sheen and Lou Diamond Phillips in the 1988 Hollywood blockbuster, *Young Guns*.

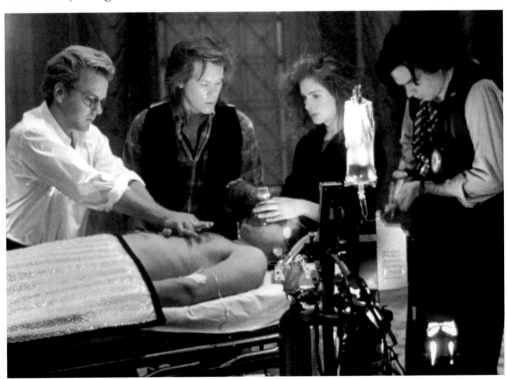

With co-stars Kevin Bacon, Julia Roberts and Oliver Platt in the 1990 thriller, *Flatliners*.

Kiefer turns in a chilling performance as Hart in the 2004 thriller, *Taking Lives*.

In January 2002, collecting the coveted Best Actor Golden Globe for his portrayal of Jack Bauer in the hit drama *24*.

Flanked here by *24* cast members Kim Raver and Elisha Cuthbert, Kiefer celebrates the drama's 100th episode in January 2006.

'The screen hums whenever Sutherland's on it. He transcends *24*, creating Bauer's bitterness and nobility out of pauses and hard-eyed stares.' – *Time* magazine

a lot of time on the road. We got further and further apart. I got more involved in my life than I got involved in ours. All those things over a period of time wear thin.' Though Kiefer has been candid about his second marriage biting the dust, he does not display dirty linen in public. Asked to name the worst thing he had ever done to someone he loved, Kiefer confessed to having lied to Kelly. Did that lie involve him being with another woman? Kiefer economically replied: 'Yes.' He went on to say that the 'lie' was that he had promised to behave in a particular way in this second marriage and he did not do so. 'The lie was way at the beginning,' he said. Bluntly he stated that the marriage failed because *he* had failed it, castigating himself for not having been man enough to be a truly great husband.

He made no bones about the fact that he continued to love Kelly, but the couple separated in March 1999. 'Sometimes, things don't quite work out right,' he said. The couple needed time to figure out what to do, and in the 12 months that followed their separation they made two attempts to reconcile, but these were not successful and divorce number two for Kiefer looked likely. Having tried marriage twice and run aground both times, Kiefer came to the conclusion: 'Marriage is apparently something that I am not very good at but I'm a great friend, honestly!' He was not flippant about it, however. It concerned him deeply that he had screwed up a second time. Having wed way too young the first time around, he saw now had just been a mistake in not knowing at 20 what he'd wanted to do with his whole life. This second failure was harder to quantify. It could, he conceded, quite simply come down to the fact that the institution of marriage was not right for him. 'Because I can't fault Kelly for any reason why it didn't work,' he admitted. In 2004 Kiefer stated firmly that walking up the aisle was not something he wanted to do again. He reckoned he'd had a couple of swings at it and struck out.

In 1999, officially separated from Kelly, Kiefer melted back into the rodeo circuit, planning to bide his time and see which way the wind would blow him, but in this world now, things didn't feel the same. He had reached a level of success in team roping that sated him, and although roping would continue to give him pleasure, he knew subliminally that it was not pushing the buttons for him as before. Then his life came into drastically sharp focus one dark night on the road, when he suffered a near-death experience.

Along with John English and another guy, Kiefer was in transit across America, heading to their next competing event, when their truck headlights shone on to a Road Ends traffic sign. 'We didn't realise that it literally ended right there,' recalled Kiefer. The road abruptly fell away beneath them and the gigantic truck was sent suddenly into midair. It landed several feet below with an almighty crash, and only by the grace of God did not turn over. Along with the others in the vehicle, Kiefer was shaken almost to shattering, and shocked out of his wits. 'It was one of the scariest moments of my life,' he revealed. 'My heart was pounding. It really was a miracle escape.'

This heart-stopping fright helped Kiefer to re-evaluate his life. Rodeo riding is a sport for a lean and hungry young buck at his physical peak. If he immersed himself for too long in this world, he could also run the risk of staying out of the acting loop for too long to be able to come back as leading man material. Kiefer was waking up of a morning now, wondering what else there was, or ever could be, to challenge him to the right degree in rodeoing and ranching. He was also starting to miss acting, remembering the great times he had sometimes had making films. He is a man willing to broaden his horizons, but acting is his intrinsic passion. After two years, it was clear to him what he wanted to do. In 1999 Kiefer actually had a film release – a German-made movie that had been in the can, called *After Alice* (otherwise known as *Eye of the Killer*). Written by Jeff Miller and directed by Paul Marcus, *After Alice* was a crime thriller in which Kiefer had the lead role as Detective Mickey Hayden. As the new millennium approached, however, Kiefer set his sights on making a bigger splash. It would not be easy, though.

In his inimitably frank fashion, Kiefer recently reflected on this period when he had decided to return to the movie world. He recalled how he had fondly imagined that when he went knocking on doors again, introducing himself as Kiefer Sutherland, Hollywood filmmakers would welcome him with open arms. He confessed: 'Reality is, they went, "So?"' He tried to view this philosophically as a sign that if it was not meant to be, so be it, but acting meant far too much to him for that. In the last quarter of 1999, back in Los Angeles, Kiefer carefully considered his options, maybe widening the parameters, and soon he was in negotiations about starring in a proposed television series adaptation of the 1997 Oscar-winning movie, *L.A. Confidential*. He would take the role of Hollywood cop Sgt Jack Vincennes, which Kevin Spacey had filled in the big-screen version. A pilot show is said to have been made, and was awaiting sale to a TV network.

In December, Kiefer gladly took time out from trying to kick-start his film career to take part in another pro-celeb charity ice hockey game, this time at Madison Square Garden, New York, in aid of the Chistopher Reeve Foundation. Meanwhile, back in LA, moves were afoot in his private life to shift to the next stage. Several months had now passed since separating from Kelly, and Kiefer had decided to put his Tudor-style Los Angeles home on the market. Having been unable to reconcile, both he and Kelly had to look to sorting out their futures. Divorce papers would be filed in the New Year, when matters took an unexpected and upsetting twist.

CHAPTER 14

THE PENDULUM SWINGS AGAIN

O N 13 MARCH 2000, Kiefer and Kelly Sutherland filed for divorce. They had been separated for a year, two attempts at reconciliation had failed, and both had come to the decision that divorce was the next step in dissolving their short-lived marriage. Having had no children together, the couple anticipated that the legal procedure would be routine. Through a business acquaintance, Kiefer had hired the services of a family law lawyer. That morning he went to the lawyer's office and signed the papers, prior to leaving Los Angeles as planned. That evening, however, he received a telephone call that something really bizarre had happened.

A journalist for *People* magazine had called Kiefer's publicist, Annett Wolf, to draw her attention to a document that had been filed in Kiefer's name. Urging the publicist to check it out, the journalist said: 'There is something terribly wrong with it. It doesn't make sense.' Soon after, Kiefer discovered that Kelly had just had a similar phone call from a friend of hers in the media. It turned out that, inexplicably, a document had been filed in Kiefer's name requesting the court to issue a restraining order against Kelly. Both Kiefer and Kelly were completely baffled by this. Kiefer was quickly on the warpath. It was a ludicrous error, but potentially damaging to his estranged wife's reputation. First thing next day, an amendment was filed on Kiefer's instructions, but the genie was out of the bottle. As restraining orders are public documents, someone somewhere along the chain had leaked it to the Associated Press wire service, and news of this application for a restraining order against Kelly Sutherland was already flashing across the media. Said Kiefer: 'Stories started to be told on morning TV in Los Angeles and on Canadian TV saying the most outrageous things, such as my wife was a stalker, that she was crazy, that she was a peeping tom – really, the most outlandish stuff. I could not stand idly by.'

In the hysterical and gossip-hungry showbiz circles, no one was interested in discovering that a retraction document had been lodged, that it had all been an extraordinary mistake. Kiefer despaired and grew ever more angry that the woman he described as being the most decent, kindest person he had ever known was being attacked in this way. He had learned to roll with the punches, but he was furious that Kelly had been targeted. She wasn't in the business, and had no experience of how to handle the overwhelming barrage of press attention that she was suffering. She was deeply embarrassed, and felt so humiliated that she could not face leaving her house to collect her boys from school as usual, since the pack were ready to descend in full cry. Kiefer spoke with Kelly straight away; and her feeling of defencelessness in the face of this unfair onslaught only fired his protective sense even higher. The next day, 15 March, Kiefer agreed to be interviewed by *Entertainment Tonight*, when he took the opportunity to set the record straight. He could not have praised his wife more highly, and he stated categorically: 'In no way, shape or form have I ever asked for, have I ever filed, nor do I want to file, any kind of restraining order.' He also apologised for the acute embarrassment this entire fiasco had caused to everyone concerned. Kiefer went on to state publicly that the error in filing a restraining order had not been intentional on any level. He released a statement to that effect, but it seemed certain that, behind the scenes, somebody's head would roll for it.

The storm would blow over and Kelly would recover and get on with normal life, but it did not help an already tense and unhappy situation. Kiefer called it a very difficult time. The *Entertainment Tonight* interviewer had asked Kiefer whether, if he thought Kelly was so wonderful, there was any chance that they could avoid divorce and sort out their marriage. Kiefer responded that over time too many things had been said and done, occasionally out of anger, to be forgotten or forgiven. More than that, he would not say. Years later, admitting that he had not coped very well with his second marriage going under, he called this divorce 'one of the worst experiences of my life'. He hoped that in time it would be possible for him and Kelly to be friends.

It had not been quite the fresh start that Kiefer had hoped for from the new millennium, but he put this turbulence behind him and before long was ploughing his energies into another area in life he feels passionately about – Canada's national health service. His mother had already begun a six-month campaign across Canada to highlight publicly the danger of sleepwalking into the government's plans to privatise part of the public health care system. In the summer, Shirley would take her protest to a Summit of the Americas meeting held in Windsor, Ontario. For now, in April, she had helped organise a series of public meetings and street protest marches. On 15 April, Kiefer was happy to join 2,500 street protesters at a rally in Calgary. Three days later, he was the feature speaker at another massive Friends of Medicare rally in Edmonton, where he denounced plans by the Conservative premier, Ralph Klein, to amend Bill 11 in manner. Kiefer maintained that proposals to allow private operators to provide certain health services would result in direct competition with public health care – creating a two-tier health service in Canada, whereby the public system would inevitably deteriorate. Along with his outspoken mother and hundreds of thousands of equally concerned Canadians, Kiefer feared the systematic dismantling of the Medicare system pioneered by his grandfather, Tommy Douglas, and which worked well in the interests of all, not just the wealthy.

Work-wise, 2000 saw the release of some films Kiefer had in the pipeline. At the recent Sundance Film Festival *Beat* had been screened, a drama billed as the true life story of events that helped shape the lives of some of the most influential artistic figures of the 1960s beat generation, including William Burroughs, Jack Kerouac and Allen Ginsberg. In the 1960s, Morocco was to American literati what Paris had been in the 1920s. William Burroughs lived in Tangier, the nucleus of a clutch of talented expatriates including the composer and novelist Paul Bowles, and painter-cum-writer Brion Gysin. Americans and Europeans flocked to sample Morocco's more licentious delights, such as kif and male prostitution. *Beat* was written and directed by Gary Walkow, and Kiefer starred as writer and junkie, William S Burroughs. Joining him on the film shoot in Mexico in 1999 were Courtney Love, who plays Burroughs's wife, Joan Vollmer, Ron Livingston as Allen Ginsberg, and Daniel Martinez as Jack Kerouac. Director Gary Walkow recalled of working with Kiefer: 'Kiefer encouraged me to shoot the rehearsal and he was right. He nailed things on the first take. He is a very skilled actor on every level.'

Also released in 2000 was *Woman Wanted*, which Kiefer directed as well as taking one of the lead roles. Joanna Glass had based the screenplay on her novel, which told the story of an attractive young woman who starts work as housekeeper for a widower and his adult son. She ultimately becomes intimately involved with both father and son, creating enormous strain, jealousy and animosity between the men; the situation is further complicated when she becomes pregnant. She settles for neither man but, consequently, both are tied in some way to the child she carries. *Woman Wanted* had been filmed two years earlier in Winnipeg, Canada, mainly at a house in Wellington Crescent. Kiefer's character was a disillusioned poet, Wendell Goddard. His screen father was Michael Moriarty, while Holly Hunter played the woman at the centre of this complex threesome. Other cast members included Carrie Preston, Allegra Fulton, Sean McCann and Shirley Douglas.

As Kiefer's third time in the director's chair it should have been an exciting endeavour, but during the post-production stage problems had set in. Kiefer's preferred cut of the film was deemed by others to be too long, and a series of meetings ensued to discuss re-editing. *Woman Wanted* premiered in spring 2000 at the art house Carlton Cinema in Toronto, and when Kiefer saw what had been done with his film he promptly removed his name as director from the credits. Alan Smithee was substituted – Smithee being the pseudonym commonly employed when a director wants his name deleted from a movie's credits. Some industry figures felt it was a shame that Kiefer reacted this strongly. The consensus was that he had made a really good fist of directing the movie, and had drawn powerful performances from his co-stars. Kiefer, however, felt it had all gone wrong. He hadn't imagined *Woman Wanted* being re-cut in its final form, and he felt, as he put it, 'beaten up badly'. Distribution was not as he had understood it was going to be either, and he called the result 'a mess'. Though the film opened to moderate reviews, it had all gone sour for Kiefer.

In May, Kiefer appeared as Sheriff Bobo, a supporting role in *Picking Up the Pieces*, a movie that the *New York Post* dubbed 'a thoroughly outrageous religious spoof'. Written by Bill Wilson, directed by Alfonso Arau and starring Woody Allen, David Schwimmer, Cheech Marin and Elliott Gould, with an unaccredited appearance by Sharon Stone, this satirical screwball black comedy was damned by *Variety* as 'a tawdry misfire of the lowest order'. It went to Cinemax, a sister cable channel to HBO in lieu of a theatrical release.

Kiefer came back as the leading man in the romantic thriller, *The Right Temptation*, penned by Larry Brand, with Lyndon Chubbuck at the helm. The movie involved a triangle comprising Michael Farrow-Smith, a high-flying business-man, his jealous wife, played by Dana Delaney, and a female private detective hired to get close to him, a role taken by Rebecca De Mornay. Joanna Cassidy and Adam Baldwin completed the core cast. As Michael Farrow-Smith, Kiefer was yet again cast in a cleverly manipulative role, and it gave him his fourth screen appearance in 12 months. He was committed to a further two movies, for release in 2001, that could hardly be more different from each other.

Cowboy Up was a romantic drama-cum-western, written by James Redford and directed by Oscar winner Xavier Koller. Alongside Kiefer in the lead role as Hank Braxton, were Marcus Thomas, Daryl Hannah, Molly Ringwald, Melinda Dillon and Pete Postlethwaite; since it was set in the rodeo world, it was naturally up Kiefer's street. According to one of the film's unit directors, Richard Martini, Kiefer went to great lengths to treat half a dozen of the professional bull riders who worked on set. He said: 'During the Bull Riding finals in Las Vegas, Kiefer took these guys out to dinner, then took them to a casino and gave them each a thousand bucks to gamble with. Kiefer has cowboy in his blood.' *Cowboy Up* was released in early 2001, by which time Kiefer had swapped the rodeo ring for the arena of World War II to make *To End All Wars*.

Ernest Gordon's bestseller, *Through the Valley of the Kwai*, told the true story of 4,000 prisoners in a Japanese prisoner of war camp, who where forced to build the infamous Railroad of Death through Thailand. *To End All Wars* concentrated on nine men, including Ernest Gordon himself, who survived the appallingly brutal horrors of psychological and physical torture that were meted out daily to prisoners in the camp deep in the jungle of Burma-Siam. Brian Godawa had adapted a powerful screenplay from the book, and David L Cunningham directed. Robert Carlyle, Kiefer, Ciaran McMenamin, Mark Strong, James Cosmo and Adam Sinclair joined other cast members and crew to film on location in Scotland, Thailand and the jungles of Kauai. The movie starts at the coast of Thailand after the fall of Singapore in February 1942, when captured soldiers, blindfolded and bound, are being violently herded around, even cruelly subjected to mock executions; the story that unfolds is disturbingly vile, leaving the audience in a state of revulsion for the Japanese captors.

In the terrifying prison camp, no possible way to break a man was left untried. A Scottish commanding officer had a water hose forced down his throat until he literally almost drowned on dry land, while one of the gentlest, most humanitarian of prisoners was actually crucified by a chillingly callous commandant, who was seemingly threatened by the placid prisoner's Christian faith in God. The newly captured soldiers are all from the Scottish regiment, the Argyll and Sutherland Highlanders, with one exception – Lt Jim Reardon, a US Merchant Marine on attachment, nicknamed 'Yanker'. As Lt Reardon, Kiefer plays a guy not yet broken by the Japanese, and who from the moment of his capture is plotting his escape, if possible, if not then to find a way of surviving. He has his own code of self-preservation, and is scared witless to see the numb acceptance in the dulled eyes of those who have spent untold months in the camp.

It was a good role for Kiefer who, in the early scenes of the film reminded the audience that he has the dirtiest laugh in Hollywood. Over the course of the film Kiefer's character, however, goes from being a would-be black marketeer jack-the-lad, to a crippled, broken man, running about bowing and scraping in a coolie hat, meekly willing to take savage beatings even for things he did not do. Kiefer gave a compellingly moving portrayal of a strong man who metamorphosises this way, and many felt that among several good screen appearances Kiefer's was the strongest. It had not come easy sometimes. For one torture sequence, Kiefer had to be tied to a stake with his legs forced into the most painful position possible, and he had to train rigorously for weeks to have the necessary muscle tone and suppleness to endure filming it. During shooting, Kiefer lost almost a stone in weight. Five hundred actors were drafted in to play scenes that required a collection of emaciated prisoners, and Japanese actors played the brutal camp commandant and guards. Said Kiefer: 'We were concerned that certain scenes would offend them, but we had respect for each other as actors.' The final scene showed an 83-year-old British real-life survivor of the camp meeting up with one of his former Japanese guards, at a World War II POW cemetery. 'It was a profound moment,' recalled Kiefer of watching this scene being filmed. 'Out of this immense suffering came an amazing feeling of hope and forgiveness.'

To End All Wars, released in 2001, had at times been arduous to film, but there had been lighter moments, and Kiefer had especially enjoyed it when his stepdaughter, Michelle Kath, had visited him on set. Now in her mid-twenties, she had turned into a slender beauty, with long, dark hair and a warm smile that lit up her eyes. Protective stepdad around or not, when Michelle was there she met and subsequently fell in love with one of Kiefer's co-stars, East Kilbride actor Adam Sinclair, who played the prisoner nicknamed Jocko.

In 2001, once back in Los Angeles, one of 34-year-old Kiefer's greatest sources of happiness was spending time with his daughter, Sarah. Newly a teenager, she lived with her mother, Camelia Kath, literally just along the road from her father. The pair continued to have a very special relationship, even if Kiefer, suffering the pangs most dads do, thought his little girl was growing up too fast. Naturally, they were never destined to share musical taste. She teased him for still listening to 1970s progressive rock; he was bemused by her passion for hip-hop. Together, they went to an Incubus concert, and Kiefer was stunned by Sarah's release of enthusiasm. 'She screamed in a way I never knew she could,' he declared. 'That was a wake-up call.' Determined to be there for his daughter in every way, Kiefer wanted to be ready to tackle anything that came his way during her development. Under no illusions that teenagers any longer need the birds-and-bees chat, Kiefer still maintained: 'I hope I'm smart enough with my daughter to understand when those questions come up, what they really mean.'

Just as Kiefer is committed to being a good father, his own parents in turn were not unaware that their son was not exactly satisfied with the path of his career since returning to acting, and they decided to do something to help. Kiefer revealed: 'They both still have contacts in the industry. I never asked them for anything, but they guessed what I was going through. They started throwing parties and inviting producers over. They recommended me.' Kiefer appreciated his mother and father's belief in him and their support, but he was about to turn a corner professionally that would give him the biggest role of his life and bring him the international fame and respect he deserved.

CHAPTER 15

THERE IS A GOD

'KIEFER SUTHERLAND WAS BORN to play Jack Bauer.' So said Joel Surnow, co-creator of one of the most electrifying screen heroes ever, the star of *24*, one of the best, ground-breaking television drama series of our time. This stark statement was well understood by those who had taken a keen interest in Kiefer's career since it began 15 years earlier. The combination of his intense energy, natural ability and screen presence was always going to coil itself around a high-octane character of dynamism and maturity. Bauer was it, and with inimitable modesty Kiefer was openly grateful. 'When something like *24* happens,' he said, 'you bow your head and say thank you.'

Sharp writing from Joel Surnow and Robert Cochrane created this gritty, explosively nail-biting action thriller, which centred on the events of a single day, with the novel premise that each of the 24 one-hour episodes be played out in real time. Surnow first came up with this unique idea for a drama in summer 2000, but when he pitched it to Cochrane, his friend's initial response was: 'It can't be done.' End of conversation. However, Joel and Robert came back to the notion just days later, and both were intrigued to see if they could pull off the project. They knew it was ambitious in the realms of television, but they cracked it. Originally intended as a one-off mini-series, *24* generated such word of mouth excitement, coupled with rave critical reviews, that its rabid core fan base mushroomed into an international audience and the appetite for the award-winning hit show continues to grow.

In 2001 riveted viewers were introduced to CTU, a fictional Counter Terrorist Unit based in Los Angeles, whose commanding head, renegade federal agent Jack Bauer, is about to have the worst day of his life. Bauer's quickly established back story is that his unswerving commitment to his work, operating in the deadly shadow world of covert operations for the US government, has taken its toll on his private life and led to an estrangement from his wife and teenage daughter. America is in the throes of a presidential election campaign. It is the day of the California primary, and in Los Angeles the life of David Palmer, an African-American Democratic candidate, has been threatened. The plot quickly thickens. Within hours, Jack Bauer's daughter and wife are kidnapped in a move that ultimately ties in with a fast-paced but convoluted chain of events unfolding over 24 hours to a startling and breathtaking climax.

Jack Bauer is a hero with compelling steel and hypnotic authority. 'That's what is appealing about Jack,' declared Kiefer, 'he takes charge.' Bauer also distinguishes himself by his loyalty to his country and his unlimited resourcefulness. He has a sixth, seventh, even an eighth sense, and in terms of TV entertainment he seems to have come along at the right time. Howard Gordon, one of *24*'s executive producers, said: '*24* taps into the public's fear-based wish for protectors such as Jack Bauer who will do whatever is necessary to save society from harm, but it shows a dark side too. Jack Bauer is a tragic character. He doesn't get away with it clean. He's got blood on his hands. In some ways, he is a necessary evil.'

For Kiefer, the Jack Bauer role was a godsend. It came his way via a friend, director Stephen Hopkins, who urged him to read the script for the pilot, which he himself was due to helm. The 43-year-old director had known Kiefer for years. Said Hopkins: 'Kiefer has grown up a lot. He's a stronger, clearer man. He's got a teenage daughter and has reached a point where he knows what he wants.' Kiefer read the pilot for *24* on a plane on his way to Vancouver for a hockey tournament, and by the time the aircraft touched down he couldn't believe his luck. He felt in a no-lose situation. The pilot show was clever and different, with the potential to be a vastly invigorating project, but at the same time, to Kiefer's way of thinking, its unique concept stood little chance of being picked up by a major US TV network. In any event, he reckoned he would be well paid to film it, and if no network ultimately weighed in, then his career would not be harmed by a dud show at this critical comeback point.

The ticking countdown clock, nerve-shreddingly omnipresent, was something that initially Kiefer did not try to get his head around. Written across the front page of the script were the words: 'All events happen in real time,' but he ignored that and cut quickly to the dialogue; the appeal of Jack Bauer hit the spot at once. Kiefer loved the fact that here was an extremely capable hero with a special forces background, in charge of a nation's security, but who can't control his rebellious 16-year-old daughter. A very reactionary federal agent, everything he does has a consequence. Sometimes his impulses are right, other times they are wrong. He is fallible. On arrival at Vancouver airport Kiefer straightaway telephoned Stephen Hopkins with the words: 'Okay, I'm in.'

It is now inconceivable to imagine any other actor than Kiefer in the role of Jack Bauer, but he was offered the part almost by chance. Joel Surnow recently looked back: 'We had no idea who we wanted when we started casting. Then one day someone just said: "What about Kiefer Sutherland?" It was like: "Bingo!" Teenagers can relate to him from his movies, yet he's a man now. Kiefer has the anger and intensity to be a great villain. If you take that energy and give it to a good guy, you've got a really volatile, potent character.' It was a feeling Surnow became wedded to. He already admired Kiefer as an actor. 'He reminds me of Gene Hackman,' said Joel. The writer's only faint reservation had been whether Kiefer could be accepted as the father of a 16-year-old, but that doubt fast faded. Over the months of development, *24* was highly organic, and soon Joel was declaring: 'Kiefer as Jack Bauer is such a compelling combination, it draws you to write that character deeper and deeper.'

In March 2001, with *24* picked up by Fox TV, Kiefer secured the challenge of becoming the show's anchor. 'When I was offered *24*, it came like a saving grace. I owe it a lot,' he said. At that point Kiefer sold his huge cattle ranch in Santa Ynez and made Los Angeles his working base. He wanted his whole concentration to be on Jack Bauer, a complex character with myriad dimensions, some of which did not dovetail with his personality in real life. Kiefer consciously got very close to Jack Bauer to assume that skin. 'It's funny,' he said, 'because I'm strongly opposed to the death penalty and I don't believe in "acceptable losses". It's complicated for me to play this character. Yet one of the big draws was, here is a guy who is ordinary in a lot of ways but due to his profession he's placed in extraordinary situations that he has to make right with action and with thought.'

The plight Bauer finds himself in when his dedication to his demanding job conflicts with his responsibilities as a husband and a father, was a factor that Kiefer deeply identified with. 'It's an aspect of Jack, I really felt connected to,' he maintained, and he firmly believed it was a personal dilemma that would resonate with many viewers. 'By the end, Jack realises how important family is to him but isn't completely forgiven for all he's done. That sounds like life to me,' he said. The breathless pace of the show also appealed to Kiefer's energetic nature. When he later learned that the first series was picked up by Britain's BBC channel with no adverts he declared: 'Man, without breaks *24* moves like a racehorse!' Kiefer had already been aware of passing through the in-between stage as an actor – deemed too young for some roles and too old for others – and the days of playing even university dropouts was long gone. 'With my face, I realise I am difficult to cast,' he confessed. He relished even more then being given this golden opportunity. 'Jack Bauer possesses a dynamic range. I'm not sure I've ever played anyone like him before,' he said.

What Kiefer had certainly never considered before, was working on a television series. In a sense it was an in-built resistance to a medium that had been influenced by his father's attitude to the distinction between the worlds of film and television. 'I remember my father explaining it to me,' recalled Kiefer. 'He said: "If you want to see an actor like Robert Redford or Paul Newman, you have to pay the five bucks to go see them. You have to make a commitment to leave your home. If you do television, you take away that mystery."' Kiefer also never forgot Donald once saying that there were actors and then there were TV hacks. This went way back to a time when American television comprised less than a handful of channels. Even when Kiefer had started out in the mid-1980s, there was little crossover between actors of the small and big screen, but by the turn of the millennium TV had changed out of all recognition. Old-style thinking was no longer applicable, and the lines had become blurred. Now, huge film stars had had their start in television. Whereas a decade earlier, Kiefer confessed that he would have laughed at the very notion of doing a television series, in the past four years he had watched the quality of programming soar, with hit shows such as *The West Wing*, *The Sopranos* and *ER*. 'TV was now often better than a lot of movies,' he explained. 'So if you're trying something new and fresh, the stigma of swapping medium is not nearly what it used to be.'

It helped, too, that some of Kiefer's closest friends had

successfully crossed over to make regular appearances in hit TV shows. Robert Downey Jr had gone into *Ally McBeal*, Charlie Sheen made his mark in *Spin City*, and Sean Penn guested on *Friends*. Having spoken to Penn once about this transition, Kiefer said: 'I loved Sean's reasoning. He said: "It was the only show my daughter cares about and I wanted to do something she'd really like me in, so I'd be cool."' Kiefer's compass then had to be the quality of the material. He bluntly pointed out that he had sweated blood for some movies that few people got to see, and that an actor needs to know that his work is appreciated. He insisted forthrightly: 'An actor would be lying if he told you that there wasn't a difference between a full and a half empty house and what that will do to your performance. The fact that [on TV] you know that on any given night 20 million people are going to watch what you do makes you excited when you're working.' Comparisons between *24* and other hit television series were something Joel Surnow had particular views on. He said: 'This is not *The X Files* or Oliver Stone. *24* also isn't really about terrorists as such. It's more of a revenge story about one guy.'

On 19 July, news broke that Fox TV would be presenting a ground-breaking new drama series, with Kiefer Sutherland as its star. By this time, filming for the episodic thriller was well under way, and joining Kiefer to make up the central cast were Leslie Hope as Jack Bauer's wife, Teri, and Elisha Cuthbert as their high-maintenance daughter, Kim. At CTU, Jack's main cohorts were Tony Almeida, played by Carlos Bernard, and Nina Myers, a role taken by Sarah Clarke. David Palmer, the African-American presidential candidate, was played by Dennis Haysbert, with Penny Johnson Jerald as Sherry, his scheming wife. Xander Berkeley portrayed George Mason, a by-the-book type who is drafted in to assume Jack Bauer's post as head of CTU when it appears that Bauer has gone off the rails. As the new kid on the block, *24* was not shot in a Beverly Hills studio lot. Instead, the set was built in less glamorous surroundings in the LA suburb of Woodland Hills, in the San Fernando Valley. CTU's offices were constructed inside a disused warehouse in a nondescript business park that appeared to have no address. A chain-link fence and two layers of security ringed the set, mainly to ensure airtight secrecy for the gripping drama's edge-of-your seat plotlines.

Filming began around spring and would spread over the next ten solid months. The schedule was gruelling – 12 hours a day, five days a week. For Kiefer, weekends entailed preparation work, sitting for interviews and doing photo shoots. 'Towards the end, we were into hard nights, 5.00 p.m. until 5.00 a.m.,' he said. They would get through around eight script pages a day. As Kiefer pointed out, working on a season of 24 is the equivalent of making 12 movies back-to-back. 'There are so many things I have to worry about,' he confessed, 'from the script to technical things, to my performance. I certainly don't have time to be bored.' As production steamed ahead at this furious pace, writers Joel Surnow and Robert Cochrane were working their fingers to the bone to maintain the highest level of suspense and surprise. Half way through the 24 episodes Kiefer recalled: 'I remember thinking, these guys better slow down or there'll be nowhere left to go, but it's amazing how they have been able to turn the story in on itself, back out and back in on itself again.' The co-creators admitted that this knife-edge pressure was a little scary at times, but as Joel Surnow said, although various crisis situations in the plot kept suddenly rearing up – ultimately, they had in their heads what the last act of the last hour should be.

An added responsibility was accommodating the real-time aspect. The actors worked constantly to a stopwatch. 'If you were in a fight in the last filmed scene which is supposed to be two minutes ago, when they come back to you, you've still got to be breathing hard,' said Kiefer. Once he saw how it all looked on screen he fully appreciated its value. 'When there are 15, then ten, then five minutes left, it creates a level of anxiety for viewers that, for some reason, is pleasurable.' The other feature synonymous with *24* is the use of split screening, when every so often the picture breaks up into boxes to help remind viewers of what stage all the subplots are at; against the ominous ticking of the clock, this also ups the ante. Kiefer thought this device ingenious. 'That wasn't in the script, that was Stephen Hopkins,' he explained.

The secrecy surrounding the plot was not just for prying outsiders; the show's cast and its hands-on star only got to know the story so far ahead, and everyone eagerly awaited getting their hands on the next script – not least to find out if their character was still alive by the end of the next episode. No one was safe, and it created an edge that was more than enough to keep all the actors on their toes. Reading an early script for series one, Kiefer's eyes almost fell out when he read how Jack Bauer apparently guns down his colleague and ex-lover, Nina Myers, to comply with the demands of the ruthless kidnappers who are holding his wife and daughter hostage. 'Oh my god,' he burst out loud to no one in particular, 'Sarah Clarke's just been fired!' Twenty pages later, he discovered that Jack had surreptitiously ensured that Nina was wearing a bullet-proof vest, which saved her.

From the beginning, Kiefer had a certain degree of input into *24*, but at times his views were overruled. Such was the fascination with Jack Bauer that the show's devoted fans started debating the tiniest detail of his behaviour. Kiefer himself began querying things like: when does Bauer get to grab something to eat? He is careering from one crisis to another from midnight without food, drink, sleep – anything. When Kiefer suggested a moment in the show when Jack buys a hot dog from a burger van, the writers downed him – they believed viewers would think that was funny. According to Kiefer, he and the powers that be got into an argument over this eating issue. A compromise was found when, more than half way through, having rescued his family, the exhausted federal agent gets to bolt a tray of food while waiting at CTU to be debriefed on his renegade behaviour over the past few hours.

It may seem a small matter to feel so strongly about, but Kiefer had so immersed himself in this role that his attention to detail shone through. His presence on screen was almost always required, but he did have times to slink away to his trailer, which from the outside was so unprepossessing that a journalist later invited to the set for an interview described it as 'grungy'. It was comfy inside, and had everything Kiefer needed, including the company of his pet dog, Molly, always affectionately happy to see her master during his breaks. Meticulous attention had to be paid to every aspect of Kiefer's appearance. Although 24 took 10 months to film and would be shown on TV over almost six months, the action supposedly happens in a single 24-hour period, which meant that facially and bodily Kiefer had to stay exactly the same throughout. He also had the most action sequences to undertake, so fitness was an issue. Since signing on the dotted line to become Jack Bauer, Kiefer had not taken part in rodeo riding. Between his passion for rodeo, skiing and ice hockey, he had in the past broken his collarbone, a knee, an elbow, both wrists, one ankle and all his fingers, but the producers had no need to worry that he would forget his duty to take care of himself.

He had never been more conscious of the need to be in shape. 'Not for vanity,' he insisted, 'just simple survival.' He continued to smoke, which made all the running about he had to do on screen more than a little arduous. On camera it never looked as if he struggled at all, though, and the cameramen were amazed that a man who lit up as often as Kiefer could sprint to order like he did. As Jack Bauer, Kiefer had somehow to maintain an almost manic energy level throughout all 24 episodes. Not surprisingly, after a long shoot, he went home tired to his LA apartment. After walking Molly, the pair would then crash in front of the television for a while. Kiefer often fell sound asleep, while Molly, curled up at his feet, would happily chew on a bone. With such a demanding workload Kiefer lived alone, had no special lady in his life and scant time to socialise. At one point the only people he met outside 24's cast and crew were shift workers breakfasting at Denny's at dawn.

24 was destined to be the hottest show on TV, and Kiefer felt the fact that director Stephen Hopkins had not worked on a television series before played a massive part in helping to create that success. 'Although things are changing, particularly in network television, there are creative limitations, but Stephen was unaware of them so he rode right over them,' said Kiefer. Kiefer had never before had the opportunity to work on something unremittingly for so many consecutive months, and 24 threw up the chance for cast and crew to become well acquainted. Kiefer and Carlos Bernard hit it off from the first day of filming. The darkly handsome actor, who would accrue his own personal fan base portraying CTU agent, Tony Almeida, played a joke on Kiefer within minutes of arriving on set. Carlos describes his hair as resembling a rat's nest, and he walked straight up to Kiefer and asked him, apparently anxiously, if he thought that his hair looked dreadful. 'Can you tell?' he asked repeatedly, until a bewildered Kiefer discreetly asked Carlos if he was wearing a wig. Carlos recalled: 'I said: "Oh my god, you *can* tell!" I feigned a mini breakdown and Kiefer, who is the sweetest guy in the world, was so upset that he'd upset me. He kept reassuring me: "No, no, you can't tell at all!" I was just screwing around, but I couldn't keep it up for long because he got all flustered.'

Dennis Haysbert, with whom Kiefer would have a close on-screen interaction as would-be president and federal agent, has also recalled happy times. He described working with Kiefer as being akin to working with his best friend, calling Kiefer a genuinely good guy. Said Dennis: 'It's a fun set to be on and Kiefer has fun, but fun just for the sake of it? No.

When the work needs to be done, Kiefer's right there to do it.' Almost every actor in 24 was new to one another, and in those circumstances there can be a tendency to arrive on set with preconceived ideas. Elisha Cuthbert, who took on the role of Bauer's headstrong daughter, Kim, arrived knowing that her mother had really liked Kiefer for years as an actor. Elisha knew all about how Kiefer had been a Hollywood golden boy when he'd been about her age, which made her a little unsure of what the actor playing her father would be like. 'When we met, he made it very easy,' she recalled. 'He was really down to earth.'

The other corner of the Bauer family triangle was Jack's wife, Teri, played by Leslie Hope, whose respect for and friendship with her screen husband is very apparent. She quickly chalked up that Kiefer is one of those actors a crew adores working with, which on an arduous shoot oils the wheels for everyone. During filming, Leslie declared: 'I may be having the best time of my life. It's like going to work on the best movie set every day. Kiefer is gracious and generous, has the patience of a saint, is a good listener and his butt looks awesome in his Wranglers!'

Penny Johnson Jerald had the task of playing devious and dangerous would-be First Lady, Sherry Palmer, who is too shrewd ever to underestimate Jack Bauer. Off set, Penny found Kiefer a surprise in some ways. Describing him as 'absolutely adorable', she spoke of a time when the cast and crew had moved from the San Fernando Valley south to Long Beach to shoot the assassination attempt on David Palmer, and some people stayed overnight there. She said: 'Someone was looking for Kiefer because we were all hanging out and enjoying each other's company. He was finally found in the laundry room, folding laundry with the maids. He was having a great time hanging out with the help. That's Kiefer. He's cool!'

Kiefer's intensity was the other striking factor for those around him. 'It's an honour to get to watch Kiefer work,' said

Karina Arroyave, the elfin actress who played traitor CTU operative, Jamey Farrell. 'I was trying to figure out what makes him so good and I realised it was that everything he does is so specific. Every single line has so much meaning. He takes everything to a heightened level.'

To the cameramen, Kiefer's actorly precision was manna from heaven. It made acting out even the toughest, fastest fight sequences go smoothly, because once Kiefer and the director of photography had worked out the physicality in a scene, no matter how many takes it took to complete, Kiefer never varied from the plan. From a cinematographer's point of view, that is a rare quality in an actor. Kiefer's commitment to 24 was more complete than his co-stars had ever expected. He would not go back to his trailer when his part was off camera, leaving a script girl to stand in for him, as stars frequently do. In November, the cast and crew were allowed a rare weekday off for the annual Thanksgiving Day celebrations. On the day before, Tamara Tunie, the statuesque, power-dressed boss, Alberta Green, thought she was the last actor left on set. She had to film her final two scenes, both phone calls her character had with Jack Bauer. 'It's about 6 o'clock in the evening on the Wednesday,' she said, 'I go on set, ready to pick up the phone and Kiefer walks in.' Kiefer had finished filming his scenes by mid-day and was thought to have long since knocked off. Startled, Tamara asked him what he was doing there. Kiefer replied: 'I'm doing my phone calls with you.' Again, it may seem an insignificant detail, but Tamara Tunie didn't think so. She declared: 'Nobody can give me the excuse that they can't be off camera, ever again. Kiefer is a class act.'

Long before November, the director, producers and writers felt fully vindicated in their choice of Kiefer Sutherland as Jack Bauer. Robert Cochrane enthused: 'Kiefer brings a dark side with him, and it's a tremendous sense of three-dimensionality, layers and complexity.' Executive producer Howard Gordan declared: 'Kiefer elevates everyone else's game. He insists on a certain level of commitment. The urgency that he creates informs the entire show and the quality of acting among the ensemble. He is the single best actor I've ever had the privilege of working with.'

Xander Berkeley, as George Mason, had his run-ins with the renegade Jack Bauer before ending up a sneak fan of the daringly reckless hero. Off camera, Xander did not hide his respect for Kiefer. He was aware of Kiefer's reputation for having an edginess, and maintained: 'That creates great veracity for Jack Bauer. Kiefer's not an apologist. He likes to have fun and live hard. If he acts crazy sometimes, that's what makes him fun to be around.' Kiefer could certainly prove that that wild spirit had not entirely deserted him, as was witnessed one off-duty evening in summer when, having downed a few drams of his favourite whisky at a swish Beverly Hills hotel, he suddenly jumped fully clothed into the deserted, shimmering swimming pool. Director Stephen Hopkins said of his friend: 'On the rare occasions when we got drunk together, Kiefer was a charming drunk, not at all a bad tempered person.' Next morning, up early with a banging head, Kiefer would look in a mirror and tell himself that he was getting too old for these carousing capers.

By now, Kiefer had bought a home in Toronto quite close to where his mother lives, but mainly he stayed at his LA apartment, where he enjoyed chilling out in a variety of ways. His prized guitar collection had risen to 37 instruments, and he enjoyed quietly strumming away. He had also acquired a taste for cooking. 'I'm not a very complicated chef,' he admits, 'but I find it incredibly relaxing.' Kiefer and Kelly's divorce had not been finalised – a situation that would inexplicably stretch on for some time. There had been newspaper speculation some months back that the couple had rekindled their romance, but that was never confirmed by either party. What was clear by 2001 was that they had found at least a friendly footing, for it was Kelly who had diplomatically suggested to Kiefer that since he was living alone, he really ought to get himself some cookery lessons. By his own admission, when he started those lessons he was something of a pain. It was his first time back in a classroom in 19 years, and initially he lurked at the back ready with a few funnies for the teacher. He quickly realised he was being daft, moved up front and concentrated on learning the basic cooking and baking skills.

When he wasn't running lines of dialogue through his mind as he sifted flour through his nimble fingers into a baking bowl, he loved as ever spending time with Sarah. They played chess and liked reading together. 'Something I enjoyed was reading *To Kill a Mockingbird* aloud with Sarah and talking about what it meant to be in the South at that time.' Kiefer recently declared proudly: 'She's pretty clever and not half as rebellious as I was at her age. I'm very impressed.'

Despite being careful off set not to endanger life and limb, Kiefer's exuberance once led after all to an accident on set when he shattered a kneecap pulling off a stunt. 'Fortunately when it happened we had three weeks left to shoot before the Christmas break and there were a lot of car scenes,' he said. 'Still, we had to scramble and figure out all the scenes where I'd be prone, which weren't that many.' It was an accident that threw up extra challenges for the writers, and left Kiefer hobbling around with a walking cane for a while.

Some time back, Joel Surnow and Robert Cochrane had indicated that they knew how the show's convoluted plot would end, but when the cast got their final scripts, there was a shock in store. Robert Cochrane said: '*24* never gave out a "don't worry, be happy" vibe. After all the stuff that happened, if everyone had ridden off into the sunset it would have felt false.' Kiefer conceded: 'We knew something was going to have to give. We knew there was no way everyone was going to walk out of this fine.' What no one expected was that Teri Bauer would end up being shot dead. When Kiefer discovered his screen wife's fate, at first he was vehemently against the decision to kill her off, and indeed many of the show's vociferous fans would not much like it either, but Kiefer's objections were overruled without appeal. It showed Kiefer that in 24's pecking order, as at 2001 he ranked roughly fourth. It was hard, he said, for he rated Leslie Hope very highly as an actor, and had been able, throughout the ten-month shoot, to depend upon her in every professional way. On a personal level, too, he described this development as: 'I lost my right hand.'

Once he could take his emotional reaction out of the equation, however, he could see that he had been wrong to oppose the decision to ice Teri Bauer. Cochrane called the shock true to 24, and Kiefer now believes that Teri's death was the first marker to both cast and audience that no character was safe, including his own. 24 without Jack Bauer is unthinkable, yet Kiefer made a valid point when he said that if the audience is so sure that no matter what peril he is in, he will win through, it would harm the dramatic tension, perhaps fatally. People care about Jack Bauer, and it matters what happens to him.

By the time filming finally finished, it had been some ride for Kiefer. He had turned 35 in December 2001, and was a calmer person. Now when he was tired, he would consciously slow down rather than think himself invincible and so end up burning out. He had a sense of perspective when it came to work, that felt better balanced, and he was not being emotionally drained by having to cope with a turbulent love life. Asked if he had regrets about having two failed marriages behind him, Kiefer replied: 'How can I? I have a beautiful daughter and many happy memories.'

Throughout 24 Jack Bauer has the US President's ear, and people sometimes wonder if, considering his Douglas family background, Kiefer would in real life be tempted into politics. When Republican George W Bush had squeaked into the White House in 2000 for his first term of office, some US motorists stuck stickers on their car bumpers which read: 'Don't Blame Me – I Voted For Bartlett!' (a reference to the

Democratic President depicted by Martin Sheen in *The West Wing*). An actor *had* made it to the White House before, with Ronald Reagan. So, could it be Jack Bauer for President? Kiefer found such suggestions hilarious. He has strong political views but – entering that particular minefield? He answered: 'With my past? Are you kidding?'

Although Kiefer was living the lion's share of his life in Los Angeles, he maintained off duty that, in his head, he was often at home in Toronto. Trying to explain the difference between Canadians and Americans was something Kiefer found impossible. However, he hinted that Canadians maybe had more benign natures, when he told the story of how he was walking along a street in Los Angeles one day, busy chatting with a friend, and not looking where he was going. He said: 'I walked into a parking meter. Before I knew it, I'd said: "Sorry" to this inanimate object. If I'd had any change on me, I'd probably have given it some!'

Filming for series one of *24* carried on long after the first episodes aired, but by autumn, the programme makers had roughly the first eight episodes in the can. The PR machine had long since geared up to swing into action, and advance programme pilots had been doled out to the media. In summer 2001, *24* had already become the talk of Hollywood. On 9 September, Fox TV officially announced that *24* would make its debut on US television on 30 October. Two days later, the terrorist atrocity of 11 September 2001 numbed the whole world, and plans to launch *24* on the announced date changed. On 7 October, the new date was given as 6 November 2001. Like billions of people, Kiefer was devastated by the scale of the appalling acts of terrorism. TV images of brave firefighters determined to get upstairs in what was left of the collapsing World Trade Center towers in New York were permanently burned onto his brain. He felt useless, he said, insignificant in the scheme of things. It was a natural reaction to the scale of the death toll and the examples of the real-life heroism that emerged. Kiefer's intense feelings of inadequacy made him a little tetchy when in the following weeks people came up to him, excited at the prospect of 24 starting. They'd read glowing critical previews and couldn't wait to see the show. Kiefer's first inner response was to be appalled or even angry at the facile outlook, until it dawned on him that he was being too harsh. People *needed* normality, escapism, some relief from the oppressive grief and the suffocating air of tragedy and fear.

For a time, it was bandied about that huge changes had had to be hastily made to 24's first few episodes in the light of the terrorist attack, but Kiefer took time out to set the record straight on that front. He explained clearly that in 24 a terrorist, on board a plane, sticks a hypodermic needle into a stewardess's throat, which was similar to what had happened on one of the four real-life aircraft that were hijacked on 9/11, but 24 makers did not take that out. What the programme makers did delete was a scene of the fictitious aircraft exploding and coming apart. They did not, however, change the story line. On *Entertainment Tonight* Kiefer said: 'We had shot our pilot [episode] and quite a few episodes before the terrible tragedy of 9/11. We were very clear that 24 is a fantasy and it is never to be confused with the terrible reality of what happened on that horrific day.'

As 6 November 2001 approached, public anticipation over 24 mounted to a high degree. Indeed, it was the best-previewed drama of the year's new shows. The *Boston Globe* called 24 'an innovative and expertly executed hour of suspense.' The *Washington Post* hailed it 'gripping from the get-go!' The *Los Angeles Times* simply settled for 'smashing'. Of Kiefer as Jack Bauer, the *New York Post* praised: 'He is so good, it's like he's not acting!' and the *San Francisco Chronicle* could take or leave the ticking clock feature but said of Kiefer that he was 24's 'star it couldn't afford to lose'. Britain's *Maxim* magazine later weighed in with: 'There is only one troubled existentialist hero role worth its salt these days: confused, in the dark, paranoid and desperate, Jack

Bauer is a role model for our times!' Joel Surnow joked that he hoped the show wouldn't air, believing that the critical reaction could never again be so good! He, of course, wanted *24* to air and achieve great success, but he warned: 'The media have a way of building things up to a fever pitch and there's only one place to go from there. You flame out.'

24 would only go from strength to strength, accruing millions of new devotees every season, and Kiefer would be staggered by the response to it. Interaction with the show's audience simply took off, and sometimes fans have chosen the most inappropriate times to try to engage the star. Once, Kiefer was driving along and a motorist drew parallel, recognised Kiefer and began avidly discussing *24* with him instead of concentrating on the road. Kiefer recalled: 'I'm thinking: I can't do this, right now! I'm going to run into someone.'

Kiefer Sutherland was again the name on everyone's lips, but he said of his career at that point: 'I've been up and down the ladder so many times, it's a relief I didn't hit the ground.' He had said a decade earlier that the really good work for an actor does not start until he is in his thirties. Shirley Douglas said of her son: 'Kiefer's whole life is now concentrated on *24*. Those bags under his eyes are not just for the character! He's always short on sleep, but he's extremely happy and that's all that matters.' Kiefer's father may have once had a distinct aversion to television, but Donald too had kept abreast of the huge changes in this medium. He said: 'I have no objective viewpoint of Kiefer's career. *24* just takes your breath away. You're immediately sucked into the vortex of it.'

Kiefer was still working hard on the show. With its release on air he was now red-hot professionally, and the clamour for interviews with him was deafening; despite being choc-a-bloc at work, he made what time could be spared for the press. Journalists were often surprised that while Kiefer was front cover material all over again, he was not a prima donna who needed a list of demands to be met before he would sit down for an interview. There was no phalanx of protective publicity people to be waded through, no rigmarole at all. Most times, Kiefer would drive himself to an appointed hotel for an interview with only his dog for company.

24 was a solid gold hit, and success the second time around was certainly very sweet for Kiefer. Yet he remained genuinely modest. 'On a career level, I have to say that this has been the most important year for me. I thank 24 all the way home and all the way back to work every day,' he said. His stunning, critically acclaimed portrayal of Jack Bauer catapulted Kiefer back into Hollywood's A-list. He was now also affectionately labelled Tinseltown's latest comeback king. This bright spotlight brought a deluge of attention from all quarters, which steadily increased the number of unusual situations Kiefer had to cope with. On a ski lift once, a real life CIA operative jokingly tackled him for being an impossibly capable federal agent. Apparently, the CIA operative's mother thought that Jack Bauer was so much more efficient than her son.

Because smoking in Los Angeles restaurants is not allowed, Kiefer could often be found lighting up on the pavement outside elegant eateries in areas frequented by autograph hunters. He has claimed that some autograph hunters only found out who he was when he had obligingly signed their pieces of paper legibly, but his face was very well known. About being approached by strangers, Kiefer said: 'I'm not really comfortable with people coming up to me wanting to talk, but signing is fine.' He resolutely refuses to have minders, though. He does not believe in barricading himself off from the public. 'People in the street pay money to watch me,' he said. 'Without them, I'd be no one.'

He is able to take a similarly relaxed view about the paparazzi. Out dining one day when series one of 24 was riding high, a friend with him grew extremely irritated that a photographer was snapping away at Kiefer from across the way. The friend heatedly insisted that no one should be allowed to do that. Kiefer's response was to shrug and say: 'It's part of what I do, so he can if he wants.'

24 series one premiered in Britain on BBC2 in March 2002. Before that, recognition came Kiefer's way when he received an Emmy nomination for Outstanding Lead Actor in a Drama Series, and a Golden Globe Best Actor in a TV Drama nomination. *24* was nominated for a Golden Globe in the Best New TV Show category, and the show received the Television Critics Association Award nomination for Individual Achievement in Drama. It was a busy award season, and Kiefer picked off the Golden Satellite Award for Best Performance by an Actor in a Series – Drama.

Then on 20 January 2002, at the Golden Globe Awards ceremony in Los Angeles, he won the coveted Golden Globe, beating off stiff competition from Simon Baker for *The Guardian*, James Gandolfini for *The Sopranos*, Peter Krause for *Six Feet Under* and Martin Sheen for *The West Wing*. On the glitzy evening, before an international television audience, Kiefer was overwhelmed as he clutched his Best Actor trophy. He later said: 'My mind went totally blank and my body went numb. It was a very surreal moment. It was a great night. I admit, I felt really cocky for about twenty-four hours and then I had to go back to work.'

CHAPTER 16

JACK BAUER IS BACK

WHEN THE DIGITAL CLOCK-style '24' first scorched its way on to British television screens in spring 2002, in America work on series two of the hit drama was already under way. Keeping his eye on the show's reception abroad, Kiefer was thrilled with its success in the UK. 'It was phenomenal,' he said. 'It was the biggest show the BBC has ever had. It became the number one DVD in the UK, knocking off *The Lord of the Rings*.'

Series one of 24 had set the bar so high that some wondered if a second season could live up to expectations. Privately, Kiefer too had faint moments of concern. Not a fan of film sequels, his first instinct had been that 24 was such a breathtaking triumph, maybe the smart thing might be to leave it at that – untarnished. The risk of being unable to equal series one, or to better it, was very real to him. He adored the show and his character, but was aware that decisions made under pressure can be regretted with hindsight. However, when the programme makers went over what series two would embrace, he became 'terribly excited'.

Series two of 24 would be a lot harder edged, even more action-oriented than its predecessor and in some ways Jack Bauer would not be the man he was. This new longest day in the tough federal agent's life occurred 18 months on from the previous day, and the threat this time comes from a group of terrorists aiming to detonate a nuclear bomb in Los Angeles. The threat appears initially to emanate from an Arab American, but this changes over the course of the labyrinthine plot. In the post-9/11 climate, there was heightened awareness among the programme makers not to blur the lines between reality and fantasy. Kiefer confessed: 'Unfortunately, there is a lot for our writers to take from the headlines but we would certainly like that to become less and less.'

As before, the scripts for 24 were among the most tightly guarded in television, with the actors only receiving a week's notice of any major plot twists. What was obvious from the opening minutes was that Jack Bauer is in a very dark place emotionally, which makes him an extremely dangerous man in different ways. He is not working for the government, and feels that his job has cost him everything. With his pregnant wife murdered, his daughter is keeping her distance from him, because he is too painful a reminder of what happened before. Operating on a very short fuse, when CTU need him back Jack is very unpredictable. In series two, the violence level rises substantially from the beginning, and it is a two-way street. Later, Bauer is captured by the villains and tortured so brutally that he 'dies', in the sense that his heart stops, and he has to be revived by a defibrillator. He appears ready to sign his own death warrant at one point, too, when he volunteers to fly a plane with an unstoppably activated nuclear bomb on board into a crash landing in the desert.

The thrills and spills came head-spinningly thick and fast, and it was often arduous for Kiefer, who was already on a killer work schedule. The torture scene alone took a draining five hours to shoot. 'It was a really difficult sequence,' he said, 'compounded by the fact that I was naked. It's the first time I've ever had to do something like that.' This different Jack Bauer, however, was precisely what energised Kiefer. He stated upfront: 'I wanted Jack to be very cold, very hard and mean.' Kiefer also approved of the difficulties portrayed between Bauer and his daughter, for it showed that a deep core connected both explosive days. He revealed: 'Personally, I was also satisfied with what the show examined from a political perspective.'

Just as *24* attracts extraordinary devotion from its fans, so it extracts a high level of dedication from its cast and crew. While injecting new blood, series two also welcomed back familiar characters including George Mason, Tony Almeida, Kim Bauer, David and Sherry Palmer and Nina Myers; for everyone involved it meant bravely pulling out the stops. Co-creator Robert Cochrane had this to say: 'Once you have a show that is set in the world of anti-terrorism, you can't shy away from the things that people are afraid of. It'd be like a cop show with no murders.' Joel Surnow reflected of this new series: 'He is struggling to keep it together, fighting to stay noble. We're talking about Jack Bauer and Kiefer Sutherland both.'

Being such a complex undertaking, *24* required the involvement of a team of writers working constantly. One of them was Evan Katz, who said: 'I joined the show during the second season as a consulting producer, which generally means you are a part-time writer/producer. Typically on *24*, we have about five guys who are writer/producers. We all make stories together in a room, again and again. Then we'll go off and write episodes alone or in pairs.' Katz wrote the episode in series two where Bauer, during an intense interrogation, seemingly has the young son of an Arab-American terrorist killed. It was a difficult scene to put down on paper and to enact, but Katz ended up delighted all round, especially with Kiefer. 'Kiefer is critically important to *24*,' declared Evan. 'He is really fascinating to watch – a real sort of edgy, believably ruthless presence.'

Kiefer had come to this new season geared up to explore further his dynamic character's multi-faceted personality.

'Jack is certainly loaded with a great deal of conflicts this time around,' he said. He called himself privileged to be back as Jack Bauer, and was proud of many satellite aspects of the show. 'I think if you show on television that a black US President exists, then people will accept that that's a possibility, which is a huge step forward.' The ever-present danger of Bauer being killed was also very successfully maintained, adding to the spice. Kiefer opined: 'This show is effective as long as you think I could potentially die.' Evan Katz likened *24* to Hitchcock's *Psycho*: 'In *24*, we'll kill anyone, which adds to the audience's discomfort.'

Before the fans got the chance to be upended, the actors themselves were back living on a knife-edge, and those new to *24* quickly learned to take nothing for granted. Laura Harris, a 26-year-old actress from Vancouver, thought she had been cast as the beautiful, blonde Marie Warner, fragile daughter of a wealthy businessman, who is set to marry her Arab-American fiancé when he suddenly becomes suspected of being a terrorist. Things turn upside down when *she* proves to be part of the ruthless terrorist cell behind the nuclear bomb plot. When this twist landed in Laura's lap she grew incredibly excited. 'I read the script and I rolled it up and I threw it across the room,' she confessed. 'I was so energised. I couldn't believe it!'

Another newcomer to *24* was Reiko Aylesworth, who would establish herself as CTU agent Michelle Dessler. Talking of Kiefer's rampantly rising sex appeal she said: 'It's funny, you read what's posted on all of these websites and you would think they'd have to have smelling salts on the set to revive all the ladies, but it's not like that.' Reiko had admired Kiefer as an actor for a long time, and found him as professional on set as he was fun off it. She revealed: 'We all look to him to set the standard. It's the best set I've ever worked on, and a lot of that is due to Kiefer.'

Sarah Wynter, as Kate Warner, completed the trio of

glamorous actresses new to the *24* cast. Kate is on the side of the good guys, and although she only meets Jack Bauer for the first time that day, there is a romantic spark between them. Off camera, Sarah found Kiefer one of the most unusual leading men she had ever encountered. 'He's definitely unique,' she gaily declared, 'with a wicked dry sense of humour and a real cowboy side to him.' According to Sarah, if Kiefer noticed her off in a corner of the set, fretting about an upcoming scene, he would walk up to her, push her playfully over and carry on his way. 'It was his way of saying: "C'mon, get on with it!"' she explained. Other cast members were also grateful that no one stood on ceremony, and that there was no precious behaviour from the show's leading light. It was universally agreed, on the contrary, that Kiefer had a knack for bringing everyone together.

As was the case the first time around, Kiefer's heavy commitments to *24* left him very little free time. Even then it was sometimes difficult in certain ways to distinguish between Kiefer Sutherland and Jack Bauer. Both were impetuous, as was proved one day when Kiefer was driving home through LA. He saw what looked like an old lady being beaten up by youths bent on stealing her purse. In such a high crime city, this was hardly an unusual sight. However, Kiefer angrily stopped his car, jumped out and descended on the would-be muggers. The sight of an enraged Jack Bauer bearing down on them was enough to panic the guys, who were only spared retribution for their 'assault' when it was frantically pointed out to the livid actor helping the lady to her feet, that he had just inadvertently interrupted the shooting of a scene for a student film!

By May 2002, with sleep deprivation once again looming, Kiefer had taken up running in an effort to look after himself better. 'When you get past 30, everything in life is about abstaining and giving up and everything is about discipline,' he acknowledged, adding ruefully that, at least in the meantime, he continued to hang on to smoking. He still had to restrict himself to watching ice hockey, rather than playing the fast-action sport of hard knocks, and for a screen agent who handles the most sophisticated hi-tech gadgets, Kiefer was bamboozled by the internet. He was not particularly impressed by the World Wide Web when he did go looking for a detailed picture of a Scottish thistle, which he wanted to have replicated in a tattoo. His personal screen charisma and heart-throb status only strengthened over the course of the year, and that summer in Britain's *Daily Mirror* poll of television's Sexiest Men, Kiefer ranked fifth. In private, back in America, he still lived alone but was by now quietly dating a 28-year-old artist named Catherine Bisson.

Kiefer still kept in touch with his stepsons, Julian and Timothy, and with Michelle, and fatherhood was something he confessed he could go on about forever. He remained sensitive to what he felt had been his initial failings as a very young dad, and admitted to having heart-to-hearts with Sarah about this. He revealed: 'I apologised to my daughter when she was about 14, saying: "I'm sorry we had to raise each other." She replied: "Dad, it's all right. I wouldn't want it any other way."' Sarah once made her father a clay cup, writing on it: 'My daddy is a saint.' Kiefer commented drily that that was when he realised that his little girl had a good grasp of sarcasm!

Kiefer's parents in turn continued to take stock from afar of how much their son was working. Said Shirley Douglas: 'No matter how tough things have been, Kiefer always turns up for work and works hard. There's something in him – his tenacity. He just keeps going.'

While Kiefer's low-key love life was conducted away from work, on the set of *24* love had blossomed between the actors portraying CTU boss George Mason and traitor Nina Myers, and on 7 September 2002 Xander Berkeley and Sarah Clarke got married. Xander later recalled that during one scene in series two, when Bauer takes over the forceful interrogation of Myers, bearing in mind that Nina murdered Jack's wife

Teri, Kiefer's performance of an agent already on the edge, on the verge of committing murder, was so realistic that as a loving new groom he was momentarily anxious for his wife. It was only acting, however, but Jack Bauer's star as a believable screen hero was in the ascendant. On 18 October 2002, Kiefer was named Man of the Year in a TV Drama at the *GQ* Awards.

On 29 October 2002, series two of *24* premiered on American television. Everyone connected with this electrifying drama, which hadn't dipped an inch, knew right away that it would be another copper-bottomed smash hit, for this debut episode posted ratings that were 11 per cent up on the premiere episode of series one. Over the course of series two, *24* notched up the biggest audience gains of any drama shown on America's four major TV networks. Said Kiefer: 'On any given Tuesday night, more people watch *24* than watch any single film I have ever made.' The show and Kiefer continued to excel critically. In November, *Time* magazine said: 'The screen hums whenever Sutherland's on it. He transcends *24*, creating Bauer's bitterness and nobility out of pauses and hard-eyed stares.'

Once again, the bright spotlight shone squarely on the hero of the moment, and interest in all things Kiefer Sutherland was intense. Kiefer and Kelly were not yet divorced. Back in spring, the only news on this front had been that the estranged couple still had to finalise matters. As to whether he would ever marry again, Kiefer reiterated that that was a non-issue for him. He still felt that he had been burned twice, and asked: 'What's the thing you try to teach a child about going near an oven?' Yet in late November 2002, some unsubstantiated media claims emerged that Kiefer had bought Catherine Bisson a diamond and sapphire three-stone engagement ring, maintaining that he was set for a third trip down the aisle.

More clear-cut was the fact that Kiefer seemed indefatigable. 'Doing something like *24*, you end up with a short hiatus which makes it very hard also to do a movie,' he said. Yet in 2002/early 2003 Kiefer would pop up in four films. In March 2002, on America's Cinemax, came the thriller *Desert Saints*, written by Richard Greenberg and Wally Nichols. Directed by Greenberg, it starred Brent Roam, Shawn Woods, Christopher Bersh and Rachel Ticotin. Kiefer played Arthur Banks, a top-flight hit man who works as a hired gun for drug lords. Kiefer again played a character connected to the Mob when he took on the lead role of Pally Lamarr, a Boston cop with problems, in the action movie, *Dead Heat*, written and directed by Mark Malone. Kiefer's co-stars this time included Anthony LaPaglia, Radha Mitchell and Daniel Benzali. Director Mark Malone joined the ranks of those who found Kiefer's continuity as an actor almost frighteningly perfect. He declared: 'Kiefer is so precise you can actually cut from take to take, or from angle to angle without ever tripping over the fact that he is in a different spot.' *Dead Heat* was released in the US in July 2002 and earned Kiefer a Best Actor nomination at the DVD Premiere Awards.

In a change of pace, Kiefer had made the emotive drama, *Behind the Red Door*, in which a family is forced to face up to the consequences of its violent past, in order to find some peace. Kiefer played a character called Roy, who has Aids. Directed by Matia Karrell, *Behind the Red Door* was written by Karrell and CW Cressler; starring alongside Kiefer were Kyra Sedgwick, Stockard Channing and Phillip Craig. It too was released in 2002.

Kiefer's fourth film planned for release that year was the Joel Schumacher-directed potboiler, *Phone Booth*, in which, as a sniper with someone literally in his sights, Kiefer provided a sinister voice on the end of a telephone. Writer Larry Cohen had first come up in the early 1970s with a script for this tense psychological thriller, in which an adulterous, self-centred New York publicist is reduced from an egotistical smart alec to a terrified gibbering wreck when he answers a ringing telephone in a public call box, and finds himself on the line with a menacing stranger who seems to know all about his deceitful life. Decades on, in January 2001, shooting had finally got underway. Tightly scripted and slickly directed, *Phone Booth*, starring Colin Farrell as publicist Stu Shepard, lasted a lean 81 minutes and was shot in Los Angeles, filmed like *24* in real time, over just 12 days. Of that short shoot Kiefer, playing The Caller, was only required for two days. Forest Whitaker, Radha Mitchell and Katie Holmes also co-starred, but Kiefer called *Phone Booth* 'ultimately a one-man show', for he was blown away by Colin Farrell's performance.

Kiefer had known about this film project for ages, but had no idea that it was being made. Then he got a call from the director he had already worked with on three films and counted as a friend, who asked if he could spare the time to come and record the hushed voice of the sniper armed with a high velocity rifle which is trained on the phone box. The Caller menaces the publicist with a tiny infrared dot that he makes dance about the kiosk, emphasising the reality of his threat to kill him if he attempts to leave the phone booth. Kiefer agreed, showed up at the designated soundstage, and asked which type of voice they required. Joel Schumacher chuckled: 'What a voice Kiefer's got! He's great, wickedly funny and mischievous. Kiefer can do anything – the nicest guy in the world, or the most evil person alive. He has it all! Kiefer brings an intelligence and a quality of humanity, even when he's playing a bad guy.'

When Kiefer read the script, his take on The Caller was that he was someone who feels strongly about people who barge through life never taking responsibility for their nefarious actions. Said Kiefer: 'I see it in the US when people talk about the Enron scandal. They want these people held accountable for it. These people who made billions of dollars and have ripped us off non-stop.' From an artistic viewpoint, Kiefer did not set out to be obviously chilling. He preferred to portray someone in complete control. He explained: 'When someone is in control, they are calm, deliberate, focused and succinct. So I created a voice that was in control, which itself becomes menacing very rapidly.' Kiefer recorded his role separately and did not actually meet the movie's star until after production. 'Colin really makes me laugh,' said Kiefer. 'His first words to me were: "Wanna go for a beer?"'

Phone Booth was originally scheduled for release in mid-November 2002, but this was postponed when real-life snipers began terrorising people in and around Washington D.C. Eight people had been randomly killed by the middle of October, and in an already jittery nation, people once again felt under siege. Director Joel Schumacher understood the sensitivity surrounding the release of such a film in this current climate of fear, but that did not prevent him from being disappointed by the decision to postpone *Phone Booth*'s release, especially with no new date being set. He said at the time: 'There are many serial killers that haven't been caught. Should they not release *Red Dragon*?' By mid-November, two suspects for the sniper shootings were arrested and put forward for trial, and so a new release date for the film was set for February 2003.

Kiefer called it uncanny that series one of *24* and *Phone Booth* both mirror real-life events. 'I've turned into Reality Joe,' he said. 'Sometimes I think I should make a movie that ends with happiness and world peace but no one is writing stuff like that.' *Phone Booth* received high critical acclaim, and for a second time Kiefer was nominated for Best Villain at the *MTV* Movie Awards for his spookily hushed presence as The Caller. Come the award season, the biggest noise for Kiefer was for *24* series two. In the Emmy Awards, *24* was nominated for Outstanding Drama Series, and for the second consecutive year Kiefer received a nomination for Outstanding Lead Actor in a Drama Series. Kiefer again made the Golden Globe short list for Best Performance by an Actor in a TV Series – Drama, but lost out this year. He won the trophy for Best Actor in a Drama Series at the Golden Satellite Awards for the second year running, and when the Screen Actors Guild Awards were announced, Kiefer was nominated for Outstanding Performance by a Male Actor in a Drama Series, while *24* was up for Outstanding Performance by an Ensemble in a Drama Series. Once again, the show picked up the Television Critics Association Award nomination for Individual Achievement in Drama.

24's widening and international appeal began to show when Kiefer was nominated for the award for Best TV Actor – Drama/Action Adventure at the Teen Choice Awards, and he won the Best Foreign TV Personality trophy at Sweden's *Aftonbladet* TV Prize Awards. Despite garnering these plaudits and remaining on the crest of a wave, Kiefer continued to be cautious of success, for he had a healthy fear of the day he might run out of ideas. It tickled him immensely when his friend Robert Downey Jr had been blunt about being flavour of the month. When asked what it meant to him to be a huge success again, Downey had dampened: 'That I'm destined to fail.' It may seem a somewhat bleak attitude, but experience had taught Kiefer that he had to enjoy the moment, since a sharp turnaround could lie dead ahead. His game plan was simple: when work was on offer, grab it, do it and don't complain, because a huge percentage of actors are out of work.

Though Kiefer was feted as Jack Bauer wherever he went, he did not suffer from an inflated ego. Indeed, he joked: 'If Fox TV was a human body, I would be part of its left pinkie finger.' What particularly pleased him was that *24* fans had stayed loyal from hour one, day one, series one. 'We're grateful for that,' he declared. Bombarded for news of a series three of *24*, Kiefer dodged all attempts to trip him up. He was able to confirm that there *was* another season in the works, but could reveal nothing about the proposed storyline. In high spirits he was irreverent about his friends among the programme makers, saying: 'The producers know – bastards, they won't tell me!' Candidly, too, he made no bones about his desire to hang on to his lead role in a show that was becoming synonymous with ruthlessly wielding the axe, and he denied any suggestion that he had wanted Jack Bauer to die at the end of series two. 'I'd like to do the show as long as possible,' he stated. Jack Bauer had become the finest screen hero to emerge for a very long time, and 24 would build on that potent reputation as its popularity soared to even giddier heights. Why did it have such global appeal? Writer/producer Evan Katz was beautifully succinct. He said: 'Anxiety travels well.'

CHAPTER 17

CERTAIN
ASPECTS OF
LOVE

KIEFER'S LOVE OF acting, family, women and music all found expression throughout 2003, as did the value he places on friendship and his ingrained independent streak. In some instances, these elements became intertwined. That was especially true when he was able to get Ironworks Studio up and running. This is a private venture dear to his heart, in which his working partner is Jude Cole, a respected record producer, songwriter, artiste and manager, whom Kiefer has described as being like a brother. The two men had known each other for half their lives already, and their bond has always been based on a mutual love of music.

Said Kiefer: 'My guitar collection started when Jude and I first met. He's one of the most beautiful guitar players in the world, and there were just some guitars that he should have been playing but he couldn't afford.' Kiefer would buy guitars and promptly lend them to his talented young friend, as the struggling musician went on the road; one of them was an arctic white Les Paul custom-made guitar. 'When Jude started to do well, I said: "Hey, remember all those guitars I lent you? I want them back!"' joked Kiefer. Because his impressive guitar collection evolved over time, it was years before Kiefer realised its true extent and value. He said: 'All the Les Pauls are amazing. I've got a '59 Strat and a '66 Strat. It's difficult to say which are my favourites. I have a '51 ES225, which is a rare Gibson hollow body.' Some of Kiefer's guitars cost tens of thousands of dollars each, and one acoustic he is particularly fond of strumming is his John Lennon J-160E.

Kiefer's decision to do more than build up a shiny guitar collection took root around 1996, when he and Jude Cole built a home studio for Jude to make a record, but their vision was bigger than that, and Kiefer also held passionate views on the way the music scene was shaping. He declared at the time: 'The independent music scene is in real trouble. The opportunities for listeners to have a variety of music to choose from are getting smaller.' It dawned on Kiefer that he and his friend really wanted to find fresh talent and help launch new acts on to the music world, and that one way to achieve that goal would be to assist artistes to bypass the major record labels. They came up with the idea of establishing a full production facility in which to work with young bands. It would be called Ironworks Studio. Jude Cole would produce the bands and Kiefer would finance them.

'My plan,' explained Kiefer, 'is to find bands from across America and in Europe that we think are fantastic, and with whom we can set up a deal that will save them from the tragic story that you hear from so many young artistes, where they sell a million albums and don't make a dime! We built Ironworks on the principle that we'll record your album and you'll make money and we'll make money too.' In 2001, Kiefer had bought a renovated industrial warehouse in the Silver Lake area of Los Angeles, a district variously described as an arty bohemian suburb, or smack centre of LA's dodgy ganglands. Kiefer had made his home in a former ironworks foundry, which was somewhat prophetic, since for countless generations on the Douglas side, his mother's family had been foundry workers at the Carron Ironworks in Scotland. Kiefer then spared no expense in having a part of the 15,000-square-foot building turned into a recording studio.

He said: 'This building was exactly what I had wanted on the inside. There is a lot of exposed brick, and the wood trestle ceiling is something that's very hard to find in Los Angeles.' The recording studio occupies about a third of the property, and at the rear is an accommodation block where musicians working through the night can crash out if needed. Being an historic former ironworks, the place is festooned with strikingly ornate iron fittings that presented studio designer Jeff Cooper with an extra challenge. All the iron had to be specially treated, hollowed out and filled with a substance that would remove resonance. Jude Cole reflected: 'We were curious at first about the effect of this. Now it has really grown into its name, Ironworks.' Cole and Mark Somgynari, a top flight guitar technician, selected most of the studio's equipment, and finally Kiefer found a worthy home for his extensive guitar and amplifier collection.

To those who may have thought that Kiefer was a rich actor indulging a whim, he was adamant: 'I don't play in a band and I didn't build the studio so I could make a vanity record.' Mark Somgynari became the studio's manager, and by 2003 Ironworks was operating 12 hours a day, six days a week. Trying to afford exorbitant studio fees for recording time is often what completely cripples budding talent. Ironworks offers something new. 'We don't rent the studio out,' explained Kiefer. 'It's literally for bands we are developing. It's unbelievable how many fantastic bands are just not being heard. We want to make records and figure out how to get them out there.' To Jude Cole, Kiefer's vision means a great deal. There is no set budget when it comes to developing an artiste, and Cole wallows in the luxury of working with no cash constraints. He has described himself as 'humbled' by Kiefer's generosity, and by the enormous faith he has poured into this studio venture.

The fact that Ironworks is part of where Kiefer lives can sometimes be awkward. Said Kiefer: 'I have people I want in here on a musical level and I also have them come up my driveway, because that's where the studio is. So, in that sense I want it to be a really nice environment but I don't want to have a truckload of strangers walking in and out of here.' He pointed out that he would have encountered a lot more problems had he tried to have this set up in somewhere as swish as Bel Air in west Hollywood. By spring 2003, Ironworks Studio had four bands on its label, including Softcore. Another artiste Kiefer and Jude are excited about is Rocco Deluca, and Kiefer was thrilled when guitarist Mark Goldenberg was hugely complimentary about the studio's facilities.

Kiefer allows musicians to borrow his expensive guitars for recording sessions and unsurprisingly, as a would-be guitarist himself, he sometimes looks on enviously. Jude Cole recently dubbed his friend magnanimously as a 'pretty damned good guitar player', but Kiefer has since confessed to still taking as many guitar lessons as he can fit in. He's tired of only picking the same tune, over and over.

To many, it seems strange for someone in Kiefer's position to choose to live in Silver Lake but Kiefer has his reasons. 'The farther east I go, I realise that Los Angeles has an enormous amount to offer,' he said. 'It seems that inherently our mindset in LA is: "I've made money, so I need to move west." So I guess you end up at the beach, but I wasn't very happy living there and I had to figure out how and why I got there.' Kiefer's is certainly a colourful neighbourhood. To the north of his home, it is populated with Salvadorean people and Salvadorean gangs. To the south, it is all Ukrainians and Ukrainian gangs. 'And they don't cross,' said Kiefer. 'They use my building as a giant notice board. Every other day, one gang will post a note for the other.' Kiefer leads his life there, simply not getting in the middle of anything, and the gangs leave him be. Indeed, he considers the cosmopolitan mix of people in this edgy neighbourhood as being really good to him. Kiefer contentedly walks Molly of an evening, not feeling nervous that he has to watch his back; his wry sense of humour means that he appreciates the oddest distinctions. In the posher parts of LA, children will skip up to a dog to pet it. In his neighbourhood children freak out and flee behind their mothers' legs as most everyone, it seems, has a pit bull terrier trained to attack. 'I love that shift,' laughed Kiefer. 'There's an invisible line somewhere between Western and Vermont avenues where the dogs become mean!'

As an extension of the unpretentious way Kiefer leads his life, he also often rides the subway. He still drives when it is more convenient to do so for work, but in his leisure time, whether he is heading to the sandy coast or the crowded airport, he jostles up with all the other commuters. He never has liked to live in a rarefied air bubble, remote from other people. Kiefer likes to spend his spare time in a variety of ways. The Village Cafe over in Beachwood Canyon still draws him. 'I used to go there with friends, before I had children, before things became very important,' he recently mused. 'We lived with an ease that we thought was going to be with us all the time.'

Comfortable on the east side of LA, Kiefer still also likes those unvarnished environments offering beer, a pool table and a blaring jukebox. Some places, he has conceded, he might have been better avoiding, but he goes out to relax and enjoy himself. When he is in the mood to be alone, he will ride one of his horses in nearby Griffith Park, a vast expanse of luscious greenery, gorgeous azalea gardens and miles of trails to trek. When time permits, Kiefer swaps Griffith Park, Los Angeles, for High Park in Toronto, where he likes to run. Indulging his passion for skiing, in Toronto he heads for a 400-foot hill called Uplands, outside the city limits. 'Although I have a house in Toronto, I'll still go and stay a couple of nights at the Windsor Arms, for nostalgic reasons. It's right in the centre of town. It's a really old funky hotel that has a minimalist feel.' One of his favourite Toronto restaurants is Bistro 990, whose low, arched ceilings give it an intimate European underground atmosphere.

In early May 2003 came rumours that *24* might be made into a major movie. Kiefer stated: 'I know everyone is looking forward to that happening. We've got a big *Die Hard*-style spectacle planned in the back of our minds. The show is big enough in itself: but *24*, the movie? Bring it on!' Making *24*, season three for television was more imminent, but before that got under way, in early summer a movie Kiefer had filmed two years earlier finally surfaced. Called *Paradise Found*, it is a biopic of the 19th-century French post-impressionist artist, Paul Gauguin. Kiefer portrayed Gauguin, one of the most significant and influential painters of his time. Coincidentally, 17 years earlier, Kiefer's father, Donald, had also portrayed this artist at odds with conventional society in the movie *Oviri*, also known as *The Wolf at the Door*.

Paradise Found, written by John Goldsmith and directed by Mario Andreacchio, co-starred Nastassja Kinski as Gauguin's wife, Mette. Alun Armstrong portrayed Pissarro, Peter Varga was Van Gogh, and Thomas Heinze played Schuff. Kiefer relished metaphorically wrapping his arms around the role of Paul Gauguin, and threw himself into research, reading art books and a biography of Gauguin as well as tracking down films such as his father's. 'Picasso considered Gauguin the greatest painter that had ever lived, and not only for his painting skills but for what he chose to do intellectually,' said Kiefer. 'I talked to a lot of painters about how Gauguin affected them, and in the end the one thing that I derived from that was, this was a man who was very aware of trying to create his own legacy, not only while he was alive but certainly he knew that, in death, it would matter and that was a very big deal to him.'

Kiefer came to the conclusion that Paul Gauguin had been both immensely charming and extremely arrogant. 'Most truly arrogant people are sons of bitches,' he maintained, getting a firm handle on his film character. *Paradise Found*, however, reached only a limited audience, in that it aired on a cable TV channel devoted to indie or offbeat films, first showing in July 2003.

That same month, Kiefer's total concentration focused on undertaking yet again the gruelling shooting schedule for series three of *24*. This third momentous day in Jack Bauer's life was set three years after the end of series two, and Kiefer was keyed up to step up to the mark once more. Again, the plot inspired him, as did the development of his character and the ingenuity of the team of writers. He said: 'In the plot in the first series, there was a lot of intrigue and suspense about who the mole was. The second series was dominated by action and a threat that affected everybody in the country. This time, we wanted a combination of the best of both those series and we really believe that this third season is going to be very strong.'

What particularly appealed to Kiefer was that whereas in the past Jack Bauer was always straightforward in his actions, with this new season having more of a sense of espionage to it, Bauer's behaviour is not always comprehensible right away. It requires a faith, a trust in him from the show's audience, that all will unravel in time. The other plus point this time around was that Jack Bauer is actually driving the plot. Needless to say, the new plot would be strewn with shocks and surprises. Kiefer quipped of *24*: 'It's like *Dynasty* on crack!' By now, Jack Bauer had grown so firmly into the hearts of the show's fans that *he* has become, in some ways, more important than the innovative storylines. Bauer is a man who is an impossibly fantastic and capable hero when it comes to saving lives and averting national disasters, but who struggles personally. First, he struggled with a troubled marriage, and a troubled conscience over some of the covert things he had to do in the service of his country. Then, he wrestled with guilt that he had not ultimately protected his own wife, and faced a battle to reconnect emotionally with his bereaved daughter. Now, in series three, Jack has to conquer a drug addiction, acquired in the line of duty, as he had to maintain his cover with a group of criminals willing to trade with terrorists. The implication quickly surfaces that Jack's drug taking maybe had more to do with blotting out his gnawing inner pain. It added another interesting dimension to this 21st-century screen hero.

By now it was a given that Jack Bauer could handle any combat action backwards, in his sleep. The problem of opening up Bauer's personal love life was trickier. 'One of the dilemmas the writers found is that it's very hard to develop a relationship in a day,' pointed out Kiefer. 'If Jack were to fall in love that would be the entire show!' He added: 'There were times when I certainly wished my family life had worked out as well as my career. So that aspect of this story struck a very strong emotional chord for me.' Kiefer's involvement in *24* fleshed out even more as he became one of the show's co-executive producers. His impetuous nature, though, sometimes battled against him. He explained: 'I have strong feelings and I can be thinking of three things at once. I realise that you can sit and sulk over a problem, but you're going to have to fix it eventually. I can come across as curt but now inside I'm happy and fine. I can get excited, that's all and I just want to *do* it.'

Former cast members Sarah Clarke as Nina Myers and Penny Johnson Jerald as Sherry Palmer were recalled for the last time – both these characters would be killed off. Paul Schulze returned as CTU regional director Ryan Chappelle. New to *24* were James Badge Dale, who played Bauer's protégé agent Chase Edmunds, Jesse Borrego as agent Gael Ortega, Mary Lynn Rajskub as computer whizz Chloe O'Brian and Joaquim de Almeida as crime lord Roman Salazar. Along with the whole cast and crew, Kiefer was quickly plunged into 16-hour working days again. Zachary Quinto, who plays CTU staff member Adam Kaufman, recalled: 'Kiefer is there for 90% of the show and he's always half an hour early.' While filming was as secretive as ever, writer Robert Cochrane teased that a shock was in store. 'It's not Jack dying, but it's big,' he promised.

On this third series, writer/producer Evan Katz had become a co-executive producer, and he was still getting to grips with the show's now familiar real-time format. Said Evan: 'When you first get on the show, it takes a while to get used to it. You keep wanting to do things that you just can't do, but I believe it's a part of the show that forces you to be creative. We know the story, we know roughly where it's going. It's got some fantastic twists that I think will be impossible to see coming. We're doing our best to come at it from a fresh angle.' This time the now famously menacing ticking clock started from 11.00 a.m. The sword of Damocles that again hung overhead meant that 24's cast had become a tight bunch. Each year, they hold a Halloween party, and such is the camaraderie that even actors who played killed-off characters show up.

By now, Kiefer's love life had taken a new turn. He revealed bluntly: 'The show has managed to kill my personal life. There isn't time for much else than work.' It had been reported back in June 2003 that Kiefer and Catherine Bisson had gone their separate ways. Two months later, Los Angeles gossip columnists began linking Kiefer romantically with co-star Reiko Aylesworth, who plays 24's Michelle Dessler. As far as Kiefer and his estranged wife Kelly were concerned, they were *still* not yet divorced. Kiefer would not comment much on why this was the case, except to say: 'We are kind of figuring out what we're going to do.' Less complicated is his devotion to his daughter Sarah. He admitted: 'I always travel with a kindergarten picture of my daughter that has "I love you, daddy" written on it. She makes fun of me because I've never changed that photo, but it was the first thing she'd ever written to me and it means the world to me.' It's not as if Kiefer could resist facing the fact that Sarah was growing up, for her life was patently changing in all the normal adolescent ways. Fifteen years old, she was suffering the emotional pangs of her first boyfriend break-up. Her dad was on hand to take her 'pain' seriously and did not belittle her distress.

After all, dad knew all about distress! Sarah was learning to drive, and Kiefer had cosily imagined one day that he could let her have a taste of driving on the freeway, very early in the morning when he thought that traffic would be light. He was wrong. There was an incredible amount of traffic that morning, and he discovered too late that Sarah had an alarming habit of looking over her shoulder to check for cars, inadvertently, in the process, wrenching the steering wheel one way and making the car veer suddenly. They made their destination in one piece, but Kiefer seems to have been almost traumatised by the experience. He vividly recalled: 'I might play a tough guy who's not afraid to stand in front of a bullet, yet when Sarah merged on to the 101 Freeway and swept across four lanes, I looked like Garfield the cat hanging on to the side of the car screaming: "Let me out!" We stuck to lessons in our neighbourhoods after that.' Kiefer would get Sarah a job working with him on the set of 24 on an assistant director training scheme, but she enrolled at Crossroads School for Arts and Sciences in Santa Monica, California.

This was very much a family-oriented time for Kiefer. The following year would mark the centenary of the birth of the late Tommy Douglas, and plans were emerging in Falkirk, Scotland, to erect a memorial cairn to him in the town's main street. By autumn 2003, it also leaked out that there were moves afoot to portray Tommy Douglas's remarkable life in a television mini-series for the Canadian Broadcasting Corporation. Kiefer was again being headhunted to play the part of his grandfather, and Douglas's daughter Shirley would serve as a creative consultant on the project. Plans to immortalise Tommy Douglas on screen in some fashion would float about for years. With Kiefer's commitment to 24, plans for such a project to involve him could not solidify, at least not yet, no matter how much Kiefer admired and respected the grittily tenacious man. Kiefer also felt pride in abundance for his equally fiery mother when, in October 2003, Shirley was named a Member of the Order of Canada during an award ceremony held in Ottawa. In the Douglas tartan kilt, Kiefer attended the event honouring his indefatigable mother.

On 28 October 2003, series three of *24* premiered in the US. Its promotional advertising campaign drum beat out the message: 'To stop a weapon that has no cure, you need a man who knows no limits!' The threat presented in this series was of biological warfare. Early on, it involved a violent prison siege which included a nerve-wracking sequence with out of control convicts forcing Bauer and a couple of prisoners to entertain them by playing Russian roulette. Immediately after the broadcast of this episode, on 25 November, Kiefer addressed on air the issue of gun safety. He also gave a promotion for the Americans for Gun Safety Foundation. On a lighter note, it was reported around the end of the year that at a charity auction in America, one avid fan paid £14,000 ($25,000) to spend 24 hours in Kiefer Sutherland's company.

Kiefer is an actor who possesses one of the most elusive and envied of screen qualities – that of being both adored by women and admired by men. That popularity, when taking into account the accessible way he leads his life, means that he runs the risk of being confronted with all kinds of people in unguarded situations. He is dubbed the most famous man riding LA's subway system, but Kiefer takes a typically prosaic attitude. To the over-excitable fan, overawed to come face-to-face with him in the street, his style is to neuter the situation by simply responding in an everyday manner; most people, disarmed, duly calm down. Asked once what he would do if, on the other hand, some guy sought to have something to brag about and took a swing at 'Jack Bauer', Kiefer was blunt: 'That happens. It depends on my mood. Catch me on a day when I feel I don't need it, and *whack!*'

In terms of health, Kiefer continued to keep himself fit and lean, able to cope with the strains of his hectic life. Even so, he developed a kidney stone, which was agonising. 'I've broken many bones in my body, but I've never experienced pain like this,' he said. All discomfort was forgotten, however, when it came to the time of year when award nominations were announced. *24*, series three, received nominations from both the Television Critics Association and the Emmy Awards. Kiefer secured three Best Actor nominations from the Golden Globes, the Emmy Awards and the prestigious Screen Actors Guild Awards. He went on to win the Screen Actors Guild Award for Outstanding Performance by a Male Actor in a Drama Series, receiving his trophy on 22 February 2004 at a ceremony held at Los Angeles' Shrine Auditorium.

His career was riding at its highest point to date through exhilarating times, but Kiefer was always a hard man to slow down. Questioned whether he might take his foot off the pedal a touch, with inexhaustible energy he flashed his disreputable grin and announced: 'Patience is a virtue – I'm still working on that one!'

CHAPTER 18

MAKING A TIMELESS MARK

KIEFER WAS KEEN to play it down when in February 2004 the media reported that he had become embroiled in a brawl in a Los Angeles pub. At the time, a spokesperson confirmed that an altercation had taken place and stated: 'Kiefer was defending himself.' Kiefer quickly insisted that the tale had become exaggerated out of all proportion. He told reporters that he had been among friends that night, adding: 'We were out for a big night. We were wrestling about and a couple of people got cut, that's all. We were just having a fun time.' He clearly preferred to call it horseplay, but the resulting gash to his face was deep enough to require six stitches.

Until it healed, the ragged rip in his skin would have added to his other body markings; at this time Kiefer had six tattoos, gradually acquired over the years. His first tattoo was the Japanese symbol for strength, but others depict a sword, his family's Scottish crest, an ivy thistle, a Maori band of life and, his most recent marking, a depiction of Our Lady of Guadalupe, which was to represent the Hispanic influences in his neighbourhood of east LA. Kiefer quipped that these tattoos are a map of his life as he lives it. To study the markings is to read his life, apparently.

From a young age Kiefer had a wilful, independent streak. It had passed down from his grandparents, through his parents, and now Kiefer was seeing the signs of stubborn resolve in his own offspring. Sixteen-year-old Sarah was, by now, keen on following in her father's footsteps by becoming an actor. Like Shirley and Donald 20-odd years earlier, Kiefer had his reservations – more specifically, worries. He had watched his daughter appear in some amateur dramatic productions, and believed that she had talent, but inwardly he seemed to be resisting the idea. At first, he wondered if he was feeling slightly territorial – that acting was *his* gig, sort of thing – but then he realised that it was good old-fashioned parental protectiveness. Though his early days are long behind him, Kiefer has never forgotten the painful rejection that hopeful young actors constantly put themselves through. At some auditions he had felt incredibly vulnerable, enough for the experience to leave an inner mark on him, and he did not want to think of Sarah going through the same stream of disappointment. Being the son of Donald Sutherland had not profoundly helped or hindered him in the long run professionally, but at the time it had often seemed a mixed blessing. Sarah would come along as the daughter of Kiefer Sutherland, and Kiefer didn't know how that would play out for her. In the end, he knew that whatever his fatherly qualms, Sarah would ultimately choose her own path and he was determined to be supportive.

In spring, his own film career came into focus with the release of *Taking Lives*. Based on the novel by Michael Pye, this psychological thriller about the hunting of a serial killer with help from an FBI profiler was directed by DJ Caruso. Kiefer had a small supporting role as a bad guy named Hart. The film was shot in summer 2003 in Quebec, Canada, and although he had less than three minutes of screen time, he shared top billing with Angelina Jolie and Ethan Hawke. What struck Kiefer most about being involved in this movie was the huge shift in gear. *Taking Lives* was a major production, run on a normal, efficient schedule, but inured by now to the breakneck pace of *24* Kiefer revealed: 'I remember standing around going: "God! These people move *slow!*"'

Kiefer set out to ensure that his cameo appearance in *Taking Lives* made its mark. He certainly left an impression on the movie makers. Said director DJ Caruso: 'Kiefer is creepy on screen. You just close your eyes and listen to him talk and you realise he's got the coolest voice. You don't get that voice from staying home and going to church on Sundays, and his skill as an actor is phenomenal!' Producer Bernie Goldman agreed, describing Kiefer as scary, with an incredible intensity, someone who can convey spine-tingling screen menace without so much as lifting a finger. Said Bernie: 'It comes through his eyes and the way he holds his body, the way he moves. Kiefer can just look at you and you want to back away.' The delight for the producer was how different Kiefer is off set. 'He has a real gift,' he declared. The world premiere of *Taking Lives* was held at Grauman's Chinese Theatre in Hollywood on 22 March 2004.

Kiefer was not the only member of his family to be feted at this time. That spring, his mother followed her ex-husband, Donald Sutherland, by being awarded her own star on Canada's Walk of Fame in Toronto. As ever, the respect afforded to Shirley Douglas comes from a blend of her acting and activism. For now, Kiefer picked up on the latter and spoke proudly about how she had been on a relentless mission since the late 1990s, criss-crossing Canada in the cause of highlighting publicly the damage that 12 years of Conservative politics had done to the nation's health care system. Said Kiefer: 'She was instrumental in getting the first Liberal Ontario government in a very long time.'

Although Kiefer had heavy work commitments, he happily made time to walk his 27-year-old stepdaughter, Michelle Kath, down the aisle on 6 May 2004, when she married Adam Sinclair, the actor she had met while he was filming *To End All Wars* with Kiefer. The marriage ceremony was conducted at the grand City Chambers in Edinburgh's Old Town district, and Kiefer flew into the Scottish capital the day before for a whirlwind visit to do the honours. He booked into the nearby luxury Scotsman Hotel, and the night before the nuptials he went out on the town in celebratory mood, at one stage visiting Edinburgh's Opal Lounge. In one bar some Scottish *24* fans couldn't believe their eyes and began frantically nudging one another, not so quietly whispering: 'My god! That's Jack Bauer!' Fans approached Kiefer rather tentatively as he sat with friends at a table, and were thrilled to find the star so easy-going, happy to sign autographs and to chat a little. Scottish newspapers reported how Kiefer had drunk whisky and socialised into the early hours of the actual wedding day, but at the appointed hour Kiefer was rested, fresh and looking strikingly handsome in the Douglas tartan kilt, traditional jacket, white shirt, tie and with a dirk shoved inside his right sock.

Adam Sinclair, also debonair in the kilt, was attended by his best man and accompanied by his brothers. Just before 5.00 p.m. a group of 20, headed by the groom and Kiefer, stunned people going about their business by leaving the plush Scotsman Hotel and striding to the City Chambers on foot. People gasped openly as they recognised Kiefer Sutherland walking by. It created quite a stir, and some started calling out to him. Kiefer waved back and flashed them his wicked grin. Sarah was Michelle's bridesmaid; the stepsisters arrived at the wedding venue in a silver Mercedes, which drew to a sedate halt on the ancient cobbled courtyard outside the City Chambers. Stepping on to a red carpet to the skirl of bagpipes from a lone piper, Michelle was radiant. Her white, ankle length, sleeveless wedding gown was stylish, and her sheer veil streamed from behind a lavish tiara. Beaming, she reached out with both hands for her proudly waiting stepfather. Kiefer and Michelle have always been close, and it showed in their natural ease together. Although the Scottish press was out in force for the happy event, Kiefer was conscious that his fame should not obliterate the couple's special day. His comments to the many journalists were muted. He said: 'I've been walking around. It's such a beautiful city. We've all been having a great time in Edinburgh. Mainly, I have just been preparing for my daughter's wedding.'

More than one tabloid published photographs of Kiefer, who nipped outside the City Chambers to smoke a quick cigarette before the bride arrived. When one journalist asked him if he was nervous, Kiefer replied no, because it wasn't his wedding day. Kiefer had worn the kilt with style on the day, eight years earlier when he and Kelly Winn had wed with such high hopes in Toronto. Now, just four days after Michelle's wedding, when Kiefer was once again back in America, divorce papers were re-filed in the Los Angeles Superior Court on 10 May 2004 to end his and Kelly's marriage on the grounds of irreconcilable differences. There was no debacle, as had happened in 2000, and everyone preferred to keep this event low-key. Kiefer's publicist, Annett Wolf, would only comment: 'The papers [filed in court] speak for themselves.'

As those particular wheels were re-set in motion, later that summer Kiefer strapped back on his bullet-proof vest to portray Jack Bauer once again as filming for series four of *24* got under way. Having already dealt with an assassination attempt, a personal vendetta, a nuclear bomb threat and possible biological warfare, the pressure was enormous on the show's scriptwriters to surpass themselves. Kiefer has described *24* as being broken down into something akin to a very long three-act play, that the writers and producers work each season in sections of eight one-hour shows.

Series four was set 18 months on from the previous crisis, and the sequence of stomach-knotting real-time events got under way in satisfyingly explosive style with a spectacular train bombing. A bloodied survivor of this is then murdered and relieved of an attaché case manacled to his wrist; this turns out to contain an override device designed to take control of all America's nuclear power plants. CTU has a new boss, Erin Driscoll, who had previously fired Jack Bauer because of the drug habit he had acquired while maintaining his cover in the previous covert mission.

Jack is now working as special advisor to America's Secretary of Defence, James Heller. When the Secretary and his daughter are kidnapped by Muslim extremists, Jack is back at CTU, where he immediately clashes with Driscoll. Bauer's instinct that the two incidents are connected is correct, and he is set to get up to his renegade antics again until Driscoll is forced to realise that Jack is right. Fairly early on, Jack finds where Heller and his daughter are being held. Heller is about to be executed by masked gunmen, with the slaying streamed live around the world via the Internet. The episode's opening scene, when Bauer single-handedly goes in to the heavily armed compound and rescues the pair, is one of television's most breathtaking ten minutes ever. Multi-million-dollar blockbuster action movies have had less effect in their climax scenes.

Between the first and last episodes of *24* series four, the twists and turns would have the show's audience in a weekly sweat of anxiety. Said Joel Surnow: 'First and foremost you have to create the suspense, but the suspense isn't interesting if you're not invested in the characters.' To carry this new season forward, apart from Kiefer, familiar faces would return over the course of the 24 episodes, including Mary Lynn Rajskub as Chloe O'Brian, Reiko Aylesworth as Michelle Dessler, Carlos Bernard as Tony Almeida and Dennis Haysbert in his capacity as ex-President David Palmer. Alberta Watson, as stiff-necked boss Erin Driscoll, injected new blood, and Kim Raver portrayed Audrey Raines, daughter of US Secretary of Defence, James Heller, played by William Devane. Roger Cross made an impact as CTU Chief Tactical Officer Curtis Manning, while Gregory Itzin played an effectively ineffective President Logan, and Shohreh Aghdashloo played the wife of a Middle East terrorist.

This time around, Jack finally has a love life. He is involved with Heller's daughter, Audrey Raines, who is separated from her husband, Paul, only no one knows of their affair. Co-creator Robert Cochrane recalled: 'The chemistry between Kiefer and Kim Raver was excellent.' Kim Raver found working with 24's star a memorable experience. 'Kiefer is such a unique person,' she declared, 'so talented and so gracious. Kiefer really sets the tone with this company. I have never experienced a first day, the way I did working with him.'

For Kiefer, one of his character's best facets is the way in which Bauer has to cope with moral struggles, to deal with dilemmas in which it is impossible to save, or to do right by, everyone. This time, it appealed to him too that Jack has, initially at least, a reason to be smiling once more. Apart from a few smiles in the first episode of 24 series one, Jack Bauer has been perhaps the grimmest man on TV! William Devane was the biggest name to join 24 since Dennis Hopper, and as ever the actors new to the show added their own texture but, as Robert Cochrane admitted: 'Kiefer Sutherland has always anchored things.'

For millions of staunch fans, one of the early highlights of series four was the surprise return of Tony Almeida, who had been tried for treason at the end of series three. Because of the voracious rate at which dramatic storylines are eaten up, Joel Surnow is well aware that even beloved characters have to be axed, since there is just nowhere left for them to go. However, a way was devised to bring back Tony in spectacularly foot-stomping fashion, when he blasts his way in to rescue Jack. Said Carlos Bernard: 'The producers had always planned on bringing my character back. They just knew it would take a few episodes to work Tony in because of what happened last season.' Of Jack Bauer and Tony Almeida's bond of friendship, Carlos added: 'They are both hotheaded and have a lot in common. They feel they know which is the right way.' There is an undoubted working chemistry between Kiefer and

Carlos, which translates on to the screen. 'We're really protective of each other. I watch his back and he watches mine,' said Bernard.

Kiefer continued to work as a co-executive producer on *24*, and had discussions with the show's writers in that capacity, but principally he came at things from the perspective of portraying Jack Bauer, with whom he has become so absorbed that it matters immensely to him how every aspect of his character is handled. 'Kiefer's very good about bringing us ideas,' said Joel Surnow. 'There will also be one or two times a season when he will object to something we do – he maybe doesn't think Jack Bauer would do this or that – and we will fight it out and come to a place where we're all happy.'

Because Jack Bauer has lodged so firmly in the consciousness of the show's global fan base, it followed that the spotlight would personally pinpoint him more with each passing season. At the end of series three, millions of fans actually felt heartsore for Jack when, alone behind the wheel of his car, he quietly wept. Respect for his strength created great sympathy for this rare display of private weakness, a frailty that only endeared the character more. 'That's the reason the show succeeds,' confessed Joel Surnow.

In series four, Kiefer felt that the writers had specifically set out to explain Jack Bauer's feelings clearly, his take on important issues, in a way he believed had not been the case in series one to three. Though Kiefer is more and more pointed out in public as Jack Bauer, he is not in danger of confusing where Kiefer Sutherland stops and Jack Bauer starts, and he has not been changed as a person by portraying this indomitable screen hero. The experience has, however, made an impact on him professionally. He considers that he now pays even closer heed to the smallest aspects of a storyline, to the inference behind certain words, and believes it has enhanced his development as an actor.

At the end of series four, circumstances force Jack Bauer to fake his own death, and he is last seen slipping on sunglasses and heading off on foot at dawn down a highway, promptly tossing *24* fans into turmoil, thinking that, as Bauer is officially dead, this was his last hurrah. Joel Surnow offered a crumb of comfort by saying: 'I don't think *24* works without feeling like you are going to be on a personal journey with Jack Bauer.'

As fans eagerly awaited the launch of *24* series four, Kiefer kept his nose to the grindstone. Even so, there were a couple of distractions. In early December 2004, he was thrilled when Tommy Douglas was voted 'The Greatest Canadian of All Time' in a poll run by Canada's national television company, CBC. More than a million people voted nationwide, and Tommy trounced all his competitors for the accolade, including internationally famous statesmen such as former Canadian Prime Minister, Pierre Trudeau, the telephone inventor Alexander Graham Bell, and rock stars, actors and sporting legends. Kiefer was immensely touched that the father of Canada's government-funded medical system came out clearly on top. He said: 'It's almost impossible to describe what that means to our family. The fact that Canadians still hold that as one of the great fundamental aspects of their identity was incredibly moving to us.'

The choice of Tommy Douglas as the greatest ever Canadian was a big talking point in the country, and letters pages in newspapers from coast to coast filled up with people heartily endorsing this outcome. A Dr Alan Ennis wrote in: 'We did not pick a megastar or anyone with a lot of flash. We chose a quiet, dignified, hard-working individual who cared about only one thing in his entire career – Canada.' William Christian, a political science professor at the University of Guelph, said of Tommy Douglas: 'People simply respected his integrity. When he got up in the morning, he was decent. When he went to bed, he was decent. Heck, the man probably even dreamed decent dreams!'

At the end of December, Kiefer took himself off to Iceland, where his rock star friend, Rocco Deluca, was playing a New

Year's Eve gig in the capital, Reykjavik. Kiefer saw in the New Year there, and was stunned by a hair-raising fireworks display. Iceland has few laws regarding fireworks. Kiefer said: 'It's a small population, but they spend over $15 million on fireworks for that one night. There's no organisation to it. It's like a war zone!' His jaw dropped at one point to see two very young children blithely walk by, with some serious rocket fireworks cradled in their arms.

Soon afterwards, Kiefer had to return to Los Angeles to continue work on *24*, and he arrived to good news when the Screen Actors Guild Award nominations were announced on 11 January 2005, and he was included in the category for Best Male Actor in a Drama Series for his portrayal of Jack Bauer. *24* was also nominated for Best Ensemble in a Drama Series. The award ceremony itself was scheduled for 5 February. Before that, in early January 2005 the long-awaited *24* series four finally premiered on US television, not that far ahead of its UK launch at the end of the same month. The show was used to causing comment, but within weeks it ran into controversy when the Council on American-Islamic Relations raised objections to the depiction of a Muslim terrorist sleeper cell in the US. A spokesperson for the Council declared about one scene in which an American-Muslim youth is plotting to kill Americans: 'It casts a cloud of suspicion over every American-Muslim.'

The show's creators and makers had anticipated a degree of objection, even though *24* had featured Middle Eastern terrorists in an earlier season, without causing as much controversy. Joel Surnow pointed out that it was difficult to have a show all about combating terrorism in America in this day and age, and *not* address the fact that the US has to deal with terrorists who come from the Middle East. In this new series, the programme makers had been careful throughout to show that even within one family there could be different degrees of commitment to terrorism. Plus, in *24*'s history, there had been terrorists from groups other than Muslims.

However, in view of the objections raised this time, Fox TV decided to make a Public Service Announcement (PSA) on the issue, and ran it with the episode broadcast in America on 7 February 2005. Kiefer read the disclaimer, part of which said: 'While terrorism is obviously one of the most critical challenges facing our nation and the world, it is important to recognise that the American-Muslim community stands firmly beside their fellow Americans in denouncing and resisting all forms of terrorism. So, in watching 24, please bear that in mind.'

The wording of this PSA sat ill with some, who thought that such a blanket declaration, which could imply that *all* American-Muslims, without exception, stand firm in denouncing terrorism, was inappropriate, since sadly it was not true. In a wider context, too, questions were asked: how long would it be then, before the makers of a show depicting a black actor brandishing a gun or dealing in drugs would feel obliged to run a disclaimer that there was no intention to stereotype all African–Americans?

The issue of the torture scenes depicted in 24 was also threatening to become a thorny one. Executive producer Howard Gordon said: 'It goes with the 24 conceit that we need information and do not have hours, let alone days, to break this person, but 24's writers are *not* taking a political stand.' Robert Cochrane defended: 'We don't get off on it, but we [the writers] find ourselves in story situations where if you were an agent in that situation you'd really have little choice but to apply some kind of physical pressure.' An Amnesty International spokesman declared that 24 depicted 'a clearer idea of what torture involves. They do more to educate, than to desensitise.' Some seemed to be losing the fact that 24 is a work of fiction, purely for entertainment.

Leaving aside these controversial areas, 24 fans were hooked in their droves on series four, which had come up with another enthralling roller coaster; that was proved when the already top-rated show basked in a staggering 32 per cent hike in viewing figures. This reaction could only energise everyone connected with the show, although excitement occasionally got the better of some. Sarah Sutherland worked on *24* as part of her placement on a training scheme, and one day during filming she slipped up. Kiefer explained: 'One of the few things that I am very specific about on our show is that when we actually start to film, it has to be absolutely quiet. We were working on the second floor of a soundstage and suddenly in the middle of a scene you heard: "Rolling." I went: "Who the fuck . . . ? That was my daughter, wasn't it!"' On 3 February 2005, newspaper headlines shrieked that Kiefer Sutherland had sacked his own daughter. The truth was less lurid. Kiefer confessed that he did not actually yell at Sarah for the blunder, when he might have done so had the culprit been anyone else. Indeed, such was his restraint that the crew affectionately applauded him for it, and Sarah was not booted unceremoniously off the payroll. 'We got her a different job,' said Kiefer.

Away from work, come May 2005, newspapers started to link 38-year-old Kiefer with a new love interest, a 23-year-old Icelandic model named Kristin Haraldsdottir. The two were said to have met at a nightclub during Kiefer's recent New Year trip to Reykjavik, and the beauty was thought to have visited the actor twice already in America. Kristin was quoted as telling the press: 'Kiefer is a great guy. He's down to earth and fun to be with. There is a good feeling between us.' Kristin's father, Haraldur, was also said to have commented of Kiefer: 'I've met him and he is very nice.' However, it was hard to know if this was a new romance or not for Kiefer, for before the end of that same month newspaper reports were now linking him with a different lady altogether.

Keeping out of this speculation about his love life, Kiefer focused on the latest honour to be bestowed on him when, on 5 June 2005, he had to unveil his own star on Canada's Walk of Fame – making it a hat trick achievement for the Sutherland family of actors. That year, nine stars were honoured, including a ballet dancer, two music producers, and a boxer, as well as singer/songwriters Alanis Morissette and Paul Anka. The public ceremony took place at the Elgin Theatre in Toronto, where the red carpet was rolled out for the glittering occasion. Hundreds of people waited for hours in the sweltering summer heat for a glimpse of eight of the stars being honoured. Fay Wray, the heroine in the 1933 movie, *King Kong*, was being honoured posthumously. Kiefer's arrival on the red carpet triggered a deafening reception from the crowd; once inducted into the Walk of Fame, Kiefer spoke of following in his parents' footsteps: 'I can't express what a humbling experience this is for me to be able to share something like this with them.' Shirley Douglas had accompanied her son to the event and was delighted. 'It's a struggle in our business,' she commented, 'so I admire people who can do it.' With an arm around his mother, Kiefer happily posed for photographers; of his father he had recently announced unabashedly: 'As far as I am concerned, he is an icon.' Coupled to this was the glowing pride he still felt over his grandfather Tommy Douglas having been voted the Greatest Canadian of All Time; Kiefer's unadulterated love for his family cannot help but penetrate the heart of the most hardened cynic.

Kiefer's own appeal continued to grow. In July 2005, for the fourth year in a row he was among the Emmy nominees for Outstanding Lead Actor in a Drama Series, while *24* ranked among the shows up for Outstanding Drama Series. *24*, indeed, received a total of 11 Emmy nominations. Kiefer was one of the guest presenters at the Emmy Awards ceremony held on 18 September at LA's Shrine Auditorium, but he lost out on the Best Actor Emmy to James Spader, who collected it for his role in *Boston Legal*.

By then, *River Queen* had newly been released, an epic period drama that Kiefer had filmed along with Samantha Morton, Stephen Rea, Cliff Curtis and Temuera Morrison. The film was directed by Vincent Ward, and based on an original story by Ward, who co-wrote the screenplay with Toa Fraser. Set in New Zealand in the 1860s, it centres on an Irish immigrant and her family caught up in the battle between the European settlers and the Maori people during the British colonisation. Kiefer played a character called Doyle, and in summer 2004 he had flown out to New Zealand, where location filming had mainly taken place in the Wanganui region. Filming had been beset by problems, with bad weather causing disruption, sickness afflicting some people, and injuries on and off set, but Kiefer had obviously managed to remain in jovial spirits, judging by his high-spirited antics one night when he went out socialising. Along with a few friends from the film set, he had been drinking in the bar at the Cosmopolitan Club in Raetihi. In an adjoining room, roped off with a 'Women Only' sign, a male strip show was taking place, featuring a troupe of strippers called Men of Steel.

For a laugh, Kiefer slipped through security and startled the ladies, and the Men of Steel, by climbing on stage and joining in. Swiftly discarding his shoes and socks, barefoot Kiefer whipped off his shirt and to the raucous strains of the Tom Jones hit, 'You Can Leave Your Hat On', he promptly danced about swinging his shirt above his head. The delighted ladies enthusiastically egged him to go the whole way, but security staff intervened and Kiefer was politely ushered off stage. The New Zealand press ran the story, declaring that 24's star had treated the ladies to the 'Full Monty' but Kiefer had kept his dignity intact while having fun. Filming finished on *River Queen* before the end of 2004, and the movie debuted on 12 September 2005 at the Toronto International Film Festival, with its world premiere taking place in New Zealand the following January.

By summer 2005, news had leaked out that series five of *24* was already under way. Writers had been hard at work for months. Robert Cochrane revealed: 'We'll pick Jack up in a very different place, roughly a year later, and it won't be long before he's back in the saddle.' Filming commenced in late

July. By the turn of the year, Kiefer had secured three Best Actor Award nominations, for a People's Choice Award, a Golden Globe and a Screen Actors Guild Award. The main focus, however, was squarely on this new series of 24. Towards the end of 2005, a flurry of excitement had stirred when word spread that Donald Sutherland, who specialises in compelling cameo roles, had been contracted to portray Jack Bauer, senior, but Donald moved fast to douse the rumour. He said: 'I am a fan of the show. I watch it religiously. I am Kiefer's father, but I don't want to *play* his father.'

Although secrecy was paramount, details gradually began to leak out as to who was in or out of the show, and what the fifth crisis could be. Carlos Bernard, Reiko Aylesworth, Gregory Itzin, Roger Cross, Mary Lynn Rajskub, Kim Raver and Elisha Cuthbert were among those returning. New cast members included Sean Astin, Jean Smart, Connie Britton, Brady Corbet, Peter Weller and Julian Sands. Eighteen months have elapsed since Jack Bauer had to fake his own death. Calling himself Frank Flynn, he has been working at an oil refinery in the Mojave Desert in California, and is living a very different new life with a woman and her son, but when a serious breach of national security occurs he is coaxed out of hiding, fuelled by a sense of justice and with a thirst for vengeance.

The tag line to promote 24 series five was: 'To the world Jack Bauer is dead, but soon he'll become the most wanted man alive'. Executive producer Howard Gordon said: 'We'd put Jack in this position of being dead but alive, which is conceptually interesting but what does that mean in real time?' Of the top-secret plotline, Gordon revealed that rather than try somehow to top the nuclear bomb threat in series four, this new season the aim was to go smaller. The action would start with the US President meeting the Russian Premier in Los Angeles to sign an anti-terrorism treaty where the potential for international terrorists to plan sabotage is immense. This time it would be more political than ideological.

Kiefer was particularly thrilled that aspects of this fifth season would return to the show's roots, inasmuch as for Jack Bauer it contains a strongly personal element. He revealed: 'Through the first six episodes, Jack is flying through like a rocket because he's mad, and then his old life starts to catch up with him.' *24* series five launched in the US on 15 January 2006, and Howard Gordon promised that the first episode's opening minutes would 'scramble everyone's eggs!'

Proof that *24* continued to captivate audiences worldwide came at a glittering ceremony held in Los Angeles on 29 January, when Kiefer won his second Screen Actors Guild Award for Best Actor in a Drama Series. In Britain, *Arena* magazine hailed *24* as 'the most exciting, revolutionary and genre-redefining TV show of the last five years.' *24* series five launched in the UK on 12 February.

In April 2006, two films were released in which Kiefer had participated in different ways. One was the Disney animation, *The Wild*, directed by Steve Williams. Kiefer contributed his voice along with the likes of William Shatner, Jim Belushi and Eddie Izzard. It is said that for this voice role Kiefer had sometimes practised roaring like a lion while driving along the freeway, baffling passengers in passing cars.

The other role was as a Secret Service agent in the tense political thriller, *The Sentinel*. George Nolfi's screenplay was based on the novel by ex-Secret Service agent Gerald Petievich. It was filmed largely in Canada, and directed by Clark Johnson, with a cast including Kim Basinger, Raoul Bhaneja, Michael Douglas and Eva Longoria. In this tale of murder, blackmail and intrigue in the White House, Kiefer plays Agent Breckinridge, the protégé of Agent Pete Garrison, Michael Douglas's character. During filming, Eva Longoria impressed both Kiefer and Michael Douglas with her skill as a markswoman. 'She's certainly the best shot,' said Kiefer. 'At one point she fired off about six rounds and Michael gasped: "Oh my god!" They were all perfect bullseyes. This is not a woman you want to make angry,' Kiefer joked.

Jack Bauer clearly made Kiefer Sutherland tailor-made to play a Secret Service agent, and he is in hot demand for a range of film roles. Since 2001, Kiefer has been elevated to giddily popular heights, and seems set to soar even higher. In spring 2006 news broke that a further three series of *24* had been commissioned and it was a deal which, according to the trade papers *Variety* and *Hollywood Reporter*, sees Kiefer being paid a cool $40 million. *24* the movie is to be filmed in 2007 on location in London, Prague and Morocco and the show's producers have gone further and started planning a film franchise for Jack Bauer. Said Kiefer: 'It can be an amazing series of movies. I think we'd knock your socks off!'

Of his countless screen roles Kiefer has reflected: 'I would rather have had quality, than quantity. That's something that I'm working harder on now. I also hope to have the kind of longevity my parents have enjoyed.' Kiefer has certainly reached an interesting crossroads in his career. His fame this second time around is sustaining, and the full range of his acting talent is now being widely recognised. As a very young actor in the early 1990s he stated that it was the work that motivated him, and was the primary thing he enjoyed, and that so long as he kept his sights trained on that then he hoped he would have no problems.

Kiefer *has* had his problems, but he has overcome them with native resilience, and he feels he has learned much in the process. 'It's easy to take the most important thing in your life for granted,' he said. 'It can be gone before you realise how important it was.' Philosophically, he concludes that he can only get on with his life and, all round, do the best he can. 'One thing I learned during the leaner years is that acting isn't everything,' he declared.

Turning 40 in December 2006, Kiefer Sutherland already seems to have done so much in his life. Professionally, he is one of the most versatile actors in the business, and has an incredibly strong presence, playing either villain or hero. His magnetic personality is complemented by his uniquely hushed, velvety voice and his sensationally wicked laugh. Coexisting with his tangible edge is a disarming candour, and he is the first one to poke fun at himself. With two failed marriages behind him, he does not entirely rule out taking another trot up the aisle. 'I'm really a hopeless romantic at heart,' he recently insisted. 'Or,' he flashed his inimitably disreputable grin, 'maybe I'm just hopeless!

INDEX